British Nuclear Culture

British Nuclear Culture

Official and Unofficial Narratives in the Long 20th Century

JONATHAN HOGG

Bloomsbury Academic
An imprint of Bloomsbury Publishing Plc

BLOOMSBURY
LONDON · OXFORD · NEW YORK · NEW DELHI · SYDNEY

Bloomsbury Academic

An imprint of Bloomsbury Publishing Plc

50 Bedford Square	1385 Broadway
London	New York
WC1B 3DP	NY 10018
UK	USA

www.bloomsbury.com

BLOOMSBURY and the Diana logo are trademarks of Bloomsbury Publishing Plc

First published 2016

British Library Cataloguing-in-Publication Data
A catalog record for this book is available from the British Library.

ISBN: HB: 978-1-4411-4133-0
PB: 978-1-4411-6976-1
ePDF: 978-1-4411-7987-6
ePub: 978-1-4411-0924-8

Library of Congress Cataloging-in-Publication Data
Hogg, Jonathan, 1979-
British nuclear culture : official and unofficial narratives in the
long 20th century / Jonathan Hogg.
pages cm
Includes bibliographical references and index.
1. Nuclear weapons–Social aspects–Great Britain–History–20th century.
2. Atomic bomb–Social aspects–Great Britain–History–20th century.
3. War and society–Great Britain–History–20th century.
4. Popular culture–Great Britain–History–20th century. 5. Cold War. I. Title.
UA647.H66 2016
306.2'70941–dc23
2015011003

Typeset by Integra Software Services Pvt. Ltd.
Printed and bound in India

For Katy, and for Arlo. Our boy, always.

CONTENTS

LIST OF ILLUSTRATIONS

FOREWORD

Note on the map:
The British nuclear state – a snapshot

This map gives an impression of the scale and history of the British nuclear state over time. The map does not indicate the scientific centres of nuclear research (such as the Cavendish laboratory) and only indicates selected miltary and civil defence infrastructure to give a sense of the geographical spread of the nuclear state. The vast majority of these sites were, and remain, inaccessible to the public. Many of them changed uses over the Cold War period, and dates that have been provided indicate the first time the site was used as part of the nuclear state. For a full appreciation of the vastness of the British nuclear state, see Wayne D. Cocroft and Roger J. C. Thomas, *Cold War: Building for Nuclear Confrontation, 1946–1989* (Swindon: English Heritage, 2003), especially page 210 for a fuller map of the RGHQs. The website *Subterranea Britannica* contains a comprehensive list of nuclear bunkers, monitoring posts and storage facilities. Another excellent source of information can be found at the Drakelow Tunnels website: http://www.drakelow-tunnels.co.uk/rsg9.php

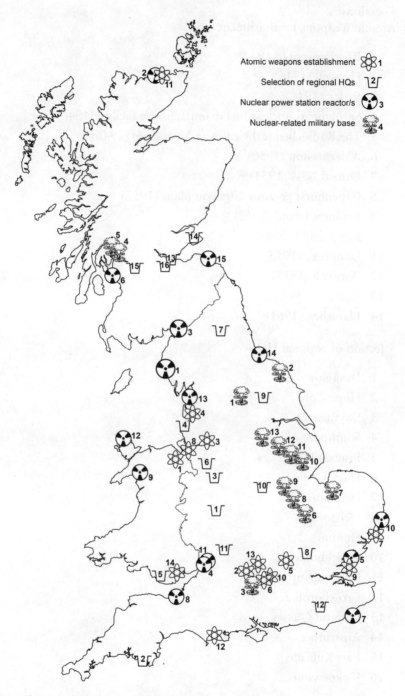

MAP 1 *The British nuclear state: a snapshot.*

Locations:
Atomic Weapons Establishment

1 Rhydymwyn (c.1942)

2 Harwell (1946)

3 Risley (1946)

4 Springfields nuclear fuel manufacturing facility (1946)

5 The Radiochemical Centre at Amersham (1946)

6 Aldermaston (1950)

7 Orford Ness (1951)

8 Capenhurst gaseous diffusion plant (1952)

9 Foulness Island (1952)

10 Burghfield (1954)

11 Dounreay (1955)

12 Winfrith (1957)

13 Culham (1960)

14 Llanishen (1961)

Selection of regional HQs

1 Drakelow

2 Hope Cove

3 Swynnerton

4 Southport

5 Brackla Hill

6 Hack Green

7 Hexham

8 Hertford

9 Shipton

10 Loughborough

11 Cheltenham

12 Crowborough

13 Barnton Quarry

14 Anstruther

15 East Kilbride

16 Kirknewton

Nuclear power stations (number of reactors)

1 Calder Hall (4) (1953)
2 Dounreay (1955)
3 Chapelcross (4) (1959)
4 Berkeley (2) (1962)
5 Bradwell (2) (1962)
6 Hunterston (4) (1964)
7 Dungeness (4) (1965)
8 Hinkley Point (6) (1965)
9 Trawsfynydd (2) (1965)
10 Sizewell (3) (1966)
11 Oldbury (2) (1967)
12 Wylfa (2) (1971)
13 Heysham (4) (1983)
14 Hartlepool (2) (1984)
15 Torness (2) (1988)

Nuclear related military bases

1 RAF Menwith Hill
2 Fylingdales
3 Greenham Common
4 Faslane
5 Coulport
6 Wyton
7 Marham
8 Wittering
9 Cottesmore
10 Coningsby
11 Waddington
12 Scampton
13 Finningley

ACKNOWLEDGEMENTS

I would like to thank Rhodri Mogford and Emma Goode at Bloomsbury Academic for their patient guidance, and Linda Jones for her shrewd and timely editorial advice. Cambridge University Press has granted permission for me to use sections of previously published material, for which I thank them. The School of Histories, Languages and Cultures at The University of Liverpool helped with some of the licensing costs for the images, for which I am thankful.

All of my third-year 'special subject' students since 2010 deserve acknowledgement here too. They made this research-led teaching module on nuclear culture a joy to teach, and they taught me many things about the nuclear age. Some students devised wonderful research projects that deserve wider recognition for their original research and novel interpretations. One such student, Sarah Hewitt, has kindly allowed me to use her interview transcripts within this book. Working closely with students on the history of the nuclear age is a constant reminder of how much work there is still to do in this area of scholarship.

Although I have taken advantage of an array of excellent digital resources now available to scholars in order to write this book, this project involved trips the old newspaper library at Colindale, the LSE archives, Merseyside CND archives, Liverpool Central Library, The National Archives and the British Library. I thank all staff who helped out along the way, with special thanks to Suzanne Yee who helped create the map of nuclear Britain. Many nuclear scholars, including Christoph Laucht, Jeff Hughes and Kirk Willis have provided friendship, support and encouragement in the past few years. At the end of this project, I view this book as a starting point, and I am looking forward to reading the future work of the many wonderful scholars who have inspired the approaches taken in this book.

Thanks to my colleagues at Liverpool for their support, especially Graeme Milne, Chris Pearson and Mark Towsey, who read through sections of this book at various stages. Special thanks to Stephen Kenny for his mentorship, encouragement and the impeccable standards he sets in teaching and research (and running), and to Joe Gilmore who has provided strong friendship as we shared, and occasionally suffered, many trips to Anfield in the last few years. I thank Mum, Dad, my brothers Richard and Alex and the Dutton family. This book is dedicated, with all my love, to Katy for her strength and unwavering support, and our little boy Arlo, who we will never forget.

CHAPTER ONE

Introduction

In the summer sky above Hiroshima, Japan, a device small enough to be carried in an aeroplane was released almost ten kilometres above the earth, fell silently, exploded low over the conurbation and in the blink of an eye released enough white-hot energy to tear life apart, incinerating untold numbers of people and creating a city of deadly firestorms, while simultaneously emitting enough radioactivity to kill and mutate living organisms for hours, months and years to come. This toxic violence was repeated over the city of Nagasaki, three days later on 9 August 1945. Two dirty, metallic, blunt and brutal weapons destroyed cities, communities, families, women, children, men and animals and polluted the skies, water and earth. These modern weapons of war were the product of decades of some of the most sophisticated and advanced scientific thinking in the history of humanity, by those who upheld the rational tradition in scientific thought. With the most brilliant scientific theories applied to military ends, American theoretical physicist J. Robert Oppenheimer, the scientific director of the Manhattan Project, in the years following 1945 decided to call repeatedly upon a quote from Hindu scripture, 'I am become death, the destroyer of worlds', in order to articulate the scientific and spiritual watershed he had overseen in the interests of national security. Now a well-worn cliché in literature on the atomic bomb, Oppenheimer's insistent quote, delivered teary eyed towards the end of his life in a television interview, can be read as solemn reminiscence, a grandiose statement of his own personal role and responsibilities, and a surreal, even irrational, statement on scientific responsibility, ethics and morality.[1] In the dust of the New Mexico desert seconds before the Trinity atomic explosion in July 1945, Manhattan Project scientists did not know if the first experimental atomic explosion would ignite the earth's atmosphere. At the heart of the twentieth century, in the mushroom cloud of bureaucratic and mechanized total war, the atomic bomb and the Nazi holocaust swirled in the world's conscience, signifiers of the gruesome extremes of modernity, political thought and human agency.

As Andrew Rotter has argued, the atomic bomb is the world's bomb.[2] It has inflicted both instant and slow violence on the world.

In 1947, a year and a half after the attacks on Hiroshima and Nagasaki, English writer J. B. Priestley offered a brief introduction to an 'atomic' focused issue of the British Broadcasting Corporation (BBC) magazine *The Listener*:

> It does not matter a rap what your work or your interest or your hobbies or your outlook may be, whether you are looking for sheep in the Grampians, rehearsing Dvořák's 'cello concerto in Kensington, getting your trousseau together in Truro, making notes for a sermon in East Anglia, running a golf club in West Kent or a repertory theatre in East Lancashire, you cannot by any amount of wriggling, squirming or running put yourself outside the sphere of these talks. It simply cannot be done. We are now living in the atomic age.[3]

Priestley was articulating a new existential reality for British citizens: everyone was involved in the atomic age. Like it or not, this was a problem *for everyone*. By identifying the individual, local and, by Priestley's logic, global nature of the freshly created atomic era, he implicitly argued for the importance of individual responsibility in responding to the world's bomb. He called for courage to be shown in the face of uncomfortable new truths, and even urged a nascent form of activism when he went on to state that to be 'indifferent' to the talks published in *The Listener* 'is to pretend you are indifferent to the fire the grate, the heat in your oven, to transport and production and the whole economic future of this and all other countries'.[4] Personal indifference carried with it a certain danger, because it abnegated responsibility for an issue of uniquely global, national and personal importance. Ideas of this kind would become increasingly common in public discourse and, as this book will explore, historians can retrieve these sentiments through analysis of a range of narratives.

Throughout the 1950s, after the British government carried out successful atomic and thermonuclear bomb tests, increasing numbers of intellectuals like Priestley would actively try to persuade people to become anti-nuclear, in an attempt to democratize the nuclear dilemma.[5] At the same time, pro-deterrence civil defence initiatives would try to convince people that to ignore nuclear issues equalled an irresponsible act towards themselves, their families, their local community and their country. Particular moments of diplomatic crisis at the height of the Cold War, such as the Cuban Missile Crisis in October 1962, meant that even individuals who refused to admit to nuclear anxiety would have experienced some realization of nuclear danger. For some, thinking the unthinkable became an everyday habit of mind, for some it became a steady, silent presence in dreams and nightmares, sometimes articulated in the waking hours, but mainly pushed aside so that life could continue as normal. So, in a way that he could not have foreseen in 1947, Priestley was right. In the years following 1945, indifference to nuclear issues became increasingly impossible.

British Nuclear Culture is concerned with the complex national story of nuclear culture in the long twentieth century, from 1898 to 2015. Exploring this central aspect of Cold War history and the history of modern Britain, this book argues that the range of responses to nuclear technology, especially in the years after 1945, must be acknowledged as a central part of how we understand everyday life in the Cold War, and how we think about the emotional history of modern Britain. Looking back at the contours of twentieth-century history, reflections upon the origins, development and use of atomic and nuclear bombs should be central to interpretations of global history, and a vast number of national histories, not least because of the huge expense involved in creating and maintaining the nuclear state. Away from the responsibilities of government spending, the physical and psychosocial consequences of the attacks on Hiroshima and Nagasaki remain to this day, and the nuclear mobilization of nation states after 1945 requires serious analysis. Focusing on Britain, this book takes seriously the different ways in which the birth of a nuclear state creates innumerable individual and collective ripple effects for generations to come and seeks to outline general trends and themes within the British nuclear century.

As I finish this book, in 2015, the British state had a stockpile of around 225 nuclear weapons.[6] In the early twentieth century, British nuclear scientists contributed to the theoretical conception, design and testing of the world's first atomic weapons as part of the secret Manhattan Project, based in America between 1942 and 1946. A decision had to be made after war ended in 1945 on the question of whether Britain should develop an independent atomic weapon. Government officials initiated the British atomic weapons programme soon after, and the long-term result is the nuclear state British citizens find themselves a part of today.

Creating atomic bombs meant creating atomic reactors, with the first British one becoming operational at Harwell, Oxfordshire, in 1947. This reactor created plutonium-239, fissile material which could be used to detonate an atomic weapon. Another reactor used for this purpose was constructed at Calder Hall, Cumbria, in the early 1950s. This site later became home to the first commercial power station in the world, opening in 1956. In the meantime, the first British atomic weapon was exploded in 1952. This would be the first of forty-four British atomic and nuclear tests. The secret creation of these reactors and weapons started the British journey down the nuclear road, and the political, institutional, physical and psychological structure of British life would be forever altered by the nuclear arms race in the Cold War era.[7] One key argument for pursuing nuclear weapons capability was to ensure national security. Hence, as Foucault stated, 'the power to expose a whole population to death is the underside of the power to guarantee an individual's continued existence'.[8]

The social and cultural history of the nuclear age has not yet been fully explored. Although scholars working on the American context started this work in the 1980s, the British context has been covered extremely thinly.

Without always stating it explicitly, the long twentieth century was full of attempts by British people to identify the main characteristics of British nuclear culture. Widespread self-reflection saw individuals, intellectuals and scientific groups, as well as political and military institutions, struggle to articulate what the nuclear age meant. What we might call 'British nuclear culture' therefore became a persistent backdrop to everyday life, appearing more visible around times of crisis, but always there as a brooding corner of British culture. We will explore definitions of nuclear culture shortly.

This book will introduce a range of primary source materials. These include institutional, journalistic and government sources. In terms of culture more generally, literature, film, music, art, television, radio, video games and cartoon will be introduced. Protest movements produced pamphlets, music, posters and other paraphernalia. Other sources include autobiographies and diaries, as well as interview transcripts and, indeed, oral history approaches offer great opportunities for nuclear scholars in the future. Also, architecture and design will be mentioned, as well as some effort to conceptualize Cold War space, such as urban planning and broader motifs that can be found in visual culture. Some of these sources have not appeared in published work before, so the book will introduce some unfamiliar source materials.

Of course, *British Nuclear Culture* offers an overview of a national nuclear history, but we will also focus upon various cities at particular moments in the nuclear century. This will lead to the idea that certain themes, trends and continuities can be mapped across the British context, but once we dig down into the idea of nuclear culture, we can see that it is much more realistic to talk about the existence of complex, intertwined and *localized* nuclear *cultures*. By identifying these cultures, we move towards a better understanding of complex historical categories of analysis, such as the existence of nuclear anxiety. In this vein, alongside London, this study will also offer case studies based in other urban centres, including Liverpool, as well as various more rural areas of Britain such as Langho, Lancashire, or the relatively remote sites where nuclear control centres, bunkers and silos were built, nuclear power stations were constructed and, in the case of Rhydymwyn in North Wales, where secret work on the fledgling atomic bomb project took place. Top-down histories of the atomic age concentrate predominantly on Whitehall and – as useful as they are – a fuller picture of the British nuclear century can only be achieved through a detailed appreciation of the complex mixture of international, national, local and personal narratives that combine to give British nuclear culture meaning.

Some distinctions

The structure of this book involves a chronological approach to the British nuclear century, with each chapter containing relevant thematic sections and explorations into wider historiographical debates where necessary.

While there is variation of thematic focus, each chapter will begin with a brief contextual section, which will map significant 'official' narratives and synthesize existing interpretations. The largest portion of each chapter will contain sections analysing 'unofficial' narratives, including explorations of journalistic narratives, fictional narratives and reflections on everyday life in the Cold War era. A range of approaches will also be introduced alongside case studies within each chapter. Throughout the book, four main interpretative strands will be introduced: British nuclear culture, the importance of language, official and unofficial narratives and nuclear anxiety.

British nuclear culture

The first interpretative strand is to be found in the title of the book itself. 'British nuclear culture' is a problematic term. In a summary of recent work centred on nuclear history in the British context, an introductory article from a 2012 special issue of the *British Journal for the History of Science* (*BJHS*) sought to offer reflections on the meaning of nuclear culture. Co-authored by Christoph Laucht and myself, the article argued that the concept, alongside *approaches* to nuclear history, must be rigorously contested. We offered a summary of different definitions of the concept, acknowledging Kirk Willis as one of the first to coin the phrase 'British nuclear culture', defining it as 'the knowledge, imagery, and artefacts of applied nuclear physics'.[9] Laucht later introduced his own definition as 'the sum of all experiences with regard to civilian and military uses of atomic energy, including such diverse layers as science and technology (both theoretical and applied), society, culture, politics, identity, gender, race, ethnicity and class'.[10] In the special issue, Hughes argued that nuclear culture must not be treated as a monolithic idea.[11] In the same special issue, Richard Maguire's work focused on the various 'nuclear cultures' that existed within government, arguing that a 'diverse, and shifting, set of ideas' defined official thinking around nuclear weapons.[12] In the introduction to the special issue, we argued that 'British nuclear culture' demonstrates 'the rich, complex and contestable nature of the interactions between nuclear science, technology and British life and [...] problematise[d] how we choose to approach the nuclear past in Britain'.[13] Catherine Jolivette's introduction to a recent collection of articles entitled *British Art in the Nuclear Age* offers an innovative way to think about nuclear culture, where 'nature and nuclear are read not as polarised opposites but part of a common, historically specific, culture in which the visual forms, rather than merely reflects, the discourses of the age'.[14]

Part of the problem with the concept of a uniquely 'British' nuclear culture is that, normally, local peculiarities are overlooked within the national historical narrative, and a small number of sources can be improperly or partially historicized. Throughout this book, there will be moments where the lens is firmly fixed on particular regions within Britain and time given to thinking about how such approaches problematize our view of British nuclear culture. This approach is influenced by Jeff Hughes, who argued in the same special issue for the necessity of a 'critical history of responses to nuclearisation' and better acknowledgement of how cultural responses to the nuclear age are 'collectively constitutive of the nuclear condition rather than passive reflections of it'.[15] Hughes suggested that writing localized histories of the nuclear age is one way of capturing what 'nuclear culture' can mean. He argued that if we are to move 'towards a more nuanced and critical history of responses to nuclearisation [...] these responses [...] should be seen as collectively constitutive of the nuclear condition rather than as passive reflections of it'.[16] He went on to argue that

> invoking a 'nuclear culture' which pre-existed any widespread understanding or even use of the word 'nuclear' quickly becomes an apologia for the bomb, a retrospectively constructed prelude to an – in effect – legitimation of what came later. The invocation of nuclear culture here performs ideological work: [...] nuclearism can be 'found' in culture long before its material realisation, partially effacing both its novelty in 1945 and, implicitly, diminishing the agency and responsibility of those who later created it.[17]

In my own contribution to the field, I argued that 'understanding the impact of atomic culture is to understand profound psychological, spiritual and social change [...] the atomic bomb has wide-reaching consequences on the lives of individual citizens, and a significant impact on national culture'.[18] Some scholars go further, pointing to the way in which the structure of the social contract changed as the nuclear age dawned, reinforced by the language used by the nuclear state. Ian Welsh has written that 'the implementation of nuclear power recasts state-citizen relations, weakening the automatic association between state and citizen welfare. The pursuit of interstate ambitions demanded the sacrifice of private citizens. Democratic states injected plutonium into vulnerable social groups and deliberately exposed civilian populations to radioactive fallout and discharges.'[19] So, in effect, scholars have instinctively resisted concrete or narrow definitions of nuclear culture, preferring to enunciate critically the broad reach of the nuclear state and problematize the politics of the term.

Of course, some aspects of British nuclear culture were secret and remain so. Writing about nuclear development in America, David Nye stated that 'the atomic bomb had come into being not as a result of open debate but as the result of a secret project that was never subjected to the normal controls of a democratic political process'.[20] This same process holds true in the British case as well. From its origins, the nuclear state was shaped by cultures of secrecy due to serious issues over national security.[21] Margaret Gowing pointed towards a 'rigid security regime' in the post-war era, and it is clear that the 'British public received partial information about nuclear technology once it was filtered through D-Notices, and other official channels'.[22] Thus, nuclear culture was at once shaped by the secret nature of the nuclear state, that state's own official narrative, and unofficial knowledges that would slowly emerge in society more broadly in the Cold War era.

> For the purposes of this book, I define British nuclear culture as the distinct corner of British culture characterized by the development of the nuclear state and the complex and varied ways in which people **controlled, responded to, resisted or represented** the complex influence of nuclear science and technology, the official nuclear state and the threat of nuclear war. As we shall see, the range of 'control, response, resistance and representation' and the influence of the nuclear state, including its material, psychosocial and spatial consequences, were considerable.

The importance of language

Second, it is argued that there was a consistent and often implicit vocabulary that expressed powerful attitudes on nuclear realities. Most significantly perhaps, the nuclear imagination meant dealing with abstractions and unrealities: for the vast majority of people nuclear weapons or nuclear reactors remained alien and distant. Yet, through the course of the twentieth century, many British citizens would feel an intimate connection to the consequences of this technology. The majority of these people would have a purely imagined connection to nuclear technology, making language itself a key component to our historical understanding of the development of these powerful imaginaries. Examining language in detail is also important. For instance, taking just one word, 'deterrence', and considering its use by politicians, we can see perhaps the best example of 'nuclear permanence'. The logic of deterrence, as a publically articulated and perceived political *idea*, depends on the belief that the condition of nuclear threat is permanent. Without this, deterrence is useless as an idea. Deterrence cannot be temporary. This political idea links up with the permanence of the scientific and military network of nuclear institutions. This is where politics and power can be read most clearly through the use of nuclear language. Loaded with meaning amassed over years of repeated assumptions and assertions, the permanence and power of the nuclear state can be read in the discourse of British culture, and, indeed, in one single word. Linked to Welsh's ideas above, the continuation of the British nuclear state was 'dependent upon the articulation of a wide range of discursive claims'.[23]

Working through the relationship between language and nuclear anxiety, I deployed the term 'nuclearity' in an article from the 2012 *BJHS* special issue to describe the 'shifting set of assumptions held by individual citizens on the dangers of nuclear technology: assumptions that were rooted firmly in context and which circulated in, and were shaped by, national discourse'.[24] I argued that because of these assumptions, individuals implicitly understood the many things nuclear danger could mean. Because nuclearity can be seen as an active component in the formation of British identity, nuclear 'knowledge' can serve to disrupt conceptions of self, nationhood and family in everyday life. In the same special issue, Dan Cordle argued that a 'politics of vulnerability', in part, defined British culture in the 1980s, with nuclear anxiety serving as a constant backdrop to culture and society.[25] The structure of language in fictional nuclear narratives served to reinforce political agendas and ideas. The importance of language in supporting the system of power that the nuclear state represents has been well articulated in the historiography and will be explored further throughout this text.

Official and unofficial narratives

Third, after acknowledging the importance of language in shaping nuclear attitudes, the notion of 'official' and 'unofficial' narratives is introduced as the main organizing concept in this book. In distinguishing between these different narratives, the contested nature of the nuclear state comes into sharper focus. So much of the history of the nuclear age has been written from the official perspective alone, and by focusing on unofficial perspectives, we gain access to a great many untold stories directly related to the nuclear age. It is in this sense that *British Nuclear Culture* takes the 'official' and 'unofficial' distinction as an *access point* to thinking about the impact of the official political institutionalization and development of nuclear weapons and nuclear reactors to British culture more widely. As my definition of nuclear culture suggests, this impact created a wide variety of 'unofficial' cultures of reflection, assent, dissent, uncertainty and resistance.[26] People were not passive during the nuclear age.

Narratives are one way to think about the past. As historians, we continually reflect upon texts which are part of wider narratives. The majority of source materials that historians come across are a product of human energy. On production, the human responsible for creating a source is influenced by any number of things, but the author of any source where ideas are constructed will have an ontological position – a worldview. Sometimes, this worldview is made explicit, sometimes not. In itself, this worldview is an individual narrative. Very often, individual narratives betray similar influences: they may converge. The types of narrative that exist in newspapers are often pitched at what is assumed to be the dominant worldview or to appeal to an assumed set of shared opinions.

Moving from deeply committed anti-nuclear activists, to nuclear-themed literature and film, to pop music hits of the 1980s that dwelt on the nuclear threat, to hidden acts of resistance and a huge variety of 'nuclear subjectivities' which are difficult to excavate, 'unofficial' responses to official government policy proved varied, widespread and powerful. Some were self-consciously and politically 'unofficial', for instance reflecting discord in the Labour party in the 1950s and 1980s. These narratives reminded the British that the nuclear state was not a natural, permanent part of life, although this was the impression often given by official narratives, as well as from histories of the nuclear century written with the illusion of neutrality and 'objectivity'.

Within this book, 'official' narratives are understood to be those source materials that have a state-institutional origin and are linked directly to political and military policy making, civil defence and foreign policy. These were normally pro-nuclear, although, as we shall see, there are examples of anti-nuclear thought in local and national government. 'Unofficial' narratives are taken to mean those source materials that were authored or created by individuals with no vested interest in the nuclear state but act as a commentary on the nuclear state. These narratives were both pro- and anti-nuclear. Clearly, it is difficult to make neat distinctions along official and unofficial lines. For instance, it could be argued that newspapers served both official and unofficial functions. With this in mind, the terms 'official' and 'unofficial' should not be taken as definitive, but suggestive of a contested terrain of meaning. This in itself is an interpretation of the broader meaning of British nuclear culture.

By looking to individual narratives for signs of wider cultural meaning, 'nuclear subjectivities' may emerge. In the American context, Brian Taylor has argued forcefully that the negative impact of nuclear technology on individuals cannot be forgotten, and that the dominant nuclear discourse, generated as it is by self-interested institutions, needs to be challenged. Exploring the photography of Carole Gallagher, Taylor argues that photo-essays are one act of rebellion that can go a long way to counteract the pervasive force of nuclear orthodoxy.[27] These counter-narratives highlight 'nuclear subjectivity' in the way that mainstream narratives cannot.[28] Of direct relevance here is the movement that became known as 'nuclear criticism' in the 1980s. In the words of Taylor, the movement proved 'uniquely concerned with how language and images shape the public experience of nuclear weapons'.[29] These thinkers viewed 'nuclear culture as a dialogic site of struggle between conflicting and interanimating discourses [...] each seeking authority over the meaning and consequence of nuclear weapons'.[30] Taylor's work analysing nuclear photography introduced the concept of 'nuclear subjectivity' which should be understood as those reminders of the physical and psychological impact the nuclear state can have on individual lives, as seen through unofficial narratives. Taylor argued that these narratives could be powerful enough to compel us to 'revise official accounts of nuclear history',[31] and that official accounts of nuclear history have still, on the whole, left nuclear subjectivities hidden.[32] Similar approaches to the links between nuclear technology and language were taken by Hilgartner et al., who sought to demonstrate that American nuclear institutions ensured that 'nukespeak' was deployed to generate a positive impression of nuclear technology throughout the Cold War period. At the most extreme end of this interpretation is that, through media dissemination, nuclear untruths are implied, facts are distorted, and, therefore, a positive image of the nuclear industry is consistently reinforced over time.[33] In the British context, Crispin Aubrey also developed these ideas.[34]

The epistemological importance of narrative rests on a set of ideas popularized from the 1980s due to the work of cultural historians and cultural theorists. At a general level, Hayden White argued that historians must be aware of the discursive force of their own work when he wrote

> those historians who draw a firm line between history and philosophy of history fail to recognise that every historical discourse contains within it a full-blown, if only implicit, philosophy of history [...] history proper (as it is called) buries it in the interior of the narrative, where it serves as a hidden or implicit shaping device.[35]

As we will see, this is especially relevant to nuclear history, as there is a long tradition of histories focused largely on the official development of the nuclear state and its small group of predominantly male decision-makers. These historians depended upon a narrow range of sources, the availability of which was defined by the state. Within this tight bubble of nuclear power, a type of historical discourse emerged which then served to shape understandings of the nuclear state. In turn, this discourse was rarely challenged in formal academic publications. Robert Jacobs deployed the term 'narrative' to good effect in his recent work, also arguing that the use of the concept as a tool for historical investigation gets us closer to the nature of discursive power of the nuclear state. He identifies the 'primary narrative of nuclear culture the *alchemical narrative* – alchemical because of the strong emphasis on nuclear weapons as signifiers of transformation or fundamental change [...] to people around the world, nuclear weapons announced that the past was gone and the future had arrived'.[36] Jacobs argues that through frantic attempts to come to terms with the nuclear age, new narratives or motifs were constructed as a way to understand and contain the overwhelming reality of weapons that could destroy life on earth. In this sense, fictional narratives play a crucial part in developing popular understandings of nuclear threat.

When it comes to concepts such as fear or anxiety, the narrative approach is a very useful one to take. For instance, we can study the different ways in which newspapers articulate a concept, often without discussing it explicitly. Perhaps a set of assumptions underlie discussions over nuclear anxiety, or opinions are advanced on how to deal with nuclear anxiety. While it is important not to over-privilege individual articles within newspapers, we can identify articles that exemplify a particular notion or betray a deep set of assumptions on a particular issue. A key part of this approach is the acknowledgement of ambiguity: nuclear narratives are messy and contradictory. This book is not an attempt to have the last word on nuclear narratives, but an attempt to open up a new set of debates on the nature of the nuclear state or to explore the nature of nuclear anxiety further. Narratives, then, can be viewed as a window into the social creation and reinforcement of meaning.

The purpose of reducing these varying experiences to official and unofficial narratives is to suggest that whether we are dealing with a diary entry, a poem, a political cartoon, a song, government policy or anti-nuclear protest, nuclear preoccupations suffused British discourse in ways that the existing historiography has not highlighted. This book is equally interested in diary entries as well as cabinet minutes or song lyrics as well as civil defence planning. As we will see in Chapter 7, the throwaway and flippant use of nuclear language that now surrounds us is the product of a normalized nuclear state of being, and it is the emergence and persistence of specific nuclear vocabularies that creates and perpetuates forms of expression.

Nuclear anxiety

It is clear that nuclear narratives, and the knowledges they created, reinforced or challenged the nuclear state and served to structure and shape everyday realities in the Cold War era. I have argued elsewhere that 'to understand the psychosocial pressures at the heart of the nuclear age we must be sensitive to the powerful role played by diverse nuclear narratives, the knowledge they created, and the individuals involved in their production, dissemination and reception. Only then can we convincingly capture histories of everyday life that reflect the full impact of the nuclear arms race.'[37] As we will see throughout this book, official narratives of the atomic age are increasingly being 'questioned, disrupted or enhanced by analysing the significance of journalistic, anti-nuclear and fictional narratives to the development of nuclear culture in Britain'.[38] We have seen a shift away from top-down histories, offering instead a broader range of voices and approaches. The systems of power at work in the Cold War context have been increasingly challenged and problematized.

More often than not, this uncovered the power and prevalence of nuclear anxiety in twentieth-century British culture and society. This is the fourth main interpretative strand in the book. Although my definition of nuclear culture is broad, there is overwhelming evidence that demonstrates the reality, power and widespread existence of nuclear anxiety across time and space. Nuclear anxiety represented and contributed to wider social and cultural change, and it could be argued that the relaxation of societal mores enabled more confident expressions of nuclear anxiety by the 1980s. I hope this book demonstrates the underappreciated significance of nuclear anxiety in British life. The ways in which individuals responded to, resisted or represented the threat of nuclear war are something cultural historians have only just started to unravel. It is to the existing histories of the nuclear age that we now turn.

Historians and British nuclear history: Systems of power

The four interpretative strands detailed above have emerged through reflection on the development of nuclear historiography. They help to highlight and unravel a system of knowledge and power inscribed in the histories and language of the nuclear century. Until recently, it was rare for historians to challenge orthodox interpretations of Cold War Britain, which had the effect of supporting the politics of deterrence. Historians rarely problematized or conceptualized the structural conditions that defined the nuclear state. Until recently, the nuclear historiographical tradition in Britain was broadly aligned with a state-centred, Whiggish historical outlook which presented the nuclear state as a permanent and natural feature of British life. Sometimes, these histories align the rise of the nuclear state with a positive sense of national identity. Rather than interrogate and analyse the existence of nuclear Britain, the majority of these histories assume a posture of apparent neutrality and objectivity while, in fact, serving to bolster and legitimize the power of the nuclear state. Speaking of these 'traditional' approaches in a book first published in 1989, Roger Ruston argued that 'apart from a few interesting asides, there is no discussion of the moral issues in any of these works'.[39]

Some recent explorations into Cold War history are moving us away from general approaches to the Cold War, some even suggesting we dispense with the term 'Cold War' altogether.[40] It has become increasingly common to disrupt and question existing categories of analysis when it comes to the Cold War era, especially for those seeking to write histories of everyday life.[41] Although scholars have made significant headway in the American and European context, everyday life in the British Cold War era is a relatively under-researched aspect of the past. Work in the last few years has started to break open new avenues of research, countering or developing the 'official' histories that have dominated Cold War scholarship for so long. Histories of the nuclear age based on official documentation are essential to students of the British Cold War experience. Among others, work by Margaret Gowing, Lorna Arnold, Peter Hennessy, Matthew Jones and Matthew Grant has laid invaluable and rich foundations to any study of the nuclear era in Britain by using government records to map decision-making. Yet, there are many stories of nuclear Britain that have not yet been told and, on reading these 'official' histories, it would seem that the

British public passively interacted with the rise and development of nuclear technology. The work of more traditional historians of the nuclear state tends to underplay, or ignore, the complexity and existence of nuclear culture beyond elite groups.

Most early British nuclear histories were written largely from the biographical perspective, offering hagiographical accounts of the 'great' male scientists of the early twentieth century. In recent years, historians have discussed the problematic nature of such accounts and suggested that 'social constructivist' models of interpretation should be introduced to consider more carefully the social and political conditions that underlay scientific practice.[42] After the creation of the nuclear state in Britain, official historian Margaret Gowing was employed by the United Kingdom Atomic Energy Authority (UKAEA) to write the history of this development. Lorna Arnold and Katherine Pyne also served in this role.[43]

Although the work of these historians acts as crucial reference texts for the early nuclear age, it requires critical examination. Privileged yet limited access to source materials meant that these historians wrote authoritative yet partial histories of the nuclear establishment. These histories were sometimes hagiographical but did occasionally problematize the existence of the nuclear establishment. However, 'the institutional and official tone set by a small number of scholars has led to a significant proportion of atomic history being focused predominantly on government and elites', and this pattern remained strong for a surprisingly long time.[44] As Jeff Hughes wrote in 2002, 'little historiographical effort has been devoted to understanding the construction of the canonical history of nuclear physics in the postwar period, with its linear, teleological narrative and, more importantly, its implicit naturalistic justification of the creation of nuclear weapons.'[45] In the years following the publication of Gowing's work in the mid-1960s, surveys and interpretations of nuclear weapons policy emerged,[46] along with detailed accounts of Anglo-American nuclear relations.[47] Historians have enthusiastically traced the history of nuclear strategy and delivery systems,[48] and research on spying and intelligence networks is a well-established field of study.[49]

Since the 1980s, historians of the American nuclear century have offered more varied interpretations of the nuclear state, mainly due to the prevalence of domestic fallout-shelter construction in the 1950s and 1960s and America's role at the forefront of the nuclear arms race. Paul Boyer's *By the Bomb's Early Light* (1985) was the first to offer a cultural history of the nuclear age in America, suggesting the power, range and diversity of reactions to the nuclear state.[50] The book proved influential, and more specialized areas of research emerged in the American context, from the work of Elaine Tyler-May and Kenneth Rose on fallout-shelter culture, to Zeman and Amundson on popular culture.[51]

Recent work on the spatial histories of cities in the nuclear age suggests that we can analyse nuclear narratives in new ways to make sense of how cities 'enable and constrain different constellations of power and knowledge'.[52] Again in the American context, work by David Monteyne suggested ways in which the Foucauldian concept of 'biopower' – governmental processes whereby bodies are subjugated and populations controlled – can be applied to thinking about the logic of nuclear civil defence. Monteyne argues that 'cold war civil defence was a discursive formation and spatial practice particularly well suited to representing the goals and powers of the welfare state', partly because it based its 'power on an underlying reference to the established institutions of the disciplinary society'.[53] Designing and building Cold War infrastructure was part of an unquestioned faith in systems of government and thinking deemed necessary to preserve peace. Recent work has examined the physical infrastructure of the British nuclear state, suggesting new ways to conceptualize the spatial aspects of the Cold War.[54] In separate articles, Sophie Forgan and Christoph Laucht have examined the different ways in which nuclear science has been exhibited in the twentieth century, highlighting the contested nature of nuclear knowledge.[55]

The Freedom of Information Act (2005) led to the emergence of new official source materials and the re-evaluation of old historical debates. Research on civil defence by Matthew Grant in *After the Bomb* and Peter Hennessy's work on the 'secret state' are good examples of this.[56] Studies on civil defence have become increasingly developed in the historiography.[57] The expansion of digital archiving has offered new research avenues, with Adrian Bingham and Christoph Laucht offering work based on digitally archived newspapers and magazines.[58] Many more studies of media discourse in the nuclear age remain to be written. Research on design in the nuclear age, while useful, still leaves many questions unanswered on the extent to which the nuclear age influenced aspects of cultural expression in general terms.[59]

The standard 'official' narrative of the atomic age can be disrupted by analysing the significance of fictional, journalistic and anti-nuclear narratives. It was arguably Tony Shaw's research on British Cold War cinema that did more than most to turn the cultural lens onto the British Cold War, and his major work was published in 2001.[60] Shaw's work uncovered the secret debates around the production of film in the Cold War. He argued that cultural production was an extremely contested and politicized process in this era. There has been a steady increase in the field of popular culture, with a special issue of *Journal of British Cinema and Television* given to nuclear-themed TV and film in 2013, and a special issue of *Cold War History* dedicated to radio broadcasting in the Cold War era.[61] An upcoming edited collection by Matthew Grant and Benjamin Ziemann promises to deepen the debate over the relevance of Cold War culture further still.[62]

Within the 2012 *BJHS* special issue on British nuclear culture, authors offered various new ways to consider the subject of nuclear culture. Dan Cordle explored the complexities of nuclear culture in the 1980s, demonstrating the ways in which fiction made 'visible a nuclear threat that had, in the preceding decades, become so commonplace as to be mundane'.[63] Existing research on anti-nuclear activism is a rich area of scholarship,[64] and Jodi Burkett's article asserted the importance of Campaign for Nuclear Disarmament (CND) in the rise of ecological thinking in the Cold War era.[65] Alison Kraft discussed 'atomic medicine' in History Today and in another article from 2006.[66] Although this book is predominantly about the destructive impact of the nuclear state, there are positive stories that come from the peaceful applications of nuclear science.

Although we are focusing on a single national context, we cannot forget the importance of those 'studies that treat aspects of British nuclear culture within a comparative or transnational framework to showcase how major international developments or movements played out on a national level'.[67] Recent work has offered strong assertions on the lasting legacies of British nuclear colonialism, finding common links with other national nuclear contexts.[68] The British atomic testing that was conducted around the world in Australia and the Pacific islands forms a complex environmental and international history that must be explored further.[69] The 'Sellafield Stories' oral history project, and the published interviews with nuclear veterans who participated in the British H-bomb tests are valuable historical narratives. More of these histories need to be collected in the coming years, including more general recollections of living in the nuclear age.[70] British nuclear decision-making was dominated by a male, white, privileged elite, which also deeply influenced and characterized British nuclear culture more generally. This elite group also shaped the historiography of the British nuclear age. Indian author and political activist Arundhati Roy believes that 'nuclear weapons pervade our thinking. Control our behaviour. Administer our societies. Inform our dreams. They bury themselves like meat hooks deep in the base of our brains. They are purveyors of madness. They are the ultimate colonizer. Whiter than any white man who ever lived. The very heart of whiteness.'[71] In the period after 1945, British nuclear weapons thinking became mixed up with anxieties over decolonization, and nuclear weapons testing in the 1950s was planned and conducted with disregard for the lives and territories of some of the most marginalized people in the British Empire.[72] In this sense, the complex political and military cultures that dictated the white use of nuclear weapons were 'the ultimate colonizer' as, for example, the Maralinga people on Australian territory were utterly powerless against radioactive contamination inflicted upon them. Paul Williams has recently published on race and the nuclear age from a literary perspective, and we will see that a conservative politics of race and gender was discursively reinforced by a variety of narratives within official nuclear discourse.[73] Often, these narratives do this work by demonstrating the complete absence of non-white people in articulations of the nuclear state and its far-reaching influence.

*

British Nuclear Culture attempts to contribute to the historiography of twentieth-century Britain by not only acknowledging the way in which the atomic bombing of Hiroshima was 'one of the truly critical moments in the history of the twentieth century world and all human history',[74] but also exploring the ways in which British culture was altered due to the varied influence and impact of nuclear technologies and the threat of nuclear war. This impact proved to be a mixture of subtle, harsh reality and horrendous imagined possibilities. This book will explore one way to make sense of Britain's nuclear century by examining the multiplicity of nuclear narratives. The methodology that underpins the approach in the book rests on the suggestion that the process of formation, dissemination and reception of narratives is key to understanding a history so complex as to encompass military and industrial power, political institutions and culture more widely.

One central argument that will be explored is that unofficial and official nuclear narratives clashed with increasing severity as the twentieth century developed, but on the whole, unofficial narratives have remained absent from the interests of historians of modern Britain. One powerful example of such an 'unofficial' narrative is the story of a married couple from Lancashire who, after citing nuclear fear in a suicide note, killed themselves and their children in 1957. As I have argued elsewhere, and as we will see in Chapter 4, the representation of the story in the national press is of particular interest, as the *Mirror* used the example of these supposedly 'mentally ill' people as an opportunity to remind readers of how to be a responsible British citizen in the face of inevitable nuclear fear. In a way that echoes official civil defence propaganda in the 1950s, the readers of the *Mirror* were being urged to be responsible, vigilant citizens in the face of nuclear anxiety. At a time just before the rise of mass anti-nuclear activism and the Cuban Missile Crisis, this stance was common. By the 1980s, I argue, cultural politics had altered due to the increase of those unofficial narratives that directly challenged the nuclear state. In ways that simply could not have happened in the 1950s, the 1980s saw an increase in cultural works that 'disrupt[ed] the passivity of viewers and implicated them in the evaluation of nuclear representations'.[75] Thus, it was more likely that forms of nuclear representation that emerged in the 1980s would 'destabilise the authority of official nuclear images and narratives by contrasting them with their unofficial counterparts'.[76]

The development of nuclear technology for military and civil uses, and the range of responses to this development, is a story of change. Expectations, scientific horizons, political strategy and public debate constituted a constantly evolving set of understandings and knowledges. The book focuses primarily on the public responses to the creation and continuation of the British nuclear state, with reference to nuclear weapons and nuclear power stations. It will be argued that these unofficial narratives changed and evolved greatly while, in contrast, the official narrative remained more stable and consistent. Therefore, this book will also chart the historical continuities that appear when surveying the nuclear century. Official narratives, emerging from institutions of the nuclear state, shaped public understandings of nuclear science and nuclear Britain. This allowed the nuclear industry to become more easily institutionally embedded in British life, often without the possibility of public scrutiny of how the process happened, and why and how it continued to happen.

The ways in which ideas on the nuclear state were expressed proved vital to the levels of support seen towards the nuclear establishment. The book will be organized by tracing the contradictions that exist between official and unofficial nuclear narratives. Like any historical survey, this process has been necessarily selective, but every attempt is made to offer balanced and clear interpretation of a range of primary source materials, many of which have never been used in scholarly work before and certainly not in the historiography of British nuclear culture. In this sense, although this book serves as a useful classroom text, I hope it also contributes in some way to the growing field of British nuclear culture studies, where analysis of unofficial narrative remains under-represented in favour of nuclear histories that privilege and describe official interests.

We will begin with the discovery of radiation in 1898 and end with reflections on nuclear culture in 2015. This book mainly focuses on the years since 1945, but the story of Britain's nuclear century in the years leading up to the Manhattan Project will also be examined.[77] Central themes include the shifting scientific understandings of the damage radiation inflicts on humans, perceptions of nuclear danger, the development of nuclear science and the various legacies of the nuclear century. Nuclear medicine does not figure prominently in the book, although the development of nuclear medicine will be covered in Chapter 1, and acknowledged throughout. One of the most difficult aspects of planning and writing this book was deciding which primary source materials to use, as there is an infinitude of possible source materials now at the disposal of historians interested in creating detailed cultural histories of each decade of the British nuclear century, let alone the entire century. With this in mind, the book is designed with a series of starting points, where students of modern British and Cold War history can pursue or build upon interesting source sets and disagree with interpretations and suggestive analysis offered. Owing to the length of this book, outlines of the 'official' British nuclear century are kept fairly brief. As you will see, most conclusions offer suggestions towards new thematic approaches to the investigation of the largely untold 'unofficial' story of the British nuclear state. Separations between chapters and arguments put forward about processes of change should be critically interrogated and challenged by the reader.

To fully historicize the wide variety of source sets at our disposal, this book invites a sensitive and thoughtful approach to the nuclear past. While this book introduces students of nuclear history to a range of new primary sources, it suggests ways to conceptualize the nuclear century, as well as some reflections on how individual British citizens experienced the nuclear age.

Through examining under-acknowledged source materials, we can begin to unravel the 'emotional history of the atomic bomb' in Britain.[78] After all, perceptions of nuclear technology influenced – sometimes profoundly – how individual British citizens lived their lives. Anxiety over possible nuclear attack is perhaps the most obvious example of how individuals framed new ways of thinking, acting, resisting and submitting to the psychological pressures at the heart of Cold War Britain. *British Nuclear Culture* is written at an early stage of our understanding of the social and cultural meanings of the nuclear age, and the history of nuclear states will continue to be a contested and significant area of historical enquiry for years to come.[79] As this introduction has argued, vast areas of the 'unofficial' story are yet to be explored. As well as giving a broad outline of the official story of the British nuclear state, the following chapters will offer new ways to think about the nuclear century, suggesting a range of thematic and analytical approaches. Ultimately, it is for students of nuclear history to study the sources for themselves and decide which aspects of this history deserve further exploration, and which existing historical interpretations and approaches to build upon, as we aim for a truly peaceful world.

CHAPTER TWO

British Nuclear Culture, 1898–1945

The period from 1898 to 1945 was the formative era for modern nuclear science and technology, during which the range and depth of understanding around nuclear science accelerated at an unprecedented pace.[1] Within half a century, scientists moved from rudimentary understandings of radioactivity and the internal make-up of atoms to a thorough understanding of how the massive amounts of energy contained within certain atoms could be harnessed to produce useable energy through the development of nuclear reactors and weapons. This is also the period when some of the central motifs of British nuclear culture in the twentieth century were formed, in a climate that enthusiastically embraced scientific progress in the name of modernity. Hope or fear came to define perceptions of nuclear science and most notably the properties of newly discovered radioactive elements such as radium. As cultural responses fixated on potential applications, public discussion of the potential benefit and harm of these applications would prove to be a central motif throughout the century.

The climate of international scientific collaboration and openness that characterized the early twentieth century switched to one of secrecy as European war became inevitable in the late 1930s. From the outbreak of war in 1939, national security and 'big science' came to dictate the path of nuclear research, as the military applications of nuclear science came sharply into focus.[2] For this reason, nuclear science and its potential applications became embedded, institutionalized and shaped around the interests of Britain and its Allies in wartime. Seen as part of an ongoing arms race, issues around democratic accountability – in terms of moral legitimacy, expense or long-term consequences – were not prioritized in discussions over the atomic bomb. Concern over the possibility that Germany was developing atomic weapons meant that moral and ethical considerations had to be weighed against perceived national vulnerability.[3] In his attempt to describe the links between atomic science, scientists and 'the public' in the early twentieth century, we have already seen that Kirk Willis has coined the term 'British nuclear culture'.[4] This period saw a flurry of nuclear-inspired activity across all levels of British society, including an increase of reportage on the topic in the national press and the emergence of a nuclear-themed popular culture. Popular responses to nuclear discoveries increased and diversified throughout the era, although it is safe to say that nuclear culture had a limited impact on everyday life in Britain during this time. But, this was the era in which the nuclear imagination was born, and particular assumptions around both nuclear danger and the promise of future benefits were developed in wider society. The relationship between science and literature was important in the early part of the period, with nuclear science only becoming politicized in the shadow of war. It was both the impact of war between 1914 and 1918 and the threat of war in the late 1930s that shaped some of the moral and ethical justifications for pursuing military applications of nuclear science. In Britain, we can trace the beginnings of the nuclear state in this period. The transition from an international, collaborative scientific community to the secretive, closed culture of the US-based Manhattan Project led to the institutionalization of a secretive, expansive and expensive nuclear state on British soil by the late 1940s. The top-secret Military Application of Uranium Detonation (MAUD) Committee, set up in 1940, was the early British atomic bomb project that led directly to the establishment of the Manhattan Project.

In the years following the discovery of radioactivity in 1898, the British public responded in a variety of ways to the idea of nuclear science. This chapter will trace the existing historiography on early British nuclear culture and then introduce a number of unfamiliar sources on the 'radium craze' in the early twentieth century. There will be a discussion on radium as a commodity, early government responses to nuclear science and discussion of the links between science fiction and nuclear science. Then, analysis of international scientific communities is followed by an analysis of international military developments and the consequences this had for British culture and society in general terms. The historical significance of the Manhattan Project will be outlined, and it will be argued that the secrecy and militarization that defined nuclear science from the early 1940s led to the 'institutionalization' of nuclear science which, in turn, amplified widespread feelings of powerlessness and anxiety in the years following 1945. Additionally, the chapter will suggest that the ambiguity defining British responses to nuclear science was deeply rooted in the national context. This chapter ends with a brief exploration of the historical controversy over the use of atomic weapons against Japan in 1945.

Approaching early nuclear history

Scholars have offered extensive analysis of British nuclear scientists and their scientific communities in the early years of the twentieth century. Many biographies of key nuclear scientists have been written, with individuals of special interest including Joseph Rotblat, Ernest Rutherford, Frederick Soddy and James Chadwick.[5] It is well known that 'alongside explorations of medical and industrial applications of atomic technology, by 1940 the international scientific community had acknowledged the possibility of a workable atomic bomb with increasing certainty'.[6] There is a vast literature surveying the broader political and social history of this period more generally. It is of interest that surveys of the era that emphasize the 'crisis of civilisation' in the interwar years, such as Richard Overy's *The Morbid Age*, do not focus on the role of British scientists in the movement towards the atomic bomb.[7] Jeff Hughes has expressed frustration with some scholarship on early nuclear science, stating 'historians have tended to be in thrall to the aura of the nuclear and its practitioners, and that this had led them to essentialize the nuclear – to endow it with supra-human agency and potency. Most problematically, this essentializing tendency has led historians and other analysts towards description rather than analysis.'[8]

It should be noted that this early phase of modern atomic history has been written about in a limited number of ways. Of the books that have been written about the progress of nuclear science in the years leading up to the outbreak of war in 1939, many discuss the links between science and literature or the changing relationship between science and the state.[9] A significant number of these histories identify this period as one of great scientific discovery, driven by great scientists. Some historical works, such as *The Making of the Atomic Bomb* by Richard Rhodes, privilege the dramatic story of scientific discovery, where startling anecdotes and 'eureka' moments are foregrounded as inevitable nuclear milestones leading to the Trinity test. There is much to be admired about the work of Rhodes, not least his splendid eight-page description of the moment of atomic detonation at Trinity, but the literature struggled to move on from this top-down, biographical approach.[10] Along these lines, *Nuclear Muse* by John Canaday also serves to 'essentialize' early atomic history by focusing on the 'prescience' of science-fiction writers and scientists. As Jeff Hughes has argued, 'the nuclear age is only now coming to be understood as a contingent accomplishment, rather than an inevitable outcome, of scientific activity'.[11] He reminds us that 'for the period up to 1939, it is becoming clear that radioactivity and nuclear physics were not self-evident or inevitable enterprises whose boundaries and goals were predefined by nature'.[12] The literature on British nuclear scientists is now heavily influenced by social constructivism. The work of Jeff Hughes is perhaps exemplified by the wish to understand the history of science 'in terms of a specific material and social setting and a specific set of experimental and conceptual practices'.[13] Hughes wishes to disturb traditional and 'circular' interpretations of science that 'put the phenomenon first', rather looking at scientists and their work in specifically defined cultural settings. In this sense, there is no 'all-seeing' mind driving research forward, but a complex set of sociopolitical practice shaping a particular cultural framework in which scientific practice should be understood. Scientists, then, are assumed to be working in ever-changing and complicated cultures specific to the set-up of laboratories. Leaning towards the social constructivist mode, historians are becoming increasingly interested in the broader social and cultural contexts surrounding and shaping science.

Beginnings: 1898–1939

Nuclear physics in the early twentieth century: The public phase

There are many readable histories of the excitement created by the collection of scientific discoveries made in Europe at the end of the nineteenth century.[14] German scientist Wilhelm Conrad Röntgen accidently discovered X-rays in 1895, and the following year, French physicist Antoine Henri Becquerel discovered (as an indirect consequence of an experiment to attempt to ascertain levels of fluorescence) 'emanations' from uranium as a result of photographic paper becoming exposed while in contact with uranium. This is what Marie and Pierre Curie would later name 'radioactivity'. An article in *The Manchester Guardian* from 1902 excitedly discussed a talk at the Royal Institution by Henri Becquerel on the links between 'X-rays' and the remarkable properties of uranium, and it became increasingly common for the advances in nuclear physics to be reported in the national press.[15]

In 1898, the Curies extracted two new elements from pitchblende (the ore in which uranium is found) and named them radium and polonium (Figure 2.1). They realized that these were new elements, yet they shared similar characteristics with uranium.[16] As Mahaffey states, 'although they did not fully realise it, the Curies had discovered products of the decay of uranium. These are the heaviest naturally occurring elements, they are very unstable, and they slowly break down into lesser radioactive elements, the last of which is non-radioactive lead.'[17] By the 1900s, the Curies had experienced physical pain in response to working with radioactive materials but, as Mahaffey argues, 'science was still in the fantasy era'.[18] Scientific culture in the early twentieth century was a period defined by optimism and international collaboration, and medical and industrial applications of the newly discovered phenomenon were quickly developed. As Jon Agar notes, 'X-rays were being used to treat cancer within two months of Röntgen's announcement.'[19] As Agar puts it, X-rays proved to be 'only one of several new rays, radiations and particles announced in the closing years of the nineteenth century, and all of them were indications of working world concerns'.[20]

Meanwhile, at the Cavendish Laboratory at Cambridge University, Ernest Rutherford had begun to identify the different types of radiation that invisibly emanated from particular elements. He named the weaker

FIGURE 2.1 *Marie and Pierre Curie, cartoon from* Vanity Fair *(c. 1904). Image published with permission of Wellcome Library, London.*

radiation 'alpha rays' and the stronger radiation 'beta rays'. French scientist Paul Villard discovered 'gamma' rays soon after. Rutherford moved to McGill in Montreal in 1899. Working closely in Canada with English chemist Frederick Soddy, the pair made quick progress in understanding transmutation, atomic decay and the huge amounts of energy involved in these invisible elemental processes. In the most basic terms, the pair discovered that radioactivity was atomic disintegration. These experiments were discussed in Rutherford's 1904 book *Radioactivity*, where he wrote 'there is reason to believe that an enormous store of latent energy is resident in the atoms of radioactive elements [...] if it were ever possible to control at will the rate of disintegration of the radioelements, an enormous amount of energy could be obtained from a small amount of matter'.[21]

In 1907, Rutherford moved to Manchester University to carry on his research. By 1908, he had refined his understanding of alpha rays, proving that the 'rays' were in fact helium atoms, and that a more fitting term 'alpha particles' should be used to describe the radioactivity. In the same year, he was awarded the Nobel Prize for Chemistry. Two years later, Rutherford, along with Marsden and Geiger (who would later develop the Geiger counter), set up the famous 'gold foil' experiment and discovered the nucleus of the atom. Badash explains that in 1911 Rutherford 'proposed that the atom is mostly empty space, with almost all its mass concentrated in a tiny nucleus [...] the nucleus, it became apparent, obeyed some laws of physics that were not familiar in everyday, human-size phenomena'.[22] In 1919, Rutherford demonstrated that certain elements could be artificially disintegrated. It became clear that extremely powerful scientific apparatus would be needed to carry out similar experiments on heavy elements. The challenge was now to build particle accelerators powerful enough to disintegrate particles artificially. In 1932, John Cockcroft and Ernest Walton at the Cavendish were the first to achieve this when they 'split' the atomic nucleus of lithium into helium. This also led to 'experimental confirmation of the famous $E=mc^2$ relationship [...] which Albert Einstein had proposed about a quarter of a century before'.[23] As Badash sums up neatly, 'Radioactivity is the natural disintegration of nuclei, while Rutherford's work described in 1919 was artificial disintegration by natural means [...] the Cockcroft-Walton experiment was artificial disintegration by artificial means.'[24]

One more significant discovery was that of the neutron. Following work from Bothe and Becker in Germany, and Joliot-Curie and Joliot in Paris on 'gamma radiation', James Chadwick conducted a number of experiments in Cambridge that went against the 'gamma radiation' hypothesis. Instead, in 1932 he suggested that the atomic nucleus contained uncharged particles: neutrons. An article in *The Manchester Guardian* made the point that 'the experiments leading up to the discovery of the neutron are international', and that the 'modern conceptions of the nature of matter and the evolution of the elements, and hence of the universe, will be profoundly affected by the new knowledge to be gained from neutrons'.[25] Following these dramatic new understandings in nuclear physics, in 1933 Hungarian physicist Leo Szilard, in a supposed 'eureka' moment that scholars often dwell upon, theorized how to 'set up a nuclear chain reaction, liberate energy on an industrial scale, and construct atomic bombs'.[26] In the same year, Ernest Rutherford claimed that 'anyone who says that with the means at present at our disposal and with our present knowledge we can utilise atomic energy is talking moonshine'.[27] Szilard would later patent his idea, placing it in the name of the British Admiralty in 1936.

In 1938, German chemists Fritz Strassmann and Otto Hahn demonstrated nuclear fission. Lise Meitner and Otto Frisch provided the theoretical explanation for this. Lorna Arnold writes, 'during 1939 it was found that when neutrons – uncharged particles from the nucleus of an atom – bombarded uranium, not only were fission fragments and an immense amount of energy released, but also some spare neutrons which could then split other uranium atoms so that a chain reaction was possible, releasing more and more energy.'[28] As Badash reminds us, 'through all of 1939, information about fission and the possibility of an explosive chain reaction appeared widely in scientific publications and the popular press'.[29] Early in 1939, this was also related to the possibility of a devastatingly powerful new weapon in *The Sunday Express*. The article was breathlessly headlined 'Scientists make an amazing discovery; stumble on a power "too great to trust humanity with"; a whole country might be wiped out in one second'. This sensationalist language continued into the article where readers are told that 'science stands on the threshold of a release of power so vast that no one knows what will happen [...] the potential energy which might be released in this experiment would be capable of blowing up the whole of England'.[30] Although the tone is sensationalist, the article contains a significant level of detail about nuclear physics. The piece demonstrates the motif of powerlessness, utilizes a language of universalism and adopts the 'hope and fear' motif which would become more common in years to come.

We have seen how the period up to 1939 proved to be transformative for nuclear science. Scientific discussions were open and international, and developments in nuclear science had mainly positive applications, for instance in the treatment of cancer. The discoveries of the early twentieth century made clear that some naturally occurring elements held enormous amounts of energy, and if methods could be devised to release this energy, this could lead to huge benefits for humanity. Military applications of radioactivity were not pursued prior to or during the First World War, although an article from 1917 dwelt upon peripheral aspects of radium and warfare.[31] In a broader context, the contravention of the 1907 Hague Convention signified by the use of mustard gas during the First World War illustrates the cracks that were appearing in the moral and ethical norms surrounding warfare, as well as the evolving relationship between science and politics.

The popularization and appeal of the exciting possibilities of nuclear science led to its growing impact on British culture more generally. Yet, narratives of disquiet and anxiety also existed in this period. Although some scientists and commentators revealed their misgivings about possible applications of nuclear science, we will see that even some darker nuclear narratives that emerged in this period were hopeful, for instance viewing a potential atomic bomb as the 'weapon to end all wars'. This period saw the birth of the 'nuclear imagination' and the beginnings of the 'benefit' or 'harm' nuclear motif. To understand how this happened, we turn first to journalistic responses to nuclear science in this period.

Journalistic narrative

In the years following the discovery of radium in 1898, there was a growing mass of cultural expression centring on radiation, radioactivity and the issues surrounding its use in society. When the news of these new scientific discoveries reached British society more widely, it is clear that there was a powerful, but limited, response. In time, the nuclear imagination would develop into a significant aspect of life for some people. It would inform stories, help sell a range of products and shape conceptions of the future. The broadsheet press enthusiastically endorsed and promoted the brilliance of the minds responsible for the scientific discoveries and dwelt on the positive potential applications of the discovery of radioactivity.

Articles were authored by specialist science journalists, or scientists themselves, such as Oliver Lodge, and were intended to be educative, promoting the ways in which intellectual and ontological horizons were shifting. *The Manchester Guardian* played a significant role in the popularization of such ideas, through the work of science correspondent J. G. Crowther.[32] The properties of the 'new' radioactive elements were seized upon and elaborated in the national press. Such speculative reportage would shape the public imagination, creating strong motifs that would persist throughout the twentieth century. The press treated discoveries in nuclear science with genuine excitement, dreaming up future uses for radioactive material.[33] A 'vocabulary of wonder' is evident in the press, with an editorial in *The Manchester Guardian* from 1903 stating that

> radium must absorb some form of ambient energy quite unknown to us, to whose action the ordinary substances of the molecular world are indifferent. This energy must be all about us; we cannot gauge its possible resources; yet we knew nothing of it till yesterday, and only know it now as transmuted by radium [...] If only there were more radium in the world we could keep the earth warm with it when the sun went out[34]

The radium phenomenon grew fast, culminating in a craze for radium-inspired products and stories. Medical uses were explored, and *The Manchester Guardian* in 1908 enthusiastically asked whether radium was the 'long-looked-for cancer cure', reminding its readers that 'it is yet too early for us to state definitely what Radium precisely is, and what are the limits of its powers'.[35] As was also the case in America, such pronouncements were sometimes aligned with advertisements for radium potions. The sale of these 'potions' eventually led to calls to regulate the ownership and use of radioactive substances. Viscount Lee of Fareham, who was at the time chairman of the Radium Commission, warned in 1932 that 'a credulous public is being flooded with advertisements of quack radium remedies [...] the preparation or sale of radio-active preparations designed for either internal or external use should be absolutely prohibited [and] it would seem desirable that its importation should be prohibited except under special licence'.[36]

Yet, on the whole, the press treated the discovery of radium as a marker on the road to a brighter, braver world. Kirk Willis outlines what could be called a 'speculative' phase in early nuclear culture, with the bold claims made by scientists like Soddy being tempered by other more cautious scientists, such as Oliver Lodge who warned of 'irresponsible speculation' in 1903.[37] One attempt to sum up the public impact of radium was offered by historian of science Lawrence Badash. From his work, it can be argued that the cultural importance of radium has been under-acknowledged, and that a more detailed analysis of the popular press, fictional texts, scientific discourse and consumer culture leads to a richer understanding of the beginnings of nuclear culture. Badash outlines five categories of analysis, offering insights into the variety of cultural references to radium in the early twentieth century. The impact of radium as both a physical substance and an imaginary construct was significant in American and British culture and shaped a peculiar aspect of the contemporary imagination.

Although Badash concentrates on American publications, his reasoning can be applied to the British context as well. Reflecting on why 'radioactivity [...] found itself a member of a select group with popular appeal', Badash concludes that radioactivity was perceived as a 'useful' science that 'promised to provide benefits for mankind'. Second, radioactivity and radium had the 'aura of surprise, mystery, even romance about it [...] with radium, what mysteries of the nature of matter would be solved? What new regions would be opened?' Badash makes the point that romance, awe and tragedy were often associated with the element, both in terms of its essential properties and human stories that followed it. Third, 'radioactivity was seen as a powerful, even lethal force of nature'. Fourth, its quick transformation into a substance of crucial importance to society meant that the monetary value of radium soared. Lastly, Badash reminds us that much of the journalistic prose 'conveyed recognition of the revolution in scientific ideas'.[38] Borrowing and expanding upon Badash's framework of analysis, it is clear that similar patterns are apparent in British popular responses.

Radium was quickly considered a valuable and precious commodity. The wish for more supplies of this expensive and rare substance was made clear early in the century.[39] The scarcity and high value of radium are demonstrated in the *Daily Mirror* in 1937, stating '£1,000,000 would buy less than half an ounce of it'.[40] Many popular science publications, such as William Hampson's *Radium Explained* (1905), Bertrand Russell's *The ABC of Atoms* (1923) and Oliver Lodge's *Of Atoms and Rays* (1924), stressed the revolution in scientific ideas that was occurring.[41] A. M. Low's 'What's in front now the atom is split', published in *Nash's Pall Mall Magazine*, provided a great deal of information and proves a good example of the amount of knowledge available to the 'lay' public.[42] Readers of the national press learned about the 'useful' applications of nuclear science in the years following the discovery of radioactive substances. In *Practical Teacher*, an article entitled 'Radium and Its Utility to Mankind' explained the possible benefits to society if the scientific discoveries of recent years could be harnessed for a variety of applications.[43] Similar ideas can also be found in cartoons and other articles in the national press. A cartoon from January 1928 in *The Evening Standard* shows a child, who represents the year 1928, looking to 'secrets of the future', which potentially include 'the harnessed atom'. Representative of the exciting possibilities of modernity, nuclear energy is presented as an enthralling and seductive secret.[44]

Radium was also advocated as a miraculous solution to a variety of problems. A report in *The Manchester Guardian* from 1903 stated 'apparently we have in radium a substance having the power to gather up and convert into heat some form of ambient energy with which we are not yet acquainted'.[45] The article was prompted by a report to the Academy of Sciences presented by the Curies and represents the excited speculation about the properties and potential uses of the 'miraculous' element. In 1903, *Daily Mail* readers were told how cancerous tumours were made to disappear after the application of radium[46] and, in 1908, *The Manchester Guardian* reported confidently on the cancer-healing properties of a radium 'salve', created by 'Dr. Shower'. As well as more cosmetic uses of the element, 'men in the London warehouse state that they use it when they have headaches or toothaches, and that the "Salve" almost instantly relieves the pain.' Furthermore, every application has a most magical effect on the skin, and 'all poisonous substances are driven away. All wrinkles are smoothed out [...] the skin becomes as white and smooth and rosy as that of a healthy child.' The readers are told that 'there is absolutely no danger – just a tingling of the skin is felt'.[47] In a less serious manner, the *Daily Mail* predicted the use of radium for nocturnal golf, and 'radium cakes' were also advertised.[48]

Radium was often described as 'a mysterious element', with 'wonderful properties'.[49] Many commentators asked, 'where does the energy come from?' As Jacobs states, 'the identification of nuclear science with alchemy and with the magical worldview (suggested by the new scientific narrative of a world beyond sensory experience) endows nuclear iconography with a profound sense of the supernatural.'[50] It was common for narratives of this era to promote the wondrous potential of the element. Many newspapers carried advertisements for the health benefits of radium, for example

'Radium Treatment'[51] or 'The Radium Cure'.[52] The wonderful properties of radium were stressed in newspapers, with headlines such as 'Is the Sun Made of Radium?' and 'Can Radium Produce Life in Dead Matter?'[53] Even into the 1930s, the benefits of radium were being sold, for instance for beautification purposes as illustrated in the advertisement 'Radium v Grey Hair'[54] (Figure 2.2), or in fashion as a descriptive term for a bright new colour.[55] In 1904, at the 'annual dinner of the New York Technology Club cocktails were served in which a little tube of radium had been dipped'.[56] The extent to which consumer culture embraced radium is striking. Companies took advantage of the seductive aura of mystery and prestige surrounding these precious elements. Fashion houses advertised new dresses containing 'radium' colours as a sign of prestige and a marker of sophisticated femininity for the aspirational middle classes. Radium was also positioned as valuable and fashionable in a more utilitarian sense with the use of radium paint in the manufacture of watches.

Ingersoll watches sold timepieces with 'Radiolite' grade luminous material and in 1917 proclaimed the watch 'The Ideal Xmas Gift' (Figure 2.3). Dwelling on the magical and mysterious properties of radium, the advertisement states, 'the hands and figures are made of Radiolite – a wonderful new substance containing real radium'.[57] Potential buyers were seduced by the image of a glow-in-the-dark dial, and with the suggestion is that life is made easier, the benefits for watch-wearers are plain to see. The advertising attempted to encourage the alignment of masculine and heroic ideals with this prestigious and desirable object. Consumer culture in its most infamous incarnation saw the appearance of 'quack' cures where radium was presented, as Spencer Weart puts it, as the 'elixir' to heal all ills.[58] From the milder extremes, such as an increased incidence of advertising for radioactive spa holidays, the production of radium tonics was fuelled by those seeking freedom from pain. The wide consumption of these tonics not only illustrates an interesting chapter in medical history, but also tells us something about the status of radium in the popular imagination and the contradictory levels of understanding surrounding the benefits and dangers of the substance. In July 1912, it was reported that 'there are immense therapeutic possibilities in water artificially rendered radioactive to a degree much higher than natural water. Apparatus for this purpose is being shown at the British Medical Association in Liverpool next week.'[59] An advert from 1936 (see Figure 2.4) claimed to have an 'inestimable boon to bestow on mankind', and as users 'bask in the energising force of these wonderful rays', they will 'absorb new strength from the rays, giving you back that normal vigour which the fatigues of the day have used up'.[60]

Narratives of mystery and drama involving radium arose within the cultural setting. Tragic stories highlighting the physical injuries suffered by scientists working on radioactive substance were fairly commonplace through the early twentieth century, yet the injuries suffered were often linked with ideas of justified sacrifice and the higher goal of scientific

Nash's—Pall Mall for August, 1934

RADIUM *v.* GREY HAIR

65—and never a Grey Hair!

65—and not a grey hair to be seen. Wonderful! Yet an absolute fact. Let 'CARADIUM' do for you what it has done for thousands of our clients in all parts of the world. 'CARADIUM' will quickly re create, right from the hair roots, the natural colour, health and beauty to your hair. You will look 10 to 20 years younger.

Write for Free Hair Book

'Caradium' is NOT A DYE
CONTAINING RADIO-ACTIVE WATER

Regular application of 'Caradium' will revivify the colour glands of the hair and cause the natural pigment to flow afresh. 'Caradium' Restorer is just as efficacious in cases of premature or inherited greyness or greyness caused by illness, worry or overwork. It is absolutely sure. So natural is the course of restoration that the use of 'Caradium' is absolutely undetectable.

Grey Hair will never appear if CARADIUM IS USED ONCE WEEKLY AS A TONIC

Olive Oil Shampoo Powders. The finest in the world for producing Soft and Glossy hair, 6d. each. Packets of twelve, 5/-.

WARNING.—Ask for Caradium Regd. and see that you get it: imitations are useless.

 REGD.

4/-

A 4/- size is now available for those only slightly grey. 'Caradium' Hair Restorer is obtainable of all good Chemists, Harrods, Whiteleys, Barkers, Selfridge's, Timothy Whites, Boots, Taylor's Drug Stores, etc., or direct in plain wrapper, POST FREE (overseas postage 2/6 extra) from :—
'CARADIUM' (REGD.), 38 Great Smith Street, Westminster, London.

Large Size
7/6

FIGURE 2.2 *'Radium v. Grey Hair'*, Nash's Pall Mall Magazine, *August 1934. Image published with permission of ProQuest. Further reproduction is prohibited without permission.*

FIGURE 2.3 'The Ideal Xmas Gift', Nash's and Pall Mall Magazine, *December 1917. Image published with permission of ProQuest. Further reproduction is prohibited without permission.*

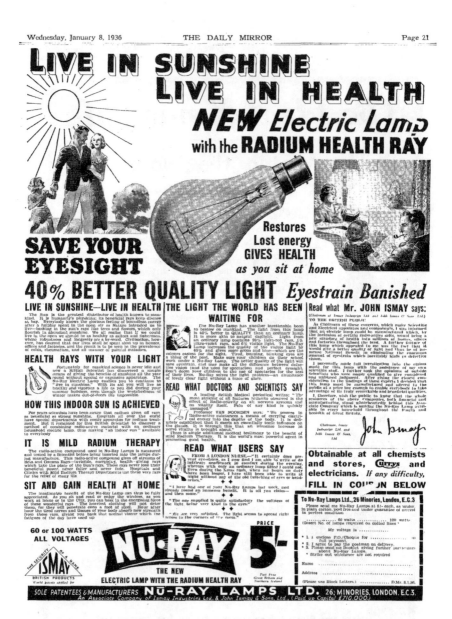

FIGURE 2.4 *'Live in Sunshine, Live in Health'*, Daily Mirror, *8 January 1936. Image published with permission of Mirrorpix.*

discovery. For example, a story in *The Manchester Guardian* spoke in respectful language for a French scientist who 'lost most parts of both arms and hands' is accompanied by the image of resoluteness in the face of terminal peril, where we are told, almost reassured, that the scientist will carry on with his work.[61] In 1929, the national press covered a dramatic story concerning twin brothers in London, Drs Arthur and Sydney Smith. The twins were radiologists who had worked to improve 'radium treatments' and who wrote *Radium in Cancer* in 1927. They committed suicide, stating 'we have given our lives to the study of cancer research. We have reduced ourselves to a state of poverty. Life is not worth living'.[62] They added, 'we pass from this world, a national awakening in radium work having been accomplished – our lives' aim achieved'.[63] *The Guardian* assumed the cause of the suicide was mental 'unbalance' due to overwork and also reported the fact that the brothers were in debt due to them acquiring a significant amount of expensive radium. The narrative echoes Badash's thesis on the dramatic properties of radium, with the national and humanitarian benefits of the work being developed by the doctors adding to the tragedy of the double suicide.

The dangers of radium healing were introduced to the readers of *The Manchester Guardian* in July 1920, when it was reported that the chief of the Department of Radiology at Salpêtrière, Paris, Charles Introut, was a 'martyr to the cause of humanity', because through his work on radium 'science and healing' he had suffered the loss of his left hand and his right arm.[64] A similar narrative appeared in the *Daily Mirror* in 1933, with a report telling the story of a doctor who was about to receive his 'forty-first radium treatment' and 'as a result of voluntarily sentencing himself to a living death in the interests of science, his hands are damaged, one eyelid has been removed, and his chest is scarred with x-ray cancers'. This reminds the contemporary reader about the dangers of radiation and its new related technologies.[65] There were other narratives that stressed the fact that radioactivity was a powerful, even lethal force of nature. In 1919, the physicist Sir Oliver Lodge wrote an article in *The Observer* discussing the 'locked-up energy of the atom' and concluded by saying:

if we found ourselves able to liberate any considerable portion of such energy in a short period of time, the explosive violence would be such that the very planet would be unsafe. It is to be hoped that no such facilities will fall to the lot of an enterprising scientific nation until it is really and humanely civilised; and is both willing and able to keep its destructive power in check. Humanity is not ripe for any and every discovery; but in due time, and when it can be applied to useful and beneficial ends, I doubt not some such power as that here foreshadowed will be attained.[66]

Thus, in this early period of nuclear culture, narratives were positive about the potential benefits of atomic science, demonstrating some optimism over future applications and excitement over the benefits this could bring to humanity. Ambiguity is also apparent, as profound questions over the broader meanings of nuclear science led to uncertainty and anxiety. It is perhaps through fictional narratives where these darker narratives were constructed with the most power.

Fictional narratives

One fascinating aspect of this period is the fact that many of the themes detailed above were also portrayed in popular fiction. Kirk Willis makes the point that almost without exception, novels in this period 'were only incidentally concerned with nuclear energy; most, instead, were either love stories, adventure tales, political satires, or future-war fables [...] all presented atomic energy exclusively as a threat'.[67] Useful scholarly works which outline early atomic fiction include work by Paul Brians and David Dowling.[68] Many histories of the early atomic era mention the links between atomic scientists and fictional authors. John Canaday, for example, attempted to examine 'atomic culture' by 'applying the tools and techniques of literary criticism to uncover the uses of literature in the development and deployment of nuclear weapons and the physics on which they most overtly depend'.[69] Canaday's work has received criticism from some scholars, yet remains a useful source in that the links between literature and atomic science are explained.

Atomic weapons were imagined in a number of early science fiction texts. *The Crack of Doom* by Robert Cromie, published in 1895, contained the first literary reference to a device similar to an atomic weapon. A translation of French author Anatole France's book *Penguin Island* was published in Britain in 1909 and contained references to a type of bomb created 'from a gas which radium evolves'. *The Radium Terrors* by Albert Dorrington (1911) is another early serialized text, while George Griffith, *The Lord of Labour* (1911), involved British scientists using radium bullets. Famously, H. G. Wells became firm friends with Frederick Soddy, and the pair exchanged ideas and influenced each other for many years. As we have seen, radium caught the popular imagination, and one of the best examples of this was within Wells's book *The World Set Free*, published in 1914. Here, Wells wrote about the possibility of an exploding atomic device. Interestingly, this was viewed as a weapon to end all future wars. He describes 'the three atomic bombs, the new bombs that would continue to explode indefinably [...] these atomic bombs which science burst upon the world that night were strange even to the men who used them'.[70] Wells painted a picture of uninhabitable cities, where 'there are stories of puffs of luminous, radio-active vapour drifting sometimes scores of miles from the bomb centre and killing and scorching all they overtook'. This nightmarish vision of modernity, the logic of the continual 'attainment of external power' Wells was so interested in, ends with another marker of modernity: the optimistic belief in a system of government perfectly designed to learn the lessons of the 'weapon to end all wars'. As Willis comments, 'Wells thus produced at once a prescient atomic Armageddon and an ambiguous nuclear millennium.'[71]

The example of Wells's collaborator Soddy sheds light on the close relationship between science and culture. Sclove argues that to understand

Soddy's unique approach to science, one has to understand that 'to achieve his insights, scientific knowledge and logical argument had, in Soddy's instance, to be supplemented by emotional involvement, intense creativity, and social awareness. In each of these respects, Soddy was unmistakably assisted by sources of knowledge entirely outside the usual domain of science.'[72] Crucially however, the example of Soddy highlights the importance of the 'role of so-called "non-scientific" factors within the content and social organisation of science'.[73] The particular combination of non-scientific and scientific factors, mixed with Soddy's personality, allowed his work to be effectively populist, but populist in a deliberate response to the strictures of the scientific community generally. This intellectual 'style' went against the grain. Soddy gave a talk to the Independent Labour Party in 1915 in which he observed that 'from a pound weight of [radioactive] substances one could get about as much energy as would be obtained by burning 150 tons of coal. How splendid! Or a pound weight could be made to do the work of 150 tons of dynamite. Ah! There's the rub. Imagine what the present war would be like if such an explosive had actually been discovered.'[74]

At the end of 'The Last Unscientific War', a 1919 publication by Civis Milesque, a pessimistic tone was struck. In the post-war era, Milesque pondered, 'in the future the objective will be the enemy's towns or munition sources [...] this will be the scientists job. Once man can mobilise natural energy, he can destroy *ad lib*. Such then is the prospect. Science will probably be the real League of Nations. Otherwise the atomic war will come.'[75] J. J. Connington's *Nordenholt's Million* (1923) told the story of a physicist who caused an accidental atomic detonation. 'The Radium Robbery', serialized in the *Daily Mirror* in 1929, used radium simply for its dramatic potential, serving as a peripheral aspect of the central plot (Figure 2.5). Robert Nichols and Maurice Browne wrote *Wings over Europe: A Dramatic Extravaganza on a Pressing Theme* (1928), a play that Charles Carpenter claims was 'the only harbinger of the Atomic Age in dramatic form'.[76] A talented but unhinged young scientist issues the government an ultimatum, either work towards a socialist utopia, or he will inflict upon the country his new discovery, which was a doomsday device capable of turning Britain into 'a whirlpool of disintegrating atoms'. We will see that the motif of the troubled scientist is a common plot device in nuclear-themed fiction and film in years to come. In the same year, a review of Benjamin Harrow's *The Romance of the Atom* featured in *The Bookman*, proclaiming excitedly that 'the atom – the basis of all we call matter – is revealed today as something immaterial, mysterious and mystic [...] the unravelling of the atom, moreover, has been the work of some of the acutest and most radiant intellects the world has seen'.[77] Olaf Stapledon was the first author to imagine the nuclear mushroom cloud. Stapledon, who taught philosophy at Liverpool University in the 1930s, wrote in his science fiction story *Last and First Men* (1930),

Page 20   THE DAILY MIRROR   Saturday, February 2, 1929

WHO IS GUILTY?

NEW SERIES OF COMPLETE STORIES
by Evelyn Johnson and Gretta Palmer

CHAPTER I.

No. 8—THE RADIUM ROBBERY

WILLIAM BASSET, M.D., author of "Pep, the Panacea," boarded the train at Chicago with the satisfaction that comes from a duty well and ostentatiously performed.

He had wound up a whirlwind drive through the Middle West, collecting a very respectable sum for the Michigan institute which was astute enough to include him among the more visionary members of its staff.

His methods, founded on the principles of the latest inspirational psychology, had left behind him a trail of bewildered philanthropists who were unprepared to meet, in a mild medico begging for donations, the high-pressure methods

There was, moreover, another strong reason why privacy was essential on this short trip.

Not the least part of Basset's mission to Chicago had been to receive, from the hands of an awed bank president, a shipment of radium valued at a quarter of a million dollars, which was destined for the research laboratories of his prosperous institution.

The event had been celebrated at a luncheon

His was a penetrating physician, Emil Jaccard, of a type which Basset, in more happy moments, would have described as "one of those backdated, old-fashioned doctors, who think their whole job is to give pills and cut out tonsils without boasting the profession."

from before his eyes, and complete unconsciousness descended on the doctor.

When he came to he found that the train was still roaring ahead. He immediately groped for his Pullman bag with a foreboding of the truth. The radium, in its lead case, had vanished.

Half turning he saw with amazement a dark brown hand . . . just as he smelt a strong whiff of chloroform.

common to insurance salesmen and the young ministers. Basset sank complacently into the green plush of his compartment and watched the porter struggling with the elaborate pigskin bags which always accompanied him on his travels. As the perspiring negro heaved three large suitcases up to the rack, Basset bit the 'end from his cigar and pointed to the remaining Pullman bag.

"Never mind that, George, just put it next to the seat here. Go buy yourself a house and lot with this," and Basset pressed a quarter into the porter's hand with all the aplomb of a multi-millionaire bestowing a new dime.

William Basset, M.D., glanced with distaste at the narrow corridor that ran on the opposite side of the car. There was something dashed unsociable about these compartment cars—they lacked the bonhomie of the smoker and the neighbourliness provided by long rows of shoes, identical with one's own, protruding from beneath green curtains.

But the Appearance of Prosperity was one of the fundamental tenets of the Basset mail-order philosophy, and its exponent dared not be caught purchasing a single berth.

at which eminent scientists were induced to doff their white jackets and attempt the tenor of "There's a Long, Long Trail," at the instigation of Basset, who earnestly assured them that "if Hippocrates had been alive to-day, fellows, he would have been a Christian and a go-getter."

The radium, when it was finally entrusted to Basset, presented a singularly unimpressive appearance.

The lead container which prevented its injuring the health of the person handling it, was about the size of an ordinary brick, and the case was finally placed by Basset in his Pullman bag, between a copy of "Salesmanship and Success" and a quart of Scotch whisky.

Radium, after all, is not a substance favoured by any burglars who have a sense of self-preservation.

Nature, to him, was merely a convenient source for sentiments appropriate to an inspirational address. After three hearty high-balls he slipped into the corner of his seat, his head half turned to the closed door, and promptly fell into a heavy sleep.

Some five hours later, only a few miles away from the town where plaudits awaited the physician, the train turned a sharp curve and puffed into sight of the lovely little lake, set about with cheap resorts, which was a favourite vacation spot with middle-class Chicagoans.

For several miles here the tracks ran along the lakeside with only a six-foot stone wall between them and the water. It was a sight which made most of the occupants of the train gasp with excitement, but Basset continued to doze peacefully.

He was rudely aroused by a gleam of light that dazzled his eyes as the sun hit a shiny object a few feet to his left.

Half turning he saw with amazement that it was held by a dark brown hand which emerged from a white sleeve that reached through the door, just as he smelt a strong whiff of chloroform.

Then the brightness of the afternoon slid

leaving a dreadful lacuna between the half-empty bottle of Scotch and the book on success.

Basset reached for the porter's bell and ran out into the corridor screaming the news that he had been robbed.

When the porter arrived he looked at the staggering medico with concern and understanding as he saw the empty glass on the table.

"What were you doing in there, you thieving devil?" thundered the irate passenger. "Call the conductor. You've stolen something out of my bag, and unless you give it back I'll murder you!"

While the negro quivered in terror, and passengers hurried from the doors of all the other compartments in the air, Basset continued to roar and threaten until the conductor arrived.

When that dignitary hastened from another he immediately had the train stopped and dispatched men of the train crew back to search the tracks for the past few miles on the chance that the radium might have been thrown overboard.

THE MAN IN THE BOAT

HE found that Basset's car was between the engine and the diner, and as no one had gone through the train in either direction for the past hour, and everyone who had boarded the car at Chicago was still present, it was logical to suppose that both the robber and his loot would be found close at hand.

Basset had fortunately a clear impression of having glimpsed the blue of the lake from the window in the moment before the anaesthetic took effect, so that the time of the robbery could be placed within the past half-hour, after the train had taken its curve and turned along the lakeside.

Suspicion naturally attached to the porter, the only negro on the car, and a thorough search of his frightened person, his cabinets, and all berths and hiding places open to him was made. Every place which could conceivably contain the lead case was probed by a dozen official fingers. The passengers were then treated to the same extravagantly careful search.

There were five other occupied compartments in the car.

In one of these was an innocuous clergyman, travelling alone, in another a young wife with her two small children, in a third a respectable middle-aged banker and his wife, and in the fourth an acidulous schoolteacher of the musical comedy spinster type.

The possessions of none of these yielded a suspicious trace.

The occupant of the fifth compartment, however, gave the investigators a chance to exchange knowing glances and warm to the search.

Jaccard had not even an old-fashioned medical requisite as a charming bedside manner. He boasted a scientifically ruthless intelligence, a great capacity for work, and an extraordinary cupidity.

It was his firm intention soon to demonstrate the fallacy of the belief that professional men are naive in matters of business, and already, by a few astute investments, he had mounted up a comfortable fortune at an age when most physicians are looking about for another year of internship.

He was setting out for a short holiday at a small lake resort a few miles farther on, and his luggage, when carefully examined, proved to consist of a very simple wardrobe including his surgeon's jacket, the most elementary of fishing tackle, a small medical kit, and a volume on the fascinating habits of the human liver under certain circumstances.

His medical kit held only such simple remedies as argyrol, novocaine and iodine and two extra-professional flasks, each half filled with brandy.

There was no trace of chloroform or of any instrument by means of which it could be sprayed across the compartment.

None the less, a guard was set to watch Jaccard's movements after he was allowed to depart to his fishing resort.

The search of the tracks had yielded only the barren information that the radium was certainly not to be found there and could only have been thrown, on either side of the tracks, into a good twelve feet of water.

Passengers on the back platform of the observation car testified that there had been no one along the tracks who could have acted as accomplice for someone on the train.

The detectives on Jaccard's trail kept out of sight as much as possible during the following days, which he spent in serenely following his programme and fishing in a rented rowboat all over the lake.

On one of his many trips, however, they saw him row rather close to the railroad track at a point near the place where the robbery was supposed to have occurred.

They saw nothing extraordinary in his movements from a little distance, and were assured that he did not leave the boat.

But as he rowed back to the hotel, his line still out, they approached him, under the guise of friendly fishermen, and managed to get a very good peep at the interior of the rowboat.

They saw nothing but an obviously empty bailing can and an extra line and bobbin.

There was not even a string of fishes on which to centre their attentions, and Jaccard's light-fitting clothing eliminated any possibility of his having secreted the radium, no matter how mysteriously obtained, about his person.

How were all traces concealed by the robber? What happened to the radium after its removal from Basset's luggage?

The solution will be published next Saturday.

FIGURE 2.5 *'The Radium Robbery', serialized in the* Daily Mirror, *1929. Image published with permission of Mirrorpix.*

For a dazzling point of light appeared on the remote cliff. It increased in size and brilliance, till all eyes were blinded in the effort to continue watching. It lit up the under parts of the clouds and blotted out the sun-cast shadows of gorse bushes besides the spectators. The whole end of the island facing the mainland was now an intolerable scorching sun. Presently, however, its fury was veiled in clouds of steam from the boiling sea. Then suddenly the whole island, three miles of solid granite, leapt asunder; so that a covey of great rocks soared heavenward, and beneath them swelled more slowly a gigantic mushroom of steam and debris. Then the sound arrived. All hands were clapped to ears, while eyes still strained to watch the bay, pocked white with the hail of rocks.[78]

In 1932, Harold Nicolson, author and diplomat, published *Public Faces*. Although, as Brians notes, 'Nicolson was less interested in technical matters than in the political manoeuvring of the great powers in which peace and British supremacy are ensured by the boldly illegal stroke of an imaginative, headstrong minister',[79] Nicolson introduces the idea of the necessity of disarmament, in this case brought about by the threat of atomic destruction. J. B. Priestley published *The Doomsday Men* in 1937, signalling an early signpost in his own nuclear century. Fictional narratives in this era not only expressed some of the difficult choices at the heart of human mastery of atomic science, but also simplified and polarized the nuclear future in their articulation of the atomic crossroads. Fictional narratives dwelt on the political and military implications of atomic science and the dangerous potential for destruction on a vast and unimaginable scale. The unbelievable scale at the heart of these fictional narratives made the nuclear future seem both imaginable and unimaginable.

Towards the atomic bomb: MAUD to Nagasaki, 1940–1945

As Europe descended into war in the late 1930s, scientists working outside Germany became increasingly concerned that an atomic project could be underway in Nazi Germany. The Einstein-Szilard letter of 2 August 1939 urged President Roosevelt to seriously contemplate the possibility that German scientists were working towards developing an atomic bomb. In a report from 1939 entitled 'Radium Danger in War-time', readers of *The Manchester Guardian* were informed that radium would be buried in the event of war 'in special boreholes fifty feet deep',[80] reinforcing the potential danger of radioactive contamination in the event of war. The 'Frisch-Peierls Memorandum' of 1940 is one of the more significant sources for nuclear historians. In this report, two Birmingham-based émigré scientists, Otto Frisch and Rudolf Peierls, offered calculations on two practical aspects of atomic bomb design. First, they argued that only a relatively small amount of uranium-235 would be needed to create a powerful atomic explosion. If the calculations were correct, a deliverable atomic weapon was feasible. Second, the scientists went into detail regarding the industrial processes involved in separating the isotope uranium-235 from the element uranium. Lastly, the memorandum discussed the severe and lasting injuries and damage that radiological weapons would inflict, the 'strategic and moral implications',[81] and the importance of keeping the report top secret.[82]

> 'The energy liberated by a 5 kg bomb would be equivalent to that of several thousand tons of dynamite, while that of a 1 kg bomb, though about 500 times less, would still be formidable [...] For the separation of the U235, the method of thermal diffusion, developed by Clusius and others, seems to be the only one which can cope with the large amounts required [...] Effective protection is hardly possible. Houses would offer protection only at the margins of the danger zone. Deep cellars or tunnels may be comparatively safe from the effects of radiation, provided air can be supplied from an uncontaminated area.'
>
> Frisch-Peierls Memorandum, March 1940

The report provided the impetus for the establishment of the top-secret MAUD Committee whose 1941 report, in turn, was offered to the American government for consideration.[83] To begin with, it appeared that the Americans were not interested in the MAUD report, but after a persuasive visit to the United States by Australian physicist Marcus Oliphant, the American Uranium Committee sought presidential approval for the development of the atomic bomb. Meanwhile, in the same year, gaseous diffusion was attempted at Rhydymwyn, North Wales, in an attempt to isolate uranium-235 as part of the secret British and Canadian atomic programme, codenamed 'Tube Alloys'. However, in 1942, British, Canadian and American atomic efforts were combined to form the Manhattan Project, and in December of that year, the first nuclear chain reaction was sustained in a nuclear pile below Stagg Fields, at the University of Chicago. Led by Enrico Fermi, the Chicago project site was one of over thirty Manhattan Project sites in America, Britain and Canada. British scientists played a significant role in the Manhattan Project, and the historical research of Ferenc Szasz excellently captures the varied contributions made by them, and James Cockcroft summed up his own early work towards the bomb in *The Listener* in March 1947.[84] Andrew Brown and Christoph Laucht are among those who have researched the contributions émigré scientists made to the atomic weapons programme.[85]

The Manhattan Project led to international agreements and eventual knowledge sharing between Britain and America. The Quebec Agreement from 1943 was an important collaborative agreement, stating 'in the field of scientific research and development there shall be full and effective interchange of information and ideas between those in the two countries engaged in the same sections of the field', but one central agreement at the beginning of the document reads:

> in view of the heavy burden of production falling upon the United States as the result of a wise division of war effort, the British Government recognize that any post-war advantages of an industrial or commercial character shall be dealt with as between the United States and Great Britain on terms to be specified by the President of the United States to the Prime Minister of Great Britain. The Prime Minister expressly disclaims any interest in these industrial and commercial aspects beyond what may be considered by the President of the United States to be fair and just and in harmony with the economic welfare of the world.[86]

'First, that we will never use this agency against each other. Secondly, that we will not use it against third parties without each other's consent. Thirdly, that we will not either of us communicate any information about Tube Alloys to third parties except by mutual consent.'

Quebec Agreement, 19 August 1943

Thus, there was some ambiguity over the leadership role Britain would play in the longer term. But, uncertainty faded when on 19 September 1944 Churchill and Roosevelt agreed that 'full collaboration between the United States and the British Government in developing tube alloys for military and commercial purposes should continue after the defeat of Japan unless and until terminated by joint agreement'.[87] In April 1945, Roosevelt died, leading to a situation that complicated the atomic relationship between the UK and the United States. The secret 1944 agreement was misfiled by the Americans, paving the way to non-cooperation in the post-war era as the agreement was not immediately acknowledged by the Americans. In May 1945, the war with Germany ended. Even as it became clear that Germany did not have the capability to build and use an atomic bomb, the Manhattan Project continued. Only physicist Joseph Rotblat left the project at this time. Prime Minister Winston Churchill's agreement regarding the use of the atomic bomb against Japan is summed up by Jones, where 'following discussion between Stimson and Wilson, in early July 1945 British assent to the bomb's use was duly indicated in a minute of the Combined Policy Committee'.[88] As Hennessy explains in *Cabinets and the Bomb*, Churchill made the decision not to include the War Cabinet in discussion over the atomic bomb before its use. Only a small handful of government officials were aware of its existence.[89]

Using atomic weapons

The creation of the atomic bomb is narrated in extraordinary detail in Richard Rhodes's *The Making of the Atomic Bomb*. In his book, Rhodes charts the complex development of the weapon and paints a vivid picture of the first atomic explosion, 'Trinity', which occurred in July 1945. Famously, scientists put bets on the likelihood of the device causing the earth's atmosphere to ignite, signifying the uncertainty surrounding the untested device. The success of the first atomic bomb test meant a decision had to be made over the use of the bomb in the war against Japan. Although Manhattan Project scientists wrote a petition arguing for a demonstration of the weapon before use against real targets, the decision to use the atomic bomb against Japan was made after consultation with a number of committees and British and Canadian officials.[90] There is little doubt that anti-Japanese sentiment within American government, and America more generally, influenced the decision.[91] The escalation and normalization of indiscriminate airborne bombing by 1945 meant that the bombing of a target city with a significant civilian population had become a common feature of warfare, and so the target list included the heavily populated cities of Hiroshima and Nagasaki. The American military prepared for the mission, with a B-29 specially adapted for the role. Colonel Paul W. Tibbets captained the plane and also renamed it the *Enola Gay*. After completing its mission to deliver uranium-235 and bomb components to Tinian Island, the USS *Indianapolis* was torpedoed and sunk on its outward journey, resulting in the death of 879 crewmen.

There is still little historical consensus over the decision to use the atomic bomb against Japan.[92] The consensus that emerged in the years following 1945 was that the bomb was used to shorten the war, saving hundreds of thousands of American lives in the process. There were dissenting voices shortly after the war including Patrick Blackett, a British physicist earlier involved with the MAUD Committee who, in 1948, argued that the use of the atomic bombs against the Japanese was the first act of the Cold War against the USSR.[93] Yet, it was not until the 1960s that a detailed historical interpretation was offered by Gar Alperovitz, who argued that the atomic bomb was unnecessary as a weapon of war and was essentially used as a diplomatic weapon to lessen the threat of the Soviet Union in the early Cold War context.[94] Alperovitz has been criticized by some historians, most notably Robert J. Maddox who charged Alperovitz with wilfully distorting the evidence to suit his argument.[95] Partly because of these debates, historical attention is often focused away from the victims of the atomic bombings. As we will see in Chapter 3, the human, environmental, political and cultural after-effects of the atomic bombings of Hiroshima and Nagasaki proved to be severe, localized and global. The world could never be the same again, but neither could the lives of nearly half a million Japanese *Hibakusha*.

ATOMIC AND NUCLEAR WEAPONS

Nuclear weapons rank as one of the most delicate, dangerous and technically advanced inventions created by humans. When detonated, they create massive blast, heat and radiation effects. The first atomic bombs were **fission** weapons, where fissile isotopes of uranium or plutonium were forced to become supercritical, creating a huge release of energy. Their 'yield' is measured in the kiloton (kt) range. The bomb used on Hiroshima was measured at 16kt, which is the equivalent of 16,000 tonnes of TNT. Although devastating on an enormous scale, these weapons were dwarfed by the development of **fusion**, or thermonuclear weapons in the 1950s which are measured in the megaton (mt) range. Like the sun, the energy produced by these weapons is created by the fusion of two isotopes of hydrogen: deuterium and tritium. This fusion is initiated by a fission reaction, making this a more complex weapon. The energy emitted by thermonuclear weapons is vast. The largest weapon detonated by the UK was 3mt, or an equivalent yield of 3 million tonnes of TNT.

Conclusion

If we are to understand British nuclear culture as the different ways in which 'people controlled, responded to or represented nuclear science and technology', then by the end of 1945, British society was beginning to be shaped by the applications of nuclear science in powerful ways. The political and military establishment had become heavily involved in the creation of the atomic bomb, and the expertise developed during this phase would carry over into the Cold War era (the subject of Chapter 3). Perhaps the most important development in this period was the *institutionalization* of nuclear knowledge during the later secret phase. Defined by an international culture of openness and pure scientific enquiry in the early years of the twentieth century, by the end of the Second World War, the secretive Manhattan Project succeeded in applying nuclear knowledge to create a weapon that surpassed the normal considerations of the military and political elite. Owing to the secrecy of the project, and the fact the war was still continuing in the Pacific, public consultation over the development and use of the weapon was, understandably, impossible. A tiny group of men decided this weapon would be used, and this set the pattern for nuclear weapons development and testing after 1945. Nuclear knowledge and infrastructure became institutionalized first in America, but other countries would soon follow. The ingredients were in place for Britain to create its own permanent, institutionalized, secret, expensive and dangerous nuclear project. As we will see in Chapter 3, the decision to pursue the British independent nuclear deterrent was made by a tiny portion of the male establishment. The absence of democratic consideration on this question meant that nuclear weapons development remained outside the remit of democratic politics while serving as the one single development that had the most potential to ruin health, happiness and life. The paradox of nuclear deterrence was created.

In terms of British culture more widely, several motifs emerged in this period which would continue after 1945. Throughout the early nuclear era there was ambiguity in popular responses to nuclear science and technology. The vast majority of these responses came from a position of partial knowledge of the status of nuclear science and medicine, and could often be placed in either a narrative of fear or hope. Knowledge of the medical applications of radiation were advancing fast, and new institutions which specialized in radiation therapy included the Marie Curie Hospital in London, which was bombed in 1944 (Figure 2.6). Yet, the unofficial narratives which emerged in this era were speculative, often emotionally charged, and played on the sensational and horrendous possibilities of nuclear science. These were dramatic narratives that reflected a sense of powerlessness in the face of the

FIGURE 2.6 *William Lionel Clause, 'Rescuing the Radium at the Marie Curie Hospital', 1944 © Imperial War Museums (Art.IWM ART LD 4045).*

new scientific discoveries that were being unlocked. Although it is possible to define the origins of 'official' and 'unofficial' nuclear narratives in the era up until 1945, it is in the years that follow that we see these narratives clashing in a sustained and public manner, creating the tensions and debates that came to define British nuclear culture.

Cultural representations of nuclear science in this early period were defined by imaginative frameworks that echoed broader social and political norms and popular scientific understanding. While nuclear-themed stories speculated about the sensational impact nuclear science could have on life, politics and society on individual and collective levels, the national press increasingly echoed and reinforced the tone and sentiment of nuclear fiction. Official narratives speak of the increasing desire and need to control nuclear knowledge and to be able to apply nuclear science to technologies that would serve military and national interests. These interests were dictated at once by the need to ensure totalitarian regimes did not develop atomic weapons, curiosity over whether an atomic bomb could be created and the longer term geopolitical advantages such technologies would give the nation. As we will see, the secrecy of the military atomic projects continued into the post-war years, where the development of the 'civilian' British atomic project was also shrouded in secrecy, with relevant official institutions filtering and shaping the public reception of atomic knowledge. Echoing Zygmunt Bauman's ideas over the pervasive 'bureaucratic culture' that is part of the logic of modernity, the technological and bureaucratic conditions for the creation of the Manhattan Project meant that scientists created an atomic weapon without being accountable for its use.[96] In the dust of the New Mexico desert, isolated from their peers, scientists worked on their segregated experiments and became divorced from the responsibility of the creation of the bomb. The use of such a weapon had still only been imagined.

CHAPTER THREE

Early Responses to the Bomb, 1945–1950

Brighter than a thousand suns

At 8.15 am on 6 August 1945, 600 metres above Hiroshima, Japan, an explosive device containing uranium-235 detonated, creating what later became rationalized as 16 kilotons of energy. Three days later on 9 August, a different 'implosion' device containing plutonium-239 exploded 500 metres above Nagasaki with an explosive yield of 21 kilotons. This convergence of scientific and military expertise initiated unprecedented levels of human violence and suffering, and devastation on a vast scale (Figure 3.1). The huge energy and heat caused by these weapons incinerated organic matter across huge swathes of land and caused metal structures to bend. Shortly after both blasts, firestorms started which decimated the cities further. For those people who survived the initial aftermath of the bombings, there followed the unknown danger of acute radiation poisoning, as radioactive fallout from the bombs fell to earth. In the longer term, *Hibakusha* – atom bomb survivors – would suffer an array of illnesses ranging from wounds with impaired healing to a range of cancers, decreased fertility and genetic mutation. *Hibakusha* would also suffer from a range of psychological disorders and would be ostracized from mainstream society in the years following 1945.[1] Between 150,000 and 246,000 women, children and men were killed by the atomic bombings of Hiroshima and Nagasaki. Controversy remains over the decision to target these two cities, with their large civilian populations. Unlike any other weapon created by humankind, atomic weapons created an unpredictable toxic, human and environmental legacy.[2]

SURVIVING THE ATOMIC BOMB

Testimony of Michie Hattori, fifteen years old when she survived the Nagasaki atomic bomb:

'When the bomb exploded, it caught me standing in the entrance to the shelter, motioning for the pokey girls to come in. First came the light – the brightest light I have ever seen. It was an overcast day, and in an instant every object lost all colour and blanched a brilliant white. My eyes couldn't cope, and for a little while I went blind. A searing hot flash accompanied the light that blasted me. For a second I dimly saw it burn the girls standing in front of the cave. They appeared as bowling pins, falling in all directions, screaming and slapping at their burning school uniforms [...] My hands and face singed, intense pain gripped my body. I tried to walk a little and stumbled over a fallen tree. I lay there, not knowing for sure where I was or whether something else may happen to me. When my sense, including my sight, began returning, I heard crying from the girls in front of the shelter. All, except one, were now standing and blowing on their skin. Looking at the one lying down, I saw her leg twisted at a crazy angle [...] the face and hands of the other girls quickly turned bright red.'[3]

Taken as a whole, nuclear histories do not focus much attention upon the victims of the atomic bombings. Why do you think this is? Does this change your opinion of nuclear historiography?

Although conventional weapons also created mass devastation and death during the Second World War, the atomic bomb introduced completely new categories of violence. The vast and indiscriminate power of the bomb meant that conventional shelters, hospitals and other vital services were rendered useless. The immediate blast effects created unimaginable destruction, including instant incineration of human beings, collapsed buildings and huge firestorms. Much of the immediate and longer term consequences of the blast were inescapable. The longer term effects ranged from acute radiation poisoning from fallout – which could cause death in a matter of days – to a range of reproductive disorders, cancers and genetic mutation in the years following the single attack. Of course, the victims of the atomic bombings had no knowledge of the dangers of fallout in the aftermath.

In the immediate aftermath of the bombing, a scientific survey of the bomb sites was carried out. In 1946, The US Government Printing Office published information on atomic bomb victims in *The Effects of the Atomic Bombs on Hiroshima and Nagasaki*. The report, compiled by the US Strategic Bombing Survey begins, 'the available facts about the power of the atomic bomb as a military weapon lie in the story of what it did at Hiroshima and Nagasaki. Many

FIGURE 3.1 *Atomic bomb damage: aftermath of the atomic bomb in Hiroshima* © *Imperial War Museums (MH 29447).*

of these facts have been published, in official and unofficial form, but mingled with distortions or errors.' The report states that 'the "fire-wind" attained a maximum velocity of 30 to 40 miles per hour, 2 to 3 hours after the explosion. The "fire-wind" and the symmetry of the built-up center of the city gave a roughly circular shape to the 4.4 square miles which were almost completely burned out.'[4] The report continues, 'in Nagasaki, no fire storm arose, and the uneven terrain of the city confined the maximum intensity of damage to the valley over which the bomb exploded. The area of nearly complete devastation was thus much smaller; only about 1.8 square miles. Casualties were lower also; between 35,000 and 40,000 were killed, and about the same number injured.' On the specific consequences of the effects of radiation, the report reads 'our understanding of radiation casualties is not complete. In part the deficiency is in our basic knowledge of how radiation affects animal tissue.' In the words of Dr Robert Stone of the Manhattan Project:

> The fundamental mechanism of the action of radiation of living tissues has not been understood. All methods of treatment have therefore been symptomatic rather than specific. For this reason, studies into the fundamental nature of the action of radiation have been carried on to some extent, the limitation being that it was unlikely that significant results could be obtained during the period of war.[5]

The report, written with the tone of scientific authority, does not attend to the suffering of the victims but attempts to understand the effects of the bomb, leading to a preoccupation with the atomic bomb as signalling the start of an experiment, whose results are not yet properly understood. A comparable report was created by British scientists in 1946, entitled *The Effects of Atomic Bombs on Hiroshima and Nagasaki: Report of the British Mission to Japan*. In a similar way to the American report, there is scientific detachment when victims are discussed (see Figure 3.2), and through the veil of scientific authority, it is clear that a great deal of uncertainty pervades scientific thinking over the effects of the bombs. Jacob Bronowski, one of the scientists who visited Hiroshima soon after the attack, wrote the following in *The Listener* in 1946.

The bombs were intentionally exploded at a considerable height, so that the ground would not be impregnated with radio-active products of the atomic fission [...] penetrating radiation had an indirect effect,

FIGURE 3.2 *In the report, the text that accompanied this image demonstrated the scientific preoccupation with textures and 'shadowing'. Rationalized material consequences are aligned with an unimaginable new form of death: instant incineration. It could be argued that the world has never come to terms with the complex meanings of atomic victimhood. Image from* The Effects of the Atomic Bombs on Hiroshima and Nagasaki: Report of the British Mission to Japan *(1946). HMSO. Crown Copyright.*

for it did not attack the blood itself, but destroyed or damaged the bone marrow which normally replenishes the cells in the bloodstream as the body naturally uses them up. Therefore irradiated people showed no symptoms for a day or two, until the cells in the blood began to be used up and not replaced. Nothing could be done for these people, and they died within one to six weeks [...] with these thousands died other thousands of unborn in the womb: there were few live births in these cities in the succeeding two months.[6]

The official articulation of Britain's role in the atomic bomb project can be found in the 1945 British Information Services report entitled 'Statements Relating to the Atomic Bomb', which was published in *Reviews of Modern Physics*.[7] This was not particularly well received by British scientists, including Chadwick, who felt it 'failed, almost completely, to emphasise the value of the British contribution'.[8]

As the post-war era progressed, there was dissent among those involved in the development of atomic weaponry. We saw in Chapter 2 that MAUD Committee member Patrick Blackett argued that the use of the atomic bombs in anger was primarily intended as the first Cold War act against the Soviet Union. Other British scientists contributed to an international anti-nuclear agenda in the years after 1945. These voices proved to be some of the more influential ones, as the British public contributed to discussions over the morality of atomic weapons. Just one example of responses to the atomic bombing of Japan was a letter written to the *Times* from January 1947, which asked why the atomic bomb was not demonstrated at sea. This letter represents one of the fragments of a growing public discourse over the morality of the use of atomic weapons in war.[9] Through detailed press reports, the British people heard the news that an atomic bomb had been dropped on Hiroshima, Japan. As we will see in this chapter, individual responses to the bomb were profoundly personal, often emotional, and rooted in a complex set of political, economic, social and spiritual anxieties in the immediate post-war era. Analysis of the period between 1945 and 1950 suggests that official and unofficial narratives were varied, and many reflected the problematic meanings of the atomic bomb, for humanity and for British life.

Historiography on the victims of Hiroshima and Nagasaki can be defined by a movement away from linear description and statistical objectification, to one that seeks to understand atomic victimhood, Hiroshima in popular and political memory, and the broader legacies and meanings of *Hibakusha*. Too often, nuclear histories do not go beyond the numerical rationalization of atomic victims, although some scholars have offered studies that problematize and conceptualize atomic victimhood and atomic survival.[10] Scholars of the nuclear age have often looked to 1945 as marking a significant juncture in modern history. From the American perspective, Jacobs writes, 'from the very start of the atomic age, nuclear narratives spilled over into the fantastic [...] whether the expectation was dystopian or utopian, the bomb affected a rupture, separating the normality of the past from the uncertainty of the future – a marker that we had entered a transformed – and transformative – landscape.'[11] Although the idea of a historical 'rupture' is a seductive one, it could be argued that as the post-war period progressed, there were also some continuities with earlier nuclear culture. The nuclear imagination dwelt on the familiar motif of the 'atomic crossroads', although it is clear that nuclear issues had a growing impact on everyday life, especially with the advent of a publicized global nuclear arms race, initiated with the American atomic tests at Bikini Atoll in 1946. We will see that there was a transformation in British government, as the nuclear state was born in secret. A huge scientific project was undertaken, with significant amounts of money invested in nuclear weapons development in an era where domestic social problems were vast. This financial investment signalled a commitment to the nuclear state for generations to come, establishing a hazardous and expensive legacy of nuclear waste, decommissioning and many other factors. Any moral and ethical questions were superseded by questions of national security and preoccupations over national prestige. The 'atomic crossroads' motif continued in public discourse, and the press became increasingly saturated with nuclear reports and opinion, British and global in focus. The British press only ever received partial information from the nuclear state due to the secrecy surrounding the British nuclear project and an effective system of 'D-Notices' which prevented certain information from appearing in the press.[12] In this sense, the 'official' nuclear narrative shaped journalistic representations of the nuclear state to a large degree.

The rest of this chapter charts the ambiguous official and unofficial responses to the dropping of the atomic bombs on Japan. It also charts the way in which the government institutionalized nuclear technology as a significant (but hidden) part of the post-war nation state. By 1949, Britain was well on the way to creating both a workable atomic bomb and a nuclear power station capable of supplying energy to the national grid. These were top-secret projects, but the legacy of Hiroshima and Nagasaki, further American weapons testing from 1946 and uncertainty surrounding global developments in nuclear technology ensured nuclear issues were a constant presence in British journalistic discourse. Groups of intellectuals, theologians, artists and scientists discussed and took the first steps towards nuclear activism of different kinds. Government thinking on atomic development was influenced strongly by the perceived loss of influence in global geopolitics due to the decline of the British Empire and the rise of the United States and the Soviet Union as the post-war superpowers. As we will see in this chapter, tensions emerged after 1945 as official narratives clashed with new unofficial narratives, and we can use a variety of primary source materials to map how this complex and ambiguous phenomenon affected everyday life. This chapter includes original research, especially utilizing the newly digitized newspaper archives, oral history testimony, fiction, film and government files. The lives and dreams of ordinary Britons began to be powerfully shaped by knowledge of the bomb.

Context and historiography

In the international context, while Britain's colonial role was diminishing, its global position would be influential in the emerging Cold War. Winston Churchill's famous 'iron curtain' speech of 1946 began to cement the polarization of ideologies. There was some optimism in the West with the creation of the United Nations in 1945 and then NATO in 1949, but when West Germany joined NATO in 1955, the Soviet Union created the Warsaw Pact to secure their geopolitical interests. This decision cemented the geographical, political, economic and military polarization that had been occurring for a decade, with notable events such as the Brussels Treaty (1948), the Berlin Blockade (between 1948 and 1949) and the Korean War (between 1950 and 1953) increasing Cold War tension. For more general background on the Cold War context, two chapters in *The Cambridge History of the Cold War* are particularly helpful. Anne Deighton surveys Britain's changing status as a global power and neatly sums up Britain's position in the immediate post-war years by reminding us that the new Labour government 'had to manoeuvre through uncharted waters, between the commitment to reconstruction, the tough geostrategy required to sustain British global and imperial interests, and the containment of Communism and the Soviet Union'.[13] Domestically, the immediate post-war years in Britain were not dominated by atomic fear, yet atomic issues had an increasingly noticeable impact. Evidence suggests that economic hardship, the national economic crisis and other social issues weighed heaviest on the British people.[14] For instance, food rationing remained in place until 1954, and housing and reconstruction continued to be a serious issue into the 1950s.[15] Britain was a country deeply affected by the experience of war. British politics and society faced a series of unprecedented challenges. There was some optimism, with the radical social reforms put in place by the Labour government elected in 1945.[16] The British Civil Defence Corps was reactivated in July 1948, and rearmament was announced in September 1950, two months before Britain agreed a uranium deal with South Africa.

Our historical understanding of official nuclear decision-making in Britain between 1945 and 1950 has been well supported. In the American context, there are a number of works that deal with nuclear culture in the immediate post-war era,[17] but cultural studies in the British context are minimal. Veldman's *Fantasy, the Bomb and the Greening of Britain* is the most lengthy work to consider the cultural aspects of the early atomic age. Recent work has also dwelt upon the existence of transnational nuclear narratives in the years following 1945.[18] Useful texts which look into post-war nuclear history in considerable detail are Peter Hennessy's *The Secret State* and Margaret Gowing's two-volume official history of the establishment of atomic policy and infrastructure in Britain.[19] More recent texts in the British context are also predominantly 'top-down' in approach, although Matthew Grant's *After the Bomb* does attend to some of the cultural aspects of the nuclear age. Because of the secrecy surrounding nuclear development, historians of modern Britain working in the 1950s to the 1980s didn't have much to say on the relevance of nuclear history and often summarized thoughts on the 'nuclear age' quickly. Arthur Marwick's words from 1968 are typical of many textbook appraisals of the impact of Hiroshima and Nagasaki, when he wrote 'in that it ushered in the age of nuclear weapons, the war was a loss to the whole of civilisation; a new, implacable insecurity entered the everyday life of millions throughout the world'.[20] Historians will often mention the enormity of the atomic bomb, referencing its effect on millions of lives, without offering detailed reflections on how this supposed turning point in history altered British culture. Additionally, historians engaging in nuclear history while public debates on nuclear weapons were raging would have been seen as engaged in highly politicized contemporary history.

When analysing the primary source material in the British context, a comparable glorification of the atomic bomb seen in sections of American society is largely absent. Something unique to the American context – perhaps the memory of Pearl Harbour, or fierce anti-Japanese sentiment more generally – led to a particular form of atomic victory culture that simply did not exist in Britain.[21] With victory secured in Europe after British citizens had endured years of aerial bombardment and the threat of invasion, the dislocation of entire families, economic and emotional hardship, the conditions were not in place for an extravagant and sustained celebration of the atomic bomb. It could also be argued that the news of the atomic bombing was received differently because of the speed with which America claimed the atomic project as its own in the post-war era.[22]

Creating the British independent deterrent

While the British population was slowly coming to terms with life after years of war, the government forged plans to develop its own atomic technology. These decisions would shape and define Britain's Cold War role and subtly influence everyday life for decades to come. After Labour came into power unexpectedly, Gen 75 (The Cabinet Committee on Atomic Energy) was created by Attlee in August 1945.[23] From the evidence, the tone in the first meeting of the committee was both anxious and idealistic, showing a willingness to reach out in international collaboration. Towards the end of the meeting, the point was made that 'no government has ever been placed in such a position as is ours today. The Governments of the UK and the

USA are responsible as never before for the future of the human race.'[24] Wittner argues that swift official movement towards nuclear-weapons development was due to preoccupations over world prestige. Minutes from later Gen 75 meetings seem to confirm this. For instance, a discussion on the expense of the atomic project turned to the fact that 'we could not afford to be left behind in a field which was of such revolutionary importance [...] our prestige in the world, as well as our chances of securing American co-operation would both suffer if we did not exploit to the full a discovery in which we had played such a leading part at the outset'.[25] This can also be read as a failure of political imagination on the behalf of British officials, mixed with paranoia and fears over national insecurity. This also explains the mindset behind subsequent efforts to present nuclear weapons as positive and peaceful. In October 1945, it was decided that the Atomic Energy Research Establishment (AERE) would be set up, and the ministry of supply would be responsible for the AERE. In November, Truman, Attlee and King met in Washington, and the Washington Declaration on atomic energy was agreed. In December, British ministers approved one atomic pile for plutonium production, and the council of foreign ministers agreed to propose a UN Atomic Energy Commission. In 1946, the first UN meeting was held in London.[26]

In January 1946, UK Chiefs of Staff produced a report which detailed how to proceed with British atomic planning.[27] In June 1946, the American 'Baruch Plan' proposed that the United States give up its nuclear arsenal to an international atomic authority. The Soviet Union refused inspection of its own project, and the Plan was vetoed in December. The anxieties of the early Cold War rendered many existing agreements and alliances defunct, and the McMahon Act in 1946 saw America formalize its separation from Britain in atomic knowledge sharing. Historians have argued this was 'a disaster' for Britain,[28] and 'between 1948 and 1958, numerous attempts were made by both Labour and Conservative governments to have the McMahon Act repealed or amended and reopen a nuclear partnership with the United States'.[29] Eventually, 'in January 1948, through the so-called *modus vivendi*, British officials agreed to rescind the "consent" aspects of the 1943 Quebec Agreement, and other areas of nuclear co-operation were placed in cold storage.'[30] Rotter has argued that it is persuasive to see this as one shaped by the 'casualness or inconsistency'[31] displayed by the American administration towards atomic cooperation.

Once it became clear that America would adopt an isolationist atomic policy,[32] the British government committed to an independent nuclear project by early 1947.[33] Baylis and Stoddart argue that it was clear that 'the deep-seated ideas and beliefs inherent in British strategic culture that emphasised Great Power status, the utility of capital weapon systems to deter threats, and the importance of staying at the leading edge of scientific and technological prowess to offset deficiencies in manpower.'[34] According to Baylis and Stoddart, 'the military Chiefs were particularly worried by the experience of the Blitz and the impact of the new technology given Britain's geographical location. These anxieties were clearly expressed in an RAF assessment of the impact of atomic weapons on Britain's future security produced in December 1945.'[35]

One important consequence of the McMahon Act was that development of both nuclear weapons and energy production would be managed by civilian rather than military departments. This was a model that was echoed in Britain. As we have seen, important decisions were taken by 'a small and active ministerial committee known as Gen 75 [and] because of its exceptional secrecy, its decisions were not even reported to the Cabinet. A still smaller group of ministers, Gen 163, took the decision in January 1947 to make an atomic bomb'.[36] A few months before, Gen 75 had 'met to discuss the feasibility of an independent British nuclear programme' on 25 October 1946. Decisions were made at this time, in part, through emotional individual responses to the global situation, for

> when faced with the tremendous cost of constructing a gaseous diffusion plant for uranium enrichment, both the Chancellor of the Exchequer Hugh Dalton and the President of the Board of Trade Stafford Cripps questioned the existence of any rationale behind an independent British nuclear deterrent. Ernest Bevin reportedly interjected, "that won't do at all, we've got to have this [...] I don't mind for myself, but I don't want any other Foreign Secretary of this country to be talked to or at by a Secretary of State in the United States as I have just had [...] We've got to have this thing over here whatever it costs [...] We've got to have the bloody Union Jack on top of it"'.[37]

The indignant passion of Bevin's statement is often commented upon, with Margaret Gowing arguing that the decision to pursue an independent nuclear arms programme was motivated, in part, by anxiety over Britain's decreasing world role.[38] As Laucht and I pointed out in 2012, there is also an interesting historiographical echo-effect caused by the repetition of Bevin's personal role 'in getting an independent British atomic arms programme under way', perhaps 'indicative of a strong preoccupation with high politics and elite personalities in the existing historiography on British nuclear history. Such approaches risk over-privileging nuclear 'moments' in the grand atomic narrative, as if Bevin's interjection was the key factor' in starting the post-war British atomic weapons project.[39] By focusing on these dramatic biographical snippets, often presented in jocular and privileged form, the birth of the nuclear state is seen as a quirky by-product of a distant age, not a system of power worthy of critical examination in the present. It should also be acknowledged that the British government was seduced by the centrality of nuclear technology to the socio-technical imaginary of the modern nation state.

In July 1947, UK atomic bomb staff met for the first time, and by August, a UK experimental pile went critical at Harwell. On 12 May 1949, A. V. Alexander, Minister of Defence, announced in parliament that 'all types of modern weapons, including the atomic weapons are being developed'.[40] This was minimally reported in the national press.[41] In April 1949, the decision to build a British atomic bomb was officially announced, and shortly afterwards, President Truman announced to the world that an explosion of a Soviet atomic bomb had been detected. As Jenks comments, 'public fears about war and atomic weapons had been increasing ever since the news of the Soviets' first atomic test emerged in September 1949. The US push to develop the hydrogen bomb, announced in January 1950, heightened public worry.'[42] In January 1950, Klaus Fuchs was arrested on charges of atomic espionage, and in April, the Atomic Weapons Research Establishment (AWRE) was formed under the directorship of William Penney, at a former RAF base at Aldermaston, Berkshire. In this period, the secret commitment to nuclear development would create complex infrastructural, political, military and social consequences for Britain.

It may be argued that official narratives in this period echoed the emotive and poetic language found in fictional narratives of nuclear war. A cabinet memorandum from 1945 contained the following words from the prime minister: 'the advent of the atomic bomb presents us with a new situation, in that there is now a weapon of transcendent power against which there can be no real defence'.[43] The language used here evokes a similar tone of urgency and portent seen in the work of some fictional authors. Using a vocabulary suffused with ultimate meaning, there is the shared assumption that humanity is using science to produce 'transcendent' forms of power over which humans have little control, and against which nations cannot defend themselves. Rather than politicians working to control its use and further proliferation, they preferred instead to emphasize and submit to a new atomic order. Politicians were making decisions that had the potential to affect lives for hundreds – if not thousands – of years, but it is clear that fears over national security, linked with preoccupations over national identity in the global context, led them to choose the path they did. It is also important to remember that specific factual information was still absent at this time, leading to partial and fragmented understandings of the consequences of Hiroshima and Nagasaki and the full meaning of atomic testing. Historians disagree over the motivational culture surrounding nuclear decision-making. Baylis and Stoddart argue that in the post-1945 era, a number of 'nuclear beliefs' were 'shared by important and influential political, military, and scientific figures in Britain'.[44] Thus, particular shared assumptions over the necessity of atomic development came to define and influence atomic decision-making. This approach is different to that of Richard Maguire, who argues that the existence of varying 'nuclear cultures' in government led to particular decisions being made.

What is clear is that the British government committed – politically, financially and morally – to a permanent military-scientific peacetime project with a range of long-term consequences it was impossible to predict or budget for, all without democratic approval. For some critics, most notably anti-nuclear activist E. P. Thompson and Labour politician Tony Benn, the birth of the British nuclear state was both profoundly undemocratic and fundamentally irresponsible.[45] Yet, politicians at the time believed that developing the atomic bomb was a necessity if Britain was to play a role in global politics. Additionally, the separation between military and civil applications of nuclear technology was presented as a clean and simple one. This is perhaps best exemplified by the fanfare surrounding the opening of Calder Hall nuclear power plant in 1956, which will be examined in Chapter 4. Paraded as the world's first commercial nuclear power station, the site was secretly established in the late 1940s to create radioactive compounds to be used in British atomic bombs. Thus, even as peaceful uses of atomic energy were promoted, an easy separation between peaceful and military applications could not truthfully be made. As we will see in the rest of the book, this enabled sections of the British population to remain consistent in their support of the British deterrent. The institutionalization of nuclear technology and its infrastructure initiated official patterns of thought and unofficial 'motifs' that would continue until the end of the century. The institutional development of the British nuclear complex occurred alongside reports of atomic espionage, political decisions over civil defence initiatives, optimistic narratives over the peaceful uses of atomic energy and profound anxieties displayed by sections of the British public. It is to these unofficial responses to the atomic age that we now turn.

A range of responses: Unofficial narratives

The bombing of Hiroshima and Nagasaki, followed by the highly publicized American atomic tests beginning at Bikini Atoll in 1946 and the explosion of the first Soviet bomb in 1949, triggered a range of responses and speculation from the British people. These reactions drew on existing nuclear motifs explained in Chapter 2 (such as the 'atomic crossroads'), but new narratives that appeared give an indication of how people responded to the reality of the atomic age and also demonstrate the emergence of nuclear subjectivity. The air of atomic mysticism and romanticism in the years preceding 1945 dissipated, and atomic realities started to become a normalized part of life. For example, people were beginning to gain a greater understanding of the effects of radiation.[46] Nuclear scholarship on this period has predominantly concentrated on elite groups of government officials and scientists, but if we take a localized, specific and historicized approach, we can start to see the nature of this cultural impact.

News of the atomic bombings spread around the world following the official announcements.[47] Paul Boyer wrote about how, following the Japanese surrender in 1945, a sustained celebratory culture developed in the United States around the use of the atomic bombs, stressing the ambiguity of these responses.[48] This ambiguity of response was echoed in Britain and would persist in the immediate post-war era as knowledge of the full impact and meaning of the use of the atomic bombings increased. Impassioned debate arose in theological circles, and individual responses to perceived nuclear danger were varied and plentiful.[49] In the American context, Jacobs argues that the advent of the nuclear age shifted traditional perceptions of life and the world, stating that 'one of the ways Americans learned to understand such atomic icons as *radiation* was as signifiers of a new vision of the physical world, a vision in which forces operated beyond perception, where time and space were not fixed'.[50] In the decade after Hiroshima and Nagasaki, the foundations of intellectual and spiritual life steadily shifted. Although there was a period of journalistic openness to this spiritual shift, this would change because, Jenks argues, 'security censorship was ostensibly about protecting vital technical secrets and military operations, but after 1947 it became expansive – banning almost all details of the British atomic bomb programme'.[51] It also promoted particular nuclear narratives. For instance, '[Leslie] Sheridan [Editorial Advisor] sometimes worked directly with newspaper management, as in 1950 when the IRD arranged for a simple story on western nuclear strategy to appear in the Sunday mass-circulation newspaper *The People* so it could be picked up and distributed overseas.'[52] As Forgan has argued, 'obsessive official secrecy prevented clear understanding of atomic power.'[53] With this in mind, it is important to note that the majority of nuclear narratives that appeared in the press in the post-war era were shaped by the restricted level of information released by the nuclear state. While it is clear that 'government censorship marked the edges of acceptable public discourse', there are still plenty of nuclear counter-narratives to analyse in the national press.[54]

The emotional and imaginative impact that the news of the Hiroshima bombing had is clear, and this was reflected in journalistic narrative at the time. On 8 August, the *Daily Mirror* included a comment from H. G. Wells on the front page which read, 'The Future? People Must Decide'. The piece quoted Wells, who said 'this could wipe out everything bad – or good – in the world. It is up to the people to decide which.' This appeared next to the main headline, 'Men in black goggles dropped first atom bomb, and said "oh my God" as CITY VANISHED IN A MUSHROOM OF FIRE'.[55] The super-weapon that Wells had imagined in 1914 was now a reality, and he left the readers of the *Daily Mirror* in no doubt over the significance of this development, both for humanity and the individual subject. Already the world-changing significance of the bomb was being acknowledged. The nuclear imaginary had combined with the real-life atomic age, and a specific vocabulary developed that spoke about the future and responsibility in the broadest terms. Early ruminations on the atomic age talked in terms of 'humanity' and 'life on earth', neatly summed up by a cartoon published in the *Evening Standard*. With this cartoon, we see the familiar 'atomic crossroads' motif in evidence, with the assumption developing that the consequences of nuclear technology in human hands will either be catastrophic or beneficial for 'humanity'. Depicted as an innocent, blonde-haired child, humanity sits threatened by, or in awe of, the looming representation of nuclear science. Humanity is hesitant at the atomic crossroad, and the overriding inference from the cartoon is a sinister choice between 'life and death' that the scientists have created. Clearly, this cartoon would contribute to a culture of uncertainty around the potential significance of atomic science and suggests the powerlessness felt by individuals in the face of this revolutionary new era.

This type of narrative appeared elsewhere. James Langdon-Davies, the *Daily Mail*'s science correspondent (who, in 1954, published *The Ethics of Atomic Research*) wrote an article subtitled, 'It Can Change Our World – Or Destroy It' on 7 August 1945.[56] On the same page, an editorial imagined the future possibilities of atomic weapons, announcing 'news which means complete revolution in our whole outlook on life and the processes of our very existence comes from the United States today [...] we only try to think what the effect of one of these dropped on London would have been – and recoil with horror from the thought'.[57] This is an early example of individual citizens imagining the consequences of atomic attack on their own city, with later speculation that the 'nation would go to "earth" under atomic raid'.[58] The editorial ends on a profound note, stating 'we stand at the threshold of a new world'. On 8 August, a personal reaction to the explosion by Captain Parsons, the military observer on the *Enola Gay*, is reported in the *Daily Mail*. Parsons said, 'the men aboard with me gasped "My God", and what had been Hiroshima was a mountain of smoke like a giant mushroom.'[59] The *Daily Mail* also reported details of the Hiroshima bombing from the crew of *Enola Gay*. Alongside the subheading 'Two Protests – "A Disgrace to the Allies"', the piece explained how 'protests against the use of the atomic bomb have been sent to Mr. Attlee and President Truman by the Rev. A. D. Belden, chairman of the "Christianity Calling" Council. The message to Mr. Attlee said: "Unparalleled terrorism disgraces the United Nations. Beg you secure veto of its use."'[60] In the same edition, an editorial entitled 'Control or Perish' stated, 'first reactions to news of the atomic bomb are threefold: Thankfulness to Mr. Churchill, Sir John Anderson, the scientists and all others responsible for making the discovery on our behalf; relief that the Germans did not discover it first, as they so nearly did; and deep anxiety as to its future application.'[61] Another article on the same day explains the atomic bomb in 'layman's terms' with an accompanying article on the nature of warfare, and an atomic themed cartoon. In the same issue, a speculative repetition of the 'London after atomic attack' scenario appears, while another article discusses peaceful applications of nuclear technology. This issue alone demonstrates multiple nuclear imaginaries, some of which are repeated from the day before. In this one edition, we can see many discursive motifs which would recur through the century and get a sense of the everyday persistence of nuclear narratives. The 9 August edition of the *Daily Mail* included a piece entitled 'Woman's Eye View', which, when discussing the advent of the atomic bomb, stated 'the instant reaction of women was a deep instinctive matriarchal fear [...] We are still reeling in contemplation of the immense potentialities of the atom bomb for good as well as evil'.[62] On 13 August, as part of an 'Atomic Age Column', John Langdon-Davies wrote 'the genie won't be put back in the bottle'.[63] This would become a common metaphor in the nuclear era, encapsulating anxieties around the capability to control the mysterious, powerful and varied forces unleashed by nuclear science.

Clearly, a range of nuclear anxieties can be seen in the British press in August 1945 alone. A cartoon published on 14 August (Figure 3.3) offers a foreboding image and dwells upon ultimate messages. Entitled, 'The 'atoms' we've overlooked', darkness and light pervade the cartoon. An ambiguous image, it seems to present 'atomic energy' as a potential saviour to humanity but the image of the atomic genie is not automatically reassuring. Stalked by brutal 'sadism', humanity, here represented again by children and a pure feminine symbol of peace, is again confronted by a choice. Again, the choice is not presented as entirely pleasant and certainly not easy. This notion of choice encouraged an early and diluted form of atomic activism. Preoccupied

The " atoms " we've overlooked

FIGURE 3.3 *'The 'Atoms' We've Overlooked'*, Daily Mail, *14 August 1945.* © *Associated Press/Solo Syndication.*

with the future of humanity, and perhaps best summed up visually by the front cover of the illustrated magazine *Picture Post* from 25 August 1945 (Figure 3.4), the choice was positioned as a key priority in the years ahead, and a responsibility to take seriously. 'Dawn – or Dusk?' the readers of the *Picture Post* were asked. With the innocent symbol of the child looking to the nuclear horizon, the readers are left with an enduring and powerful imaginary of a world altered by the advent of the atomic bomb. Recent

FIGURE 3.4 *'Man Enters the Atom Age: Dawn – or Dusk?'*, The Picture Post, 25 *August 1945. © Getty Images.*

research by Christoph Laucht systematically surveyed nuclear themes in *Picture Post*.[64]

Small-scale forms of activism were reported in the press in the immediate post-war years. In 'Words v. the Atobomb', a curious offer is made by MP Dr Mont Folleck (Labour, Loughborough) to put money into a School of Philology so that 'a reformed English language [can] be used internationally "to bring the nations of the world together"' and to counter the atom bomb.[65] On 27 August, readers of the 'Atomic Age Column' were introduced to the idea that common sense is disintegrating in the atomic age.[66] Here, the idea that ideas and values have somehow been irrevocably altered is reinforced. A cartoon entitled 'Gun Powder, Treason and Plot' was placed underneath an article on the decline of religion.[67] With the knowledge of atomic weapons came the anxiety that they could end up in the wrong hands, with one article proclaiming, 'MPs fear atom secret cannot be kept: New Men talk of "things to come."'[68] The challenge of how to respond was not always forthcoming. Elsewhere, David Nye has identified a 'transformation narrative' in nuclear discourse, which presented nuclear energy as an affordable and seemingly abundant energy source, and 'the apocalyptic narrative' that focused on nuclear weaponry.[69] This is a key tension in the presentation of nuclear narratives in the press. To demonstrate the ambiguity of early nuclear responses, we can see that some newspapers expressed optimism over the potential utility of atomic technology. Ambiguous narratives would sometimes appear on the same page. On 3 September, an article argued that atomic science could offer great benefits to humanity. On the same page, an atomic-themed cartoon appeared, again dark and brooding.[70] In many ways, this narrative and counter-narrative represents a theme that would emerge throughout the rest of the century in journalistic discourse. A piece in *The Guardian* on 8 August 1945 stated, 'we have got to see to it that the colossal energy created by the atomic bomb is harnessed for the benefit of mankind and not for destruction.'[71] The columnist Alan Moorehead downplayed the social impact of the bomb in the *Daily Express* on 20 September 1945.

> The atom bomb seems to be having a second burst of popularity (or notoriety) as a thing to talk about. I have been hearing further suggestions all week. Let's blow the ice-cap off the North Pole so that we can get at the minerals underneath. Let's disperse the clouds so that the sun will shine on the fish queues and the cities, and the British holiday-maker [...] Glancing back over recent conversations with my friends, I find all of them are living quite complacently in a world that contains the atomic bomb. No one appears to fear it. The reverse. I believe that most of them, after nearly six weeks' reflection, are definitely glad it exists, and regard it as the best possible guarantee of peace.[72]

A common-sense form of deterrence theory was emerging even in 1945, resonating with the atomic-themed stories of the 1920s and 1930s that dreamed of 'the weapon to end all wars'. Britain's role in the development of the atomic bomb was discussed in the press. Indeed, fictional narratives played a part in this contested history. An article in the *Daily Mirror* on 4 October 1945 read:

> U.S. A-Bomb film robs Britain of credit – HOLLYWOOD has made a film which fosters the impression that the atom bomb was discovered, developed and guarded by Americans – without any help at all from Britain. Americans are swallowing the fiction in this film, *The House On 92nd Street*, as fact. The commentary accompanying the film is equally misleading. British scientists are not once mentioned. Naturally American filmgoers think that British scientists had no part in producing the new weapon.[73]

After witnessing the American atomic tests at Bikini Atoll in 1946, James Cameron asked the question 'Must the world begin again?' in the *Daily Express*. He continued, 'I want to draw your attention to the fact, already it seems forgotten, and in no circumstances ever discussed at the Peace Table – that there is in existence an article known as the atom bomb…I can say that with some certainty, as I have seen it at work. If we are not pretty urgently smart, one of them will go off somewhere.'[74] The rest of the article concentrates on the horrors inflicted on the victims at Hiroshima and echoes the language used by John Hersey in his famous text *Hiroshima* which was serialized in the *New Yorker*, with fragments appearing in the British press before its release as a book in 1946. Both Britain and America were facing up to the moral consequences of atomic warfare. The *Guardian* review of the book stated 'man has either to abolish war or to accept Hiroshima's fate for his own city in the future'.[75]

Newspapers proved a solid source of education for the British people when containing detailed pieces on atomic theory, which continued throughout the twentieth century.[76] The 'Atomic Age Column' that sprung up in the *Daily Mail* is itself a statement of the widely held view that Britain was part of a new era. Such a mindset led current affairs publications and radio programmes to dedicate themed projects around the new atomic realities facing the British population. In this sense, the normalization of nuclear narratives was occurring across a range of media. For instance, as mentioned at the start of this book, in 1947 the BBC presented a series of radio programmes 'not simply to give us a lot of hair-raising dramatic stuff about atom bombing, but instead to offer us frank talks by the leading authorities in the country, on the facts, theories and problems of atomic energy […] If they cannot teach us something about atomic energy, then nobody can'.[77] *The Listener* magazine published the talks, and the introduction by J. B. Priestley summed up the permanence and inescapability of the atomic age, and reminded readers that all British people are intimately involved in the atomic predicament, writing 'you cannot by any amount of wriggling, squirming or running put yourself outside the sphere of these talks. It simply cannot be done. We are now living in the atomic age.'[78]

On New Year's Day 1946, atomic realities were not far from the mind either, as demonstrated by the cartoon 'Pilgrim's Progress, Featuring John Citizen',[79] which came a couple of months after reports that Attlee argued for the need to 'lift the spectre of fear', saying he is not 'downcast or depressed', clearly still thinking about the importance of national morale.[80] Anxieties over spying were prevalent in this period. A *Daily Mail* article from March 1946 reports on 'Atom Man Arrested at London Lecture'.[81] This was the story of the arrest of Alan Nunn May, a scientist who had worked under Chadwick as part of Tube Alloys, and then in Canada during the war who was eventually convicted of being a Soviet spy later in 1946.[82] A piece from 1946 reported on the 'London Arrest in Hunt for "Atom Thieves"',[83] with a report carrying the headline 'Russia Admits: Atom Spies Were Our Own' appearing soon after.[84] Newspapers carried atomic spy stories on their front pages. The success of the Manhattan Project was only possible through the collaboration of scientists from all around the world, including Germany. In the post-war era, these alliances came to be viewed uneasily, most famously with the Klaus Fuchs case of 1950.[85] Fuchs was accused of passing atomic secrets to the Soviet Union and was put in prison for the best part of a decade. The human drama at the heart of the stories both appealed to and appalled the British readership.

Journalistic reaction around specific nuclear events, such as the American nuclear tests at Bikini in 1946, shows the strength of feeling around nuclear issues. A report from the *Daily Mail* under the headline, 'ATOM BOMBS' read 'Over 5,000 letters, most of them protesting against the atom-bomb experiment in the Pacific, have been received at the War Department. Several hundred letter-writers want to be placed on the target ships.'[86] There was also a place for humour, as evidenced by a cartoon by Giles, published in the *Daily Express* in October 1945 (Figure 3.5). Examples of this kind of response to the atomic age signify a uniquely British articulation of the anxieties inherent in the new realities presented to the British public. Through various narratives, the British public would see the scientific community as responsible for the future direction of nuclear development. Readers of the nuclear-themed issue of *The Listener* in 1947 were reminded of 'the choice before us', and 'the very success of the work of the nuclear physicists had created the most horrible of weapons in the hands of man. That first explosion in the desert destroyed the traditional freedom of the scientist, for his work now menaced the security of the world.'[87] Yet, in the same issue, G. L. Cheshire argued that the magnitude of atomic weapons was linked to the magnitude of the responsibility in the hands of humankind:

> To try to visualise it would be a waste of time. We might as well agree
> that the bomb is bigger than our understanding [...] it spelt power of

"I don't think the boy Tom quite likes the idea of 'em building this 'ere atom bomb works at Didcot."

Daily Express, Oct. 31st, 1945

FIGURE 3.5 *Demonstrating the way in which humour was mobilized against the anxiety of the new atomic age. Cartoon by Giles,* Daily Express, *31 October 1945. British Cartoon Archive, University of Kent, www.cartoons.ac.uk. © Express Syndication Limited.*

destruction, power of delving into the realm of the unknown, power of being able to achieve our objective [...] If man persists in claiming atomic energy for himself and entrusts its custody to purely human wisdom, then I for one hold little brief for the future of civilisation.[88]

This doom-laden tone is reflected elsewhere in this issue of *The Listener*, with Thomson predicting more powerful weapons will develop in the years to come,[89] and Jacob Bronowski reflecting on atomic victims and expressing the fact that humanity had not come to terms with the extraordinary global events of August 1945. In this period before formal anti-nuclear activism emerged, the pages of newspapers and magazines can be read as confused and impassioned pleas on 'the choice': often couched in abstract and vague terms, the reader was compelled to dwell on the magnitude of the problem facing humanity and choose the right path, but this was only really possible in a soft, moralizing form. It was in the 1950s that figures such as J. B. Priestley and Bertrand Russell would become figureheads for organized anti-nuclear activism, which we will explore to in Chapter 4. Sometimes, the press did carry anti-nuclear pieces, such as a piece from September

1949 entitled 'No A-Bombs for Britain'.[90] With the ambiguity of nuclear narratives, the meaning and impact of nuclear technology was something on which individual readers would develop their own opinions.

Even British youth were appealed to in different ways. *Meccano Magazine*, in its editorial column in September 1945, stated 'This unexpected climax to a long and cruel war would be less startling to readers of the "M. M." than to most people, for reference to such a possibility has appeared in these pages.'[91] An assumption is made that eager and inquisitive British youth would have been in contact with speculative information regarding atomic possibilities. In 1949, Ronald Bedford is announced as the *Daily Mirror*'s new '"Atom Reporter", who will bring to readers from time to time a glimpse of the world we are building for our grandchildren'. His first report focuses on the first Atomic Energy School, in Lancashire. Bedford tells his readers not to 'get any Wellsian ideas about this school. There are no atomic piles as there are at Britain's Atomic City, the research establishment at Harwell, Berks'.[92] Clearly, journalistic discourse was an arena where new possibilities and questions were framed, new moral and ethical boundaries tested and new imaginary threats were negotiated and received by the public. It seems clear that individual citizens were forming complex, powerful and varied opinions on the bomb in response to journalistic discourse. With the increasing frequency of atomic-themed articles in the press, preoccupations with nuclear issues were becoming a significant part of everyday life in the post-war years. Journalistic responses were varied, due to the emotional and political impulses behind the creation of particular emphases.

Regional journalism

If we look beyond national journalistic narratives, British nuclear culture becomes more complicated still. While we can find examples of individual reactions to the newly formed atomic age on the national level, more of these can be found when different regions of Britain are examined. Recent research suggests that regional nuclear narratives demonstrate the extent to which the Cold War was experienced in different ways, depending on precise regional cultural politics.[93] A brief survey of some regional journalistic narratives will show an extra layer of ambiguity in the immediate post-war era. In many regions, there are plenty of examples of a celebratory mood. In 1945, *The Garston and Woolton Weekly News* published an article entitled 'The Atomic Bomb', which served as a celebration of Liverpool University's role in the atomic bomb project, especially focusing on the role of James Chadwick.[94] It is possible to see the ways in which opportunistic commercialism led to the use of the word 'atomic'. The *Bath Weekly Chronicle and Herald* contained an advertisement for 'Atomic Carpet and Upholstery Cleaners', an example of the ways in which businesses saw the positive potential of naming products in this most evocative way.[95]

The immediate post-war period also saw fragmented 'calls to action' in response to the atomic age. In 1946, an advertisement in the *Hull Daily Mail* reads, 'The Mighty Atom – Youth. To the Under 30s and Past Members of the Junior Imperial League. A new youth movement.'[96] For some, the advent of the atomic bomb required renewed focus on the responsibility of future generations. In 1946, *The Cornishman* cited a speech by Miss J. Harrison, headmistress of Penzance County Grammar School for Girls, who proclaimed 'It is going to be our children who are going to decide whether the atomic age will hoist itself with its own petard and precipitate mankind into a bottomless pit of destruction, or whether its infinite possibilities will be harnessed for the good of humanity.'[97] In the same newspaper in 1950, a letter to the editor from W. Arnold-Forster entitled 'Hydrogen Bomb' calls for an 'all party meeting at St. John's Hall, to consider the whole issue – not merely the outlawry of certain weapons'.[98] It is clear that people were reacting in diverse ways to the atomic age and were already mobilizing themselves in the face of future danger. Along these lines, in 1950 *The Derby Evening Telegraph* asked 'who has joined civil defence?'[99] In late 1950, Earl Bathurst, vice-president of the Association of Youth Clubs, wrote in *The Cheltenham Chronicle and Gloucestershire Graphic* of the threat of Communism. 'We stand in fear not only of the greatest war in history but of being totally wiped out by the atom-bomb', he said.[100] Here, we see common anxieties over Communism and the bomb being reinforced in a specific regional context.

An article in *The Western Morning News* from July 1950 is an example of the sense of powerlessness felt by certain individuals. The piece, entitled 'Ignorance of atom warfare breeding feeling of helplessness', cites Conservative MP Geoffrey Lloyd speaking on 'the psychological impact of atomic warfare on public opinion'. The article mentions the fact that 'The Dean of Canterbury has said that stones and rocks would melt 60 miles away from the explosion' and goes on to say that Mr Lloyd had said 'I utterly repudiate a defeatist's attitude to the defence of these islands against the atomic weapon.' Then, Emrys Hughes speaks out, saying 'this country cannot be defended in atomic warfare without a huge loss of the civilian population'.[101] The dark potential of nuclear culture, one key nuclear motif which emerged during the early period of the twentieth century, expanded in both depth and breadth of scope when we consider the appearance of such ideas in the regional press. On 1 July 1946, the *Hull Daily Mail* 'Stop Press' carried a story about an 'Atom Suicide', describing how 'a young nurse leaped to death from roof of 13 story building in Los Angeles on Sunday. Aunt told police she became visibly depressed by radio broadcast of atom bomb test, and "feared for the future of the world."'[102] The readers of the *Hull Daily Mail* would be reminded of the new reality of nuclear anxiety and all the things this could mean for individuals.

Just like the national press, language used to discuss nuclear issues was often sensationalist. On 14 October 1950, the front page of the *Tamworth Herald* proclaimed, 'Statesmen fear a third world war! Do you want to know [...] whether the atom bomb will destroy mankind [...] whether there will ever be peace [...] if you do [...] The Tamworth Christadelphians invite you to A Free Public Lecture.' On the same page, there is an advert from the Warwickshire Division of the Civil Defence Corps, reminding people about a public meeting, where there would be a 'display of films dealing with atomic warfare' along with a number of talks.[103] As would be expected, regional newspapers dwelt on national nuclear politics. In response to the Soviet bomb test in 1949, the *Hull Daily Mail* commented, 'the disclosure that an atomic explosion has taken place in Russia [...] does not really warrant the shocked surprise which has apparently been caused. [...] There is no logical ground for the fear that, as a consequence, war is just around the corner.'[104] So, it is possible to find narratives of reassurance as well as anxiety. This brief survey of the regional press in Britain demonstrates that while similar responses and assumptions emerge as part of a more general 'British' nuclear culture, we must be careful about making firm conclusions. Both national and regional journalism prove to be ambiguous, suggesting that new and unique nuclear subjectivities were being formed in different locales. How did this discursive culture echo or shape everyday life? If students of nuclear history are able to access local newspaper archives, original research can be conducted in this area. We will return to ambiguous journalistic narratives through the course of the book.

Everyday life

When conceptualizing everyday life in the Cold War era, journalistic narratives are useful sources. This section will demonstrate that diaries and oral histories provide another interpretative layer and concentrates on two main source sets. First, the Mass Observation Archive at the University of Brighton holds many diaries completed by project participants. It is a very useful resource for historians of modern Britain, and some aspects of the archive are accessible online. Second, original interview transcripts conducted by Sarah Hewitt, a postgraduate student at The University of Liverpool, will be drawn upon. Combined, these two types of source demonstrate another way in which we may access the nuclear past. The narratives that emerge are complex and speak of the variety of responses to the nuclear present and future. They project anxieties into the future, while also suggesting a degree of optimism about the nuclear present.

In Barrow-in-Furness, a ship building town in northwest England, housewife Nella Last kept a diary as part of the Mass Observation project. On Tuesday 7 August, she wrote in her diary that her husband shouted to awaken her:

'Arta waken, Lass?' I slipped on my dressing-gown and went downstairs, wondering whatever could be the matter. His thick white hair, which gets so unruly at times, seemed to be on end as he rubbed it with one hand and brandished the *Daily Mail* in the other. He said, 'By Goy, lass, but it looks as if some of your daft fancies and fears are reet. Look at this' – and it was the article about the atomic bombs. I've rarely seen him so excited – or upset. He said 'Read it – why, this will change 'allt world. Ee I wish I wor thutty years younger and could see it aw'. I felt sick – I wished I was thirty years older and out of it all. My husband began to wonder if it would influence all power – cars chiefly – in some way taking the place of petrol. I left them talking, and went back upstairs with a can of hot water, to wash and dress [...] I felt in a queer whirl as I packed.[105]

The next day Last details a conversation she had with a neighbour, commenting that 'we talked about the atomic bomb. It seems to have frightened Mrs. Howson very much. Our talk had a very Wellsian turn.'[106] She also wrote about a family friend visiting the house on 26 September 1946.

He had called to see how my husband was as he was in the neighbourhood [...] I wished him far away, as he was talking so dismally about having to give up his business, of his two daughters being out of town, one [...] in London, the other working near Preston .... Between the Labour govt being the downfall of everything ... if the daft ___ would only see beyond their own noses, the duplicity of Russia in general, Stalin in particular, and 'all this atom bomb carry on' [indecipherable] my husband's face grew longer and longer, all colour left it, except his scarlet spots on his cheek bones – a sign he has almost reached the limit of endurance.[107]

The diary entries from Nella Last indicate the complex emotional responses to the news of the atomic bombings. While her husband experienced initial excitement and awe, Nella displayed a visceral response, seemingly shared by her neighbour soon after. Then, we see how the atomic bomb joins other post-war realities as a source of anxiety.

Interviews conducted recently in the Merseyside region suggest these anxieties were common. The interviews, mainly focused on middle-class female respondents who had children in the 1940s or 1950s, suggest that the threat of the bomb induced an extension of the war mentality. One respondent, Lily, said, 'I suppose we were [frightened] but we just accepted it I think. What you can't change you have to endure don't you?'[108] This sense of powerlessness is a central feature of nuclear culture. Three of the female respondents expressed disbelief and disgust over the bombings of Hiroshima and Nagasaki, and this altered the way in which they viewed Britain. Lily stated, 'well it was science fiction really; well it was fact really wasn't it? It was so horrific that you couldn't believe that it was true. It was such an evil thing to do wasn't it? [...] Then when they dropped the second one we were disgusted with that really, you know.'[109] Another respondent, Barbara, said:

you felt guilty in a way because your country was involved in killing; alright it brought an end to the war but at the cost of thousands of innocent people [...] it made you feel guilty that you were part of that country. When you see those horrific pictures of the aftermath of the bomb you know it was absolutely awful and then you know people used to go round saying, oh, it will only take one man to have a row with his wife in the morning and go in work in a bad temper. And one turns it all and takes the rest of us with him and put his finger on the button, this is the way people used to talk you know.[110]

Doris stated, 'I was ashamed of being English and a part of that.'[110] On the specific subject of patriotism, one respondent, Vera, said, 'I was patriotic before, yes. I was so horrified ... I know there wasn't a lot of British people involved in doing the atom bomb, they were mostly Americans weren't they, but there were British on board as well. And I'm so horrified that somebody from this country could go and kill people like that.'[112] This disdain was also demonstrated by Nella Last, suggesting widespread moral revulsion to the use of the atomic bomb in war. It also suggests that Britain's role in the advent of the nuclear age compelled some people to reassess British national identity.

On 29 August 1949, the Soviet Union successfully tested an atomic weapon at Semipalatinsk, Kazakhstan.[113] Responses to the Soviet explosion of an atomic bomb were varied. One Mass Observation diarist, Holness, dwelt upon the wider ramifications of the event and also drew parallels with the lead up to war with Germany in 1939: 'I listened to the report of the United Nations Assembly, and it included a rather alarming announcement of an atomic explosion in USSR. And Viskinsky is now talking of a peace pact! What does it mean? It sounds rather like Hitler's "peace" overtures when he was getting ready to attack. Two grave announcements written within one week make it feel almost like 1939 again.'[114] Other snippets from the Mass Observation diary project include, 'I wonder whether Russia have really succeeded in making an effective atom bomb. There is plenty of room in Siberia for experiments and it struck me that the fall of several meteorites recorded in the papers may have been bits of material hurled into space from Siberia, but not far enough to escape the Earth's attraction. A bit far-fetched, but just possible.'[115] The news of the Soviet atomic bomb crept into the emotional lives of individuals. Again, Holness wrote, 'there was such a strange storm in the night. I was awakened at about 1.30 by a terrific wind and torrential rain [...] I was quite frightened – thinking we might be in for a real hurricane or cyclone – or even that it was the after effect of an atom bomb explosion.'[116] Being awoken by a loud storm and relating this instantly to nuclear danger signifies the extent to which, for some individuals, the bomb came to act as both a possible and rationalized explanation for startling everyday experiences.

Analysis of these sources has demonstrated the variety of responses to the atomic age. In a similar way to the regional journalistic narratives, we can see a range of articulations of nuclear anxiety and optimism. It is clear that these sources speak of the way in which individuals were coming to terms with the atomic age in different ways, demonstrating the various nuclear subjectivities that could exist. It is through analysis of these unofficial narratives that we can see powerful, ambiguous and articulate engagement with new nuclear realities and better understand how this engagement could evoke deeply personal and emotive responses.

Impact on intellectual, scientific and spiritual life

Through the previous sections, we have seen that the post-war era was partly defined by profound social and spiritual hardship. The economic and social costs of war were tremendous. There is also evidence to suggest that knowledge of the new 'atomic age' added to the psychological pressures on British citizens. We have already seen the emotionally charged response of Nella Last, and other participants in the Mass Observation project. Roger Luckhurst has pointed out the sense of rupture felt by intellectuals at the time, and it is certainly tempting to view the period following the deployment of the atomic bombs as one characterized by the creation of new expectations and new mentalities.[117] These psychological effects undoubtedly impacted upon discourse and created unique cultural references that would define public understanding of nuclear danger throughout the Cold War era. The role played by 'organic' intellectuals in the shaping of nuclear understanding is an area that is underdeveloped in the historiography. These were the social commentators who defined the problems of the time, often expressing more subtly the 'choices' facing humanity. Part of George Orwell's 'You and the Atomic Bomb' published in *The Tribune* in 1945 reads as a neat summation of the new atomic status quo

> Considering how likely we all are to be blown to pieces by it within the next five years, the atomic bomb has not roused so much discussion as might have been expected [...] So we have before us the prospect of two or three monstrous super-states, each possessed of a weapon by which millions of people can be wiped out in a few seconds, dividing the world between them [...] the kind of world-view, the kind of beliefs, and the social structure that would probably prevail in a state which was at once *unconquerable* and in a permanent state of "cold war" with its neighbours [...] For forty or fifty years past, Mr. H.G. Wells and others have been warning us that man is in danger of destroying himself with his own weapons, leaving the ants or some other gregarious species to take over [...] If, as seems to be the case, it is a rare and costly object as difficult to

produce as a battleship, it is likelier to put an end to large-scale wars at the cost of prolonging indefinitely a 'peace that is no peace'.[118]

Ralph Desmarais has reminded us that the role of intellectuals in Britain took on added complexity after 1945 due to the advent of the atomic bomb. He has argued that the influence and power of prominent intellectuals need to be acknowledged as another crucial layer to our understanding of nuclear culture. Desmarais has researched the role of scientist and science broadcaster Jacob Bronowski who 'became one of Britain's most vocal and well-known scientific intellectuals engaged in the cultural politics of the early atomic era' in the years following 1945.[119] Although Bronowski became best known for his documentary *The Ascent of Man*, his essay 'Mankind at the Crossroads' from 1946 is a passionate portrayal of the effects of the atomic bomb attacks on Hiroshima and Nagasaki, where Bronowski explicitly discusses the 'new forms of death' that atomic weaponry introduced. He does not flinch away from the more violent and disturbing effects of the weapons. Yet, Desmarais argues that 'Bronowski's misleading stories concerning the bomb long pre-dated *Ascent*; moreover, they were given credence by virtue of the authority which Bronowski both invoked and reaped as witness to the effects of the first atomic bombs.'[120]

Newspapers provided depth and breadth of debate around the spiritual dimension of the atomic bomb. The front page of the *Daily Mail* from 16 August 1945 reads, 'Anti-atom dean bans a peace service [...] There was no Victory peal from the bells of St Albans Cathedral yesterday and no civic service of thanksgiving there because the Dean, the Very Rev. C. C. Thicknesse, disapproves of the atom bomb.'[121] A frustrated reader wrote a letter to the *Hull Daily Mail* in January 1946, saying 'it would appear that leaders of the Church are in more fear of the atomic bomb than in fear of God. Christians everywhere would like to see a more vehement declaration of faith and trust.'[122] A letter to the *Gloucestershire Echo* in April 1947, expressing the perceived crisis of religious leadership offers the opinion that 'they might be allowed to appeal to the fear of atomic warfare, which appears now to have taken the place of the fear of hell'.[123]

In the *Daily Mail* on 20 August in an article entitled 'Bishops Talk of the Bomb', the Archbishop of Canterbury stated, 'physically, the atomic bomb is a new thing. Morally, it differs not in kind but only to a terrible degree from every other weapon of total war.'[124] On 22 August, The Very Rev C. C. Thicknesse replied to the Archbishop in vehement terms, next to an editorial on government policy on atomic technology.[125] Kirk Willis argues that 'uneasy over their ignorance of the complicated scientific and political issues involved, unwilling to embarrass their government at a time of delicate diplomatic manoeuvring and growing East-West hostilities, yet aware of the passionate, if divided, opinions of their members in all manner of atomic issues, Britain's leading churchmen preferred caution and acquiescence over boldness and challenge.'[126] In Chapter 4, we will see a similar trend in the 1950s with the publication of Toynbee's *The Fearful Choice*, where many church leaders distanced themselves from any plea for British nuclear disarmament.

Christoph Laucht has researched the social responsibility of the atomic scientists after 1945. In an article from 2012, he examined the fascinating story of the travelling 'Atom Train' exhibition which was set up by a group of scientists linked to the Atomic Scientists' Association (ASA). The exhibition travelled around Britain in 1947 and 1948, and Laucht argues that the 'organizers framed [the peaceful uses of nuclear energy] within the dichotomy of a bright, peaceful atomic future and nuclear annihilation'.[127] This meant that the exhibition 'formed a "techno-political" site where atomic scientists' plans for public education clashed with the interests of the emerging national security state'.[128] Thus, scientists and church leaders alike found it difficult to publically represent nuclear science without their efforts appearing politically charged. The politics of nuclear expression was becoming unavoidable.

Popular culture

In this early period of the atomic age, British literary and artistic responses to the atomic bombings proved to be fairly rare. American and Japanese responses proved more common and more ambitious in their imaginative rendering of the attacks.[129] One of the first responses came from C. S. Lewis, who wrote a poem entitled 'On the Atomic Bomb – Metrical Experiment' (1945).[130] The poem dwelt on dark imagery, articulating a fearful new reality for humanity, likening the world mood to a panicking horse.

Ewan MacColl's play *Uranium 235*, performed in 1946, was the subject of a recent article by Jeff Hughes.[131] J. B. Priestley's play *Summer Day's Dream*, first performed in 1947, is set in a post-holocaust setting, with 'atomicars'.[132] An atomic bomb ballet was organized by Japanese dancers for British soldiers in Hiroshima prefecture. As the *Derby Evening Telegraph* reported, 'British forces in Kure will tomorrow see a Japanese ballet troupe from Hiroshima perform "The Story of the Atomic Bomb – and its Aftermath."'[133] In 1948, C. S. Lewis wrote the essay 'On Living in an Atomic Age'. By then, his tone had changed on the atomic threat. By pointing out the inevitability of death, he makes the point that living in fear is absurd:

It is perfectly ridiculous to go about whimpering and drawing long faces because the scientists have added one more chance of painful and premature death to a world which already bristled with such chances [...] the first action to be taken is to pull ourselves together. If we are all going to be destroyed by an atomic bomb, let that bomb when it comes find us doing sensible and human things – praying, working, teaching, reading, listening to music, bathing the children, playing tennis, chatting to our friends over a pint and a game of darts – not huddled together like frightened sheep and thinking about bombs. They may break our bodies (a microbe can do that) but they need not dominate our minds.[134]

Some other responses were blasé about the new threats facing humanity. In his identically titled essay 'On Living in an Atomic Age' (1948), Walter Hooper made the point that 'we need to pull ourselves together, it's nothing new. We'll all come to nothing anyway'.[135] These arguments would later resurface as a response to attempts to persuade the population to get involved in civil defence: anti-nuclear sentiment stemming from a wish to deny any preoccupation with the shadow of the bomb.

Yet, artistic responses to the atomic age make it clear that people were preoccupied by a new raft of anxieties. In the period. after Hiroshima and Nagasaki a handful of films were made, 'each involving Nazis or criminals dabbling with nuclear apparatus'.[136] These films were *Night Boat to Dublin* (1946), *Lisbon Story* (1946), *Eyes That Kill* (1947) and *Dick Barton Strikes Back* (1949). The film *Seven Days to Noon* (1950) by the Boulting Brothers depicted the feelings of guilt suffered by one atomic scientist. The scientist decides to blackmail the government into giving up atomic weapons by threatening to destroy London with an atomic weapon. The film dealt with some complex themes and is notable for its religious dimension. Interestingly, the evacuation of London is shown as a calm and orderly exercise, which is at odds with later nuclear-themed films. David Seed has embedded the film in its wider cultural context in an article that analyses the narrative strategies employed in *Seven Days to Noon* to contain nuclear fear. Indeed, 'aligning the imagined "nuclear subject" alongside real-world civil defence planning, Seed suggests that the film implicitly presents tensions at the heart of British culture in the early 1950s. He argues that by the end of the film, particular nuclear narratives "resist closure", helping to explain why such films were likely to resonate profoundly with contemporary audiences.'[137] Cultures of design and architecture were influenced by the increased prominence of atomic imagery. Richard Hornsey argues that 'the atom itself, through its mapped configurations of space, time, movement, and repetition, also offered an implicit set of comforting messages about the foundational stability of matter and, by analogical association, the structure of everyday life'.[138] The atomic age had begun, and diverse cultural references had started to express a range of ideas about the broader meanings of this, influencing British culture in subtle and powerful ways.

Conclusion

The demonstration to the world of the effectiveness of the atomic bomb in August 1945 led to a brutal and surreal set of narratives from the media, with the imagery and scale of the new phenomenon gaining prominence. We have seen how British culture following 1945 must be defined, in part, by reference to the rise of the nuclear state, and the importance of international nuclear diplomacy.[139] We have seen that many responses to the bomb were emotional, heartfelt and not always directly related to 'official' context, but rather a generalized sense of atomic threat, or the negative aspects of the fledging British nuclear state. Many of these unofficial narratives speak of the ways in which people were articulating their understandings of nuclear policy. An appreciation of British culture in this period cannot be fully realized without acknowledgement of the power and frequency of these narratives. The imagery of innocent children was a persistent motif to emphasize the 'atomic choices' facing humanity. In many of these narratives, the individual was intimately implicated in this choice: it was a contemporary issue that could not be avoided. Stretching into the future, these narratives at once displayed an understanding of the nuclear present and acknowledged the unpredictability and uncertainty of the nuclear future. In this sense, nuclear culture was defined by existential anxiety that seeped into conceptions of home, family and nation. In some ways, the atomic age rendered citizens powerless to the future direction of their lives, powerless as they were to control the nuclear imagery of their dreams and nightmares.

This period also saw the emergence of a shared official and unofficial nuclear vocabulary. By aligning national and regional journalistic narrative, we can see that a unified culture was developing around a set of nuclear assumptions. Nuclear narratives were being articulated, reinforced and then normalized into contemporary culture. Through an exploration of a range of unofficial narratives, this chapter has offered a snapshot of the complexity of public reactions to the new atomic age. The responses were highly ambiguous, yet can be viewed as the beginning of some shared assumptions around nuclear danger. The range and unpredictability of responses demonstrate the way in which individual nuclear subjectivities were developing: everyone had a different opinion on atomic affairs.

CHAPTER FOUR

Maturing Responses to the Nuclear Age, 1950–1958[1]

The 1950s set the pattern for British nuclear culture in the late twentieth century and beyond. Nuclear developments accelerated, in terms of military and civil applications, and political policy and the sheer variety of social and cultural responses increased. By 1958, nuclear weapons testing had become a central aspect of American, Soviet, British and French nuclear programmes. By the end of that year, exactly 300 atomic and nuclear explosions had been carried out by these four countries. Increasing public anxiety over the nuclear arms race, the Soviet launch of the Sputnik satellite into space in 1957 and improved knowledge around global contamination from nuclear weapons tests led to new public debates. The unprecedented and sustained arms race, and a largely pro-nuclear political climate exemplified by the rise of nuclear civil defence, led to the emergence of a mass anti-nuclear protest movement in Britain, CND, which was established in 1958, and would influence left-wing politics for years to come.[2] A growing array of fiction and film would exemplify maturing anti-nuclear arguments by the late 1950s. Institutional permanence was also consolidated in this decade, and interpretations of British history in this period should take into account the complex ways in which nuclear culture impacted upon culture more widely. Unofficial narratives in this period matured and became more frequent, sophisticated, articulate and original in their commentary on the nuclear state.

Representations of powerlessness, uncertainty, anxiety and ambiguity increased in 1950s British nuclear culture. These stronger assertions of nuclear resistance led to the disruption of broader conceptions of self, nationhood and existence in British life. It was in the 1950s that the hidden human dramas at the heart of nuclear culture shaped the lives of British citizens more strongly. The secret-then-public trajectory of nuclear development in

Britain meant that the government needed to devise ways of articulating the necessity of a nuclear deterrent to the nation and the benefits of nuclear technology for peaceful uses. This articulation took the form of an official narrative that encapsulated complex themes of national identity, prestige, duty, technological superiority and paternal responsibility. Along these lines, nuclear civil defence initiatives were introduced. As we will see, although these were designed to reassure, educate and inculcate notions of citizenship and duty, scepticism over civil defence initiatives fuelled anti-nuclear activism, created varieties of anxiety and resistance and served to highlight the lack of power the government had in ensuring the safety of the British people.

This chapter will chart the emergence of new unofficial narratives, which clashed with official narratives with increasing severity after the British nuclear weapons state went public following the detonation of the first British atomic device in 1952, and the development of thermonuclear devices in the years that followed. Although the existence of the British atomic bomb project was acknowledged in parliament in 1948, the press did not report the fact widely. This makes the 1950s a pivotal decade, as an increase in public nuclear knowledge is linked to the realities of government involvement in nuclear weapons development. Unofficial narratives reflected a new sense of powerlessness, resignation and existential threat. But now these anxieties were based on real and rational preoccupations, such as contamination from global nuclear tests and possible nuclear attack. These themes dominated nuclear culture in the 1950s and strengthened a set of assumptions around nuclear danger. We have seen that by the end of the 1940s, the dangers of nuclear technology were perceived on a highly personal basis, yet would be intricately tied to broader national concerns. As these perceptions became more common in the 1950s, unofficial and official nuclear narratives would clash with increasing severity. By 1958, new and radical narratives were beginning to emerge that can be partly explained by the steady increase in general levels of nuclear knowledge. The chapter will argue that the late 1950s was a turning point in the history of British nuclear culture due to the extent to which individual experience became more heavily shaped by knowledge of a variety of nuclear dangers.

Domestic and international context

In 1950s Britain, significant cultural and social moments included the 'Great Smog' in 1952, which contributed to the premature death of 4,000 Londoners and an increase in anxiety over the economy, crime, delinquency and mental health.[3] In this sense, British culture more widely had entered a phase of heightened paranoia, as Cold War anxieties over communism and foreign invasion combined with persistent social anxieties. The 1950s was a period of recovery and reconstruction in British society, and rationing of many foodstuffs persisted until 1954, which influenced post-war political discourse. Housing and employment remained key government priorities, yet 8–10 per cent of GNP was spent on defence in this period, and a small group of elites proved strongly supportive of growing and consolidating the nuclear state.[4] Attlee left office in 1951, which heralded over a decade of Conservative government, until Harold Wilson became Labour prime minister in 1964.

Throughout the 1950s, there was largely cross-party support for nuclear deterrence despite dissent from the left wing of the Labour Party, which did support the growing call for nuclear disarmament.[5] The pro-deterrence line was largely echoed in the press, especially in the *Daily Express* where British common sense was aligned firmly with the futility of abandoning bomb development. The continued development of Britain's independent nuclear deterrent was seen as a key aspect of foreign policy. Peter Hennessy's *Cabinet Papers* is a great resource for tracing the official policy in this period. It is now clear that nuclear decision-making was not carried out within the cabinet or parliament, but by a small elite group working away from the democratic operation of the state.

This was also a decade where public anxiety over atomic spying was prevalent. Simone Turchetti has published work on Bruno Pontecorvo, an Italian physicist who defected to the Soviet Union after working in Britain, and it is clear from analysis of the journalistic narratives of the time that the public had significant exposure to both the Pontecorvo and Fuchs cases. In 1950, the arrest of the 'atomic spy' Klaus Fuchs led to the breakdown of talks between the United States and Britain regarding nuclear cooperation. During the 1950s, America's stance gradually changed towards nuclear knowledge sharing. Matthew Jones makes the point that in the early 1950s, 'consultation over the possible use of nuclear weapons was a highly contentious aspect of the relationship between Britain and the United States during the early Cold War period'.[6] Attlee visited Washington at the height of the Korean War.[7] At the Bermuda conference in 1953, British concerns over Anglo-American relations 'reached a climax'.[8] In 1954, the United States agreed to amendments to the McMahon Act, and the Wilson-Sandys agreement of the same year heralded a new collaborative period between America and Britain, as both countries developed long- and medium-range missiles in the belief that nuclear bombers would become obsolete.[9] The British missile programme was known as 'Blue Streak'. Lorna Arnold argued that the detonation of the British thermonuclear device in 1957 led to closer Anglo-American cooperation, with the 'Co-operation on the Uses of Atomic Energy for Mutual Defence Purposes' treaty being signed in 1958.[10] This signalled the beginning of an era of openness between the two governments, of shared nuclear information, and the eventual sharing of weapons testing facilities.[11]

Jones quotes Winston Churchill who, speaking in 1954 as prime minister, summed up the situation succinctly, stating 'the difficulty is how far we ought to go in restraining [the United States] from taking risks which we cannot share'.[12] Jones argues that America needed strong allies, and Britain's stance over nuclear consultation led to the American administration adapting and refining nuclear policy in order not to 'alienate erstwhile supporters'.[13] By the end of the decade, 'the 1958 MDA and 1959 amendment ushered in a period of nuclear interdependence'.[14] In April 1957, Minister of Defence Duncan Sandys published the Defence White Paper, which reduced defence spending, ended national service and stated that Britain's future defence strategy would be centred on the independent nuclear deterrent. Simultaneously, the report acknowledged that there was no way of defending Britain against 'the consequences' of nuclear attack.[15] We will see that this contributed to the establishment of CND.

In 1952, the first British atomic bomb was detonated, entering service in January 1955. The first British bomb test was codenamed Operation Hurricane and was carried out on 3 October 1952 at Monte Bello, off the north-west coast of Australia. The tests conducted on Australian soil at Emu Field and Maralinga created fallout which affected Aboriginal populations. The maps and concentric circles accompanying newspaper reporting on this serve to dehumanize and distance the real effects the weapons tests had. Historians have argued that the development of nuclear weapons technologies followed similar patterns of colonial thinking over where to test these dangerous weapons. In the American, Soviet, British and French examples, decisions were made to test well away from home soil. In all cases, this led to significant environmental and health impacts on indigenous populations. In America, communities that were adversely affected by those tests carried out in Nevada became known as 'downwinders'.[16]

October 1956 saw the first UK airdrop atomic test over the Maralinga test range, in Australia. ICBM technology was developing fast, and the British military was supported by American technologies as part of 'Project E' in the late 1950s.[17] The 1950s was the decade of thermonuclear weapons. The first 'H-bomb' was tested by the United States at Eniwetok in March 1952, and the Soviet Union tested its first H-Bomb just over a year later. In May 1957, the first British H-bomb test was carried out after the government's decision to develop thermonuclear weapons in 1955, and in December 1955, six months after the Warsaw Pact was signed, the Blue Streak missile project was initiated.[18] Also, in 1956, the Suez Crisis and the royal opening of Calder Hall as the first commercial nuclear power station contributed to a strong narrative linking nuclear developments to British identity. In October, a serious fire occurred at Calder Hall, the consequences of which were debated for years to come.[19] Chapelcross nuclear power station, near Annan in South West Scotland, was completed in 1959 and manufactured plutonium for the British nuclear weapons programme.

On the international stage, the American 'Atoms for Peace' programme initiated by President Eisenhower in 1953 was seen by some as 'the cornerstone of America's aspirations for the international management of atomic energy'.[20] Historians have suggested that the Atoms for Peace programme was useful Cold War propaganda, a deliberate attempt to dampen nuclear anxiety and a key strategy in America retaining 'its overall dominance of atomic energy'.[21] Eisenhower, in his famous speech to the UN General Assembly in December 1953 stated, 'The atomic age has moved forward at such a pace that every citizen of the world should have some comprehension, at least in comparative terms, of the extent of this development of the utmost significance to every one of us. Clearly, if the peoples of the world are to conduct an intelligent search for peace they must be armed with the significant facts of today's existence.'[22] Eisenhower proposed that an international agency should be set up, under the auspices of the United Nations, which would administer the international expansion of nuclear technology for peaceful means.

Perhaps of wider international significance, The International Atomic Energy Agency (IAEA) was approved on 23 October 1956 and came into effect on 29 July 1957. The 'objective' laid out under Article II focused primarily on promotion and enablement of atomic energy for peaceful means. As Hamblin points out in an article written after the Fukushima disaster in 2011, the issue of accountability was a grey area in the statute and has remained so ever since.[23] In *The Guardian*, Oliver Tickell made the point in 2009 that the IAEA quickly made an agreement with the WHO in 1959 to 'give the IAEA an effective veto on any actions by the WHO that relate in any way to nuclear power'.[24]

> 'The Agency shall seek to accelerate and enlarge the contribution of atomic energy to peace, health and prosperity throughout the world. It shall ensure, so far as it is able, that assistance provided by it or at its request of under its supervision or control is not used in such a way as to further any military purpose.'
>
> IAEA Statute, 1956

In addition, Britain also became a leader in civilian nuclear power through the establishment of the UKAEA in 1955, and it was significant that the Calder Hall reactors were the first in the world to produce electricity for the national grid. In his discussion of the Bradwell Inquiry (1956), Ian Welsh states, 'every effort was made to associate the proposed reactor with the symbolic imagery contained within prestigious documents from the national arena'.[25] As part of her work on post-war France, Gabrielle Hecht introduced the term 'technopolitics', which refers to 'the strategic practice of designing or using technology to constitute, embody, or enact political goals', as part of her analysis of civilian nuclear energy and the formation of national identity.[26] The British nuclear programme, therefore, can be viewed as a 'technopolitical' strategy to fulfil political aims at home and abroad. After all, British nuclear developments would mould the public perception of Britain's place in a world increasingly shaped by the Cold War.

This was the decade where popular understanding of nuclear weapons and their potential dangers increased significantly, as evidenced by the publication of pamphlets such as *Atomic Warfare* (1950) and *The Hydrogen Bomb* (1957) and the increased detail and number of nuclear themed articles in the press.[27] A series of Defence White Papers produced between 1955 and 1957 was discussed in the national press and, as we will see, contributed to the rise of CND. Intellectual culture linked explicitly to the politics of nuclear weapons is one aspect of the nuclear age that has not been examined in much detail by historians. It is clear that, in the broader Cold War context, political and ideological allegiance sometimes came before moral or ethical stances over nuclear weapons. In December 1957, Philip Toynbee asked members of the British intellectual elite to respond to his essay 'Thoughts on nuclear warfare and a policy to avoid it', and the responses were published in 1959. Members of Parliament, the Archbishop of Canterbury, the Bishop of Chichester, Canon John Collins, A. J. Ayer, A. J. P. Taylor and E. M. Forster were among the respondents, and many disagreed with Toynbee's idealistic vision of a nuclear-free future, which involved Britain taking the lead in dispensing with nuclear weapons.[28] Clearly, broader Cold War anxieties over the threat of communism still held sway for some of those with influence over nuclear policy. Indeed, Oxford professor Isaiah Berlin was not comfortable responding publicly to Toynbee's essay.[29] Historian Richard Maguire has offered a 'novel conceptualisation of nuclear *cultures* in government. His work deepens our understanding of how the British government and bureaucracy operated in the era of the H-bomb, and explores the actors involved in decisions concerning nuclear weapons.'[30] He argued that there were many nuclear mindsets in government, again emphasizing the deeply personal connections made by individuals to the nuclear state. There are many controversies surrounding the establishment and maintenance of secret atomic institutions in the post-war period, but it is clear that these institutions served as powerful actors between states and, as Hiltgartner et al. point out, could also serve as powerful pacifiers and propagandists arguing for the legitimacy of the atomic utopia.[31]

Civil defence in the nuclear age

Vast amounts of intellectual, political and imaginative energies were put into nuclear civil defence planning in the 1950s, which was carried out at great financial cost. Between 1953 and 1955 alone, £198 million was spent on this, although as understanding grew over the massive devastation nuclear weapons would cause, and more attention turned to making deterrence work, the annual total dropped to £22 million in 1957.[32] Although this cost was on civil defence more broadly, and not exclusively nuclear civil defence, the 1950s was the period nuclear civil defence expanded in Britain, following the rather vague Civil Defence Act (CDA) of 1948. As Grant states, the CDA 'allowed nominated ministers to issue civil defence regulations for the preparation of civil defence plans throughout Britain' after the realization that there had been no preparations in place around the Berlin crisis.[33] Recently, historians have shown special interest in the 'Strath Report' (1955), written by the head of the Cabinet Office, Central War Plans Secretariat Sir William Strath, which 'divided policy into three strands: life-saving, national survival and national recovery'.[34] As Hughes suggests, this was an example of how government ministers were compelled to 'think the unthinkable' and imagine the likely consequences of nuclear war.

'The standard of living of the reduced population, although substantially lower than at present, would still be well above that of the greater part of the world. The country would be left with sufficient resources for a slow recovery.'

The Strath Report (1955) TNA, CAB 134/940

In *After the Bomb*, Matthew Grant charts the development of civil defence in the post-war era. With the public acknowledgement of nuclear capability, the British government needed to reassure and educate the British population. Grant's main thesis is that civil defence was always viewed as a facade, but it was a 'necessary facade'. Throughout the 1950s, the British public were urged to join the voluntary Civil Defence Corps with a national recruitment campaign that started in 1950, which persuaded over 200,000 volunteers to join by mid-1952.[35] The government produced a series of campaign posters, advertisements and films that stressed the importance of national duty and responsibility.

One such film, *The Waking Point* (1951), produced by the Crown Film Unit, tells the story of an upstanding citizen who slowly concludes that he must join his local civil defence group. He joins up and is on a training exercise when the core message of the film comes through the dramatic intervention of a dream sequence. The central character awakes from a nuclear nightmare and realizes in an instant that he must join in local civil defence activity. So, the cultural logic at play is that nuclear fear exists, but this can be confronted directly, by joining the Civil Defence Corps. It is unclear whether the dream sequence was supposed to speak directly to the assumed nuclear nightmares facing all British citizens at the time, but it is an interesting – and ironic – encapsulation of everyday life in the early Cold War (Figure 4.1).

FIGURE 4.1 *A nuclear nightmare convinces one man of the necessity of civil defence. The film represents official recognition that British citizens may experience extreme emotions due to nuclear anxiety: 'It hasn't happened. There's still time'.* The Waking Point *(1951). Crown Film Unit. Crown Copyright.*

It is an example of an official government recruitment narrative that implicitly acknowledges that nuclear fear may be a reality for the watching audience, but rather than protest against a system that creates fear, the responsible citizen should join the government as a local leader in reassurance and placation. After all, 'somebody's got to do the job [...] can't blame 'em for trying to be prepared this time' and it 'wouldn't have done much good last time if everyone had stuck their head in the sand'. It is interesting that 'last time', the Second World War, is introduced as a moment of collective strength and pride, something which was designed to appeal to a British audience. The phrase 'it hasn't happened...there's still time' encapsulates an active call to engage, and remain engaged, with civil defence initiatives. Faced with a nuclear nightmare, our hero remains resolute. Although acknowledging he is just as afraid as the audience, the protagonist chooses the 'correct' path.

Civil defence adverts attempted to convince people of the necessity of nuclear preparation. It was the cornerstone of responsible, dutiful citizenship to offer reassurance and resolve against imagined nuclear attack. It was also deemed necessary to promote the idea that there were ways to combat nuclear anxiety. For instance, a cartoon from 1957 (Figure 4.2) depicts a mushroom cloud over an urban setting with 'H-bomb threat' written on it. The accompanying caption reads, 'if you think it's hopeless you're wrong'.[36] By attempting to gain support for civil defence initiatives, the mushroom cloud is mobilized as part of a normalized political imaginary, where the citizen is expected to counter future threats by acting in a reassuring and dutiful manner as a civil defence volunteer. The initiatives were an exercise in emotional management, attempting to persuade and cajole British people into positive ways of thinking and acting in response to future nuclear

FIGURE 4.2 *'If You Think It's Hopeless You're Wrong'*, Daily Mirror, *26 September 1957, p. 14. Image published with permission of Mirrorpix.*

threats. Published in 1958, a Home Office pamphlet entitled *Home Defence and the Farmer* contains stark imagery of the fallout cloud in a rural setting. A green, pastoral setting is dominated by fallout, and detail is offered over the levels of radiation that is likely to affect livestock and organic produce. Informative and educational, this literature was designed to answer questions and allay anxiety over possible nuclear attack.[37] Again, this advice served to normalize the expectation of nuclear attack, while offering rational advice on how to respond. Individuals were expected to take responsibility in their local communities in the event of nuclear attack.

Yet, as Grant states, 'beyond the Corps very little had been achieved in concrete terms. Evacuation and shelter policy were seen as central elements, but no evacuation scheme had been discussed in detail, and any shelter policy would need an enormous level of government commitment for it to be implemented.'[38] In February 1954, the first UK civil defence fallout shelter exercise was carried out, setting a pattern of controversial national, regional and local mobilization exercises, which was resisted in Coventry.[39] Resistance to these exercises, and to the nuclear civil defence ethos, would increase as the decade progressed.

It could be argued that civil defence propaganda served to reinforce nuclear anxiety, strengthening assumptions around the possibility of imminent nuclear attack. This implicit acknowledgement of nuclear fear is evident in other official narratives. Winston Churchill made a speech to the House of Commons in March 1955, where he 'packed his broodings on the terrible theme of H-bomb war, his "long-pondered observations", dominating the crowded House'.[40] He stated, 'I find it poignant to look at youth in all its activities and ardour, and most of all to watch little children playing their merry games, and I wonder what will lie before them if God wearies of mankind.'[41]

'The hydrogen bomb has made an outstanding incursion into the structure of our lives and thoughts.'

Winston Churchill, *The Hydrogen Bomb* (HMSO, 1957)

This can also be seen in a brief preface from Winston Churchill from the 1957 pamphlet, *The Hydrogen Bomb*, above. There is a real sense of foreboding, and an acknowledgement that the thermonuclear bomb has altered collective and individual lives in 'structural' ways. It seems clear that Churchill was framing these thoughts in terms of morality and responsibility. Discussing 'the structure of our lives and thoughts', 'children playing their merry games' and religious anxiety, Churchill was expressing the paradox of nuclear deterrence. While believing in the necessity of deterrence, there was official acknowledgement of the inevitable anxiety and existential worry this caused. A Gaumont British News broadcast of Operation Grapple from 1957 also expresses the inherent contradictions at the heart of nuclear deterrence, with the voice-over stating, 'as the nuclear clouds finally drift into fantastic shape, we are reminded of the cloud of doubt and fear that still hangs over the world. Another world conflict would almost certainly mean the end of our civilization. But, in the belief that possession of the great deterrent is the only way to ensure world peace, Britain has become a joint custodian of the deadliest weapon yet devised by man.'[42]

With this general idea in mind, the French scholar Michel Foucault wrote, 'the power to expose a whole population to death is the underside of the power to guarantee an individual's continued existence'.[43] This official notion of responsible nuclear citizenship would be increasingly challenged by anti-nuclear voices in British life. As we have seen, official articulations of the nuclear state, including imagery and language used in civil defence propaganda, served to normalize nuclear danger, mobilize localized imaginaries of destruction and refer to the huge psychological and ontological shift the nuclear age created for British citizens. Therefore, it is perhaps not surprising that alongside the rise of nuclear weapons and civil defence programmes, the 1950s also saw the rise of anti-nuclear thought and protest.

The rise of anti-nuclear thought and protest

We have seen already that the immediate period after 1945 saw religious leaders and intellectuals ask questions about the morality of the atomic bomb. During the Manhattan Project, nuclear scientists also voiced their concerns over the use of the atomic bomb and contributed to peace movements after war ended. It was the announcement of American plans to create a nuclear bomb in 1950 that created a groundswell of anti-nuclear sentiment in the 1950s until the formation of CND in February 1958, the same month that America began supplying Thor missiles to Britain. Its founding members included Bertrand Russell, J. B. Priestley, A. J. P. Taylor, Michael Foot, Pat Arrowsmith, Canon John Collins and Sheila Jones. The movement had varied origins, with the Peace Pledge Union and 'Operation Ghandi', the Emergency Committee for Direct Action Against Nuclear War (DAC), the National Council for the Abolition of Nuclear Tests (NCANWT), formed by Peggy Duff,[44] and the Committee of 100 all offering scattered and small-scale protest from the early 1950s. Bertrand Russell offered a broadcast on Christmas Eve of 1954 in 'an urgent appeal for efforts to stop what seemed to him to be a drift towards global war, and said that this country could be knocked out by five hydrogen bombs'.[45] Russell also worked with a number of nuclear scientists in establishing the Pugwash Conferences, the first of which was held in Canada in July 1957, to assess the dangers of nuclear weapons.[46] Holger Nehring has written about the importance of transnational anti-nuclear networks in this period.[47] The Russell–Einstein Manifesto, announced on 9 July 1955, stated,

> In view of the fact that in any future world war nuclear weapons will certainly be employed, and that such weapons threaten the continued existence of mankind, we urge the governments of the world to realize, and to acknowledge publicly, that their purpose cannot be furthered by a world war, and we urge them, consequently, to find peaceful means for the settlement of all matters of dispute between them.[48]

French theologian Albert Schweitzer broadcast his 'Declaration of Conscience' in April 1957 and called for an end to nuclear testing.[49] Schweitzer argued that 'not our own health only is threatened by internal radiation, but also that of our descendants [...] we are forced to regard every increase in [...] radioactive elements by atomic bomb explosions as a catastrophe for the human race, a catastrophe that must be prevented'.[50] Idealistic words inspired new forms of anti-nuclear action in the 1950s. For instance, in 1957 Harold Steele took to sea in an attempt to disrupt the H-bomb tests organized by Britain, which was reported in *The Manchester Guardian* on 12 April 1957.[51]

This idealism did dovetail with some sections of the British political elite. A nuclear debate in the House of Commons in April 1954 led to the creation of the Hydrogen Bomb National Campaign. However, this lacked 'a clear, unifying policy demand and could only agree on a lowest common denominator support for Mr Attlee's Parliamentary motion which asked for a disarmament conference to be convened and the UN to be strengthened'.[52] After the 1955 White Paper which announced that Britain would go ahead with nuclear weapons development, debates emerged in the Labour Party over Britain's nuclear armament, which served to divide opinion within the party for years to come.[53]

In the immediate period leading to the establishment of CND, Taylor and Pritchard point to four main catalysts for the emergence of the mass anti-nuclear movement.[54] In 1957, alongside widespread anxieties over the launch of Sputnik, American diplomat and historian George Kennan delivered the Reith lectures which warned of the dangers of nuclear confrontation, at the Labour Party conference Bevin performed a policy u-turn, rejecting the unilateralist position. As a result, J. B. Priestley wrote 'Britain and the Nuclear Bombs' published in the *New Statesman* in November 1957. Priestley's article, along with Kennan's contributions, later published as *Russia, the Atom Bomb and the West* (1958), served to illustrate the extent to which unofficial articulations of anxiety over the direction of nuclear politics could make a significant difference to the composition of nuclear culture. Meredith agrees that these two intellectuals provided 'the catalyst of CND's formation'.[55] After Priestley's article generated a huge response, key activists and intellectuals met at the home of Kingsley Martin (he was the editor of the *New Statesmen*), which led to the formal establishment of the CND in 1958 (Figure 4.3).[56]

The press had appeared largely positive over the aims and behaviour of the anti-nuclear activists, contributing to wider anti-nuclear discourse before the CND was formed. *The Spectator* offered a nuclear-themed issue in 1955, stating, 'the object of the four preceding articles is to focus attention on the grimmest reality in contemporary life which is also the central fact in contemporary politics – the existence of the hydrogen bomb'.[57] Another article from 1956 called for a halt to all nuclear testing due to the adverse health effects of such activity. The piece cited a report written by the Medical Research Council, which was also publicized in the national press more widely.[58] Debates around nuclear contamination from bomb testing developed significantly, adding to calls for nuclear disarmament.[59] The rise of CND and anti-nuclear thought in the 1950s proved to have lasting influence on a vast range of intellectuals, artists and politicians. Yet, some claimed that CND failed to affect political change due to the fragmented, disorganized and politically divided make-up of the movement, and charges of elitism and left-wing collusion served to delegitimize the anti-nuclear message.

FIGURE 4.3 *Aldermaston march, 1959. Photographer unknown. Used with kind permission from The Peace Museum, Bradford.*

Journalism

In the 1950s, journalistic nuclear narratives became increasingly complex and ambiguous. On one hand, the development of nuclear culture in this period was shaped by an official and institutional nuclear vocabulary that suffused the press in the 1950s. Because of the militarized and secretive nature of the bomb and nuclear power, the dissemination of information from government sources was always partial. This leads to the need to acknowledge the extent to which nuclear culture was shaped by the control of knowledge and by the government-manufactured 'public' face of nuclear policy.[60] Reporting over the development of nuclear technology became effected by government sensitivity over the further development of nuclear weaponry. As Jenks states, 'in late 1954 and early 1955 the government sought to limit the BBC's freedom in reporting on the hydrogen bomb [if it was] presented too abruptly or in too alarming a fashion there was a real danger that people would adopt a defeatist attitude'.[61]

Therefore, nuclear issues were treated with trepidation by broadcasters in the 1950s. In an article entitled 'This is what the B.B.C. could not let me say', Emmanuel Shinwell 'learned at the week-end that a B.B.C. discussion on the H-bomb, in which he was to have taken part, has had to be postponed because of a rule barring topics due to be debated by parliament.' On the same page, Mrs Kathleen Sparks from Cowley, Oxford, writes a letter contributing to an argument on euthanizing disabled children and states, 'if only he had the courage to advocate the "putting to sleep" of the people behind the atom and hydrogen bombs!'[62] There is also a nuclear cartoon on the same page, offering further complexity to the range of nuclear narratives readers were confronted with. It is clear that the press also contained a significant amount of counter-narratives to the official line. Nuclear narratives were becoming more varied and more ambiguous in their potential meaning.

An article from the *Daily Express* in March 1957 entitled 'The Atom Revolution', and subtitled 'Nuclear power stations boost Britain's future', quotes Lord Mills, the Minister of Power, as saying, 'I believe we are at the beginning of a new power revolution which holds for us the promise of a more glorious future.'[63] It was a common aspect of the press in the 1950s to read about the bright nuclear future. Paradoxically, only days before, the *Daily Express* ran a front-page story on how a group of Manchester University students managed to fly a banner over Calder Hall, with the headline reading 'Students Mock Atom Guards'.[64] The article is typical of many newspaper articles in that the line between nuclear power and nuclear weapons often becomes blurred in the popular imagination. Whether Calder Hall was chosen by the students because of its links to weapons production is unclear, and the writing on the banner is not referred to. The two articles mentioned are just a sample of the tendency for aspects of the press to both promote the efficacy of nuclear power and implicitly reinforce the sense of danger and controversy surrounding nuclear issues. In 1958, the *Daily Express* ran a front-page story discussing the danger of planes carrying H-bombs crashing. The headline 'H-bombers: new shock: atom dust could be scattered in crash' was followed by official advice: 'it is a good rule for the public to keep clear of an accident area'. Or, as an American government spokesman was quoted as saying, 'either stop breathing or get the hell out'.[65] This type of language reads as a precursor to the tone set by *Dr. Strangelove or: How I Learned to Stop Worrying and Love the Bomb*[66] but, more importantly, demonstrates the origins and reinforcement of nuclear uncertainty.

By the late 1950s, the increasing visibility of nuclear culture led to a heightened sense of public awareness of existing and emerging nuclear threats. Sections of the press would stress the need for Britain to lead the way in the military application of nuclear physics while implicitly reinforcing the danger at the heart of nuclear science. This is especially true when considering the way in which the tabloids dealt with the H-bomb tests. An article by Chapman Pincher[67] of the *Daily Express* from March 1957 reads,

A highly organized campaign to stop the British H-bomb tests due to take place on Christmas Island soon is being waged by certain civilians, scientists and churchmen. If it succeeds, Britain will be reduced to the status of a country which will wield no influence in world affairs because it will wield no military power. Without a stockpile of H-bombs Britain will suffer the disgrace of being reduced to a satellite of America instead of being a fully-fledged ally with Independent strength to deter aggression. And no H-bombs can be stockpiled until the Christmas Island tests have been completed.[68]

The idea of 'Britishness under threat' is promoted by Pincher, who argues that for Britain to remain powerful, H-bomb tests were inevitable. The H-bomb tests are not imbued with aggression themselves but are depicted as a deterrent, as fundamentally defensive and peaceful in the face of external threat. The article is printed next to a cartoon by Giles, itself accompanied by song lyrics styled as a parody of a Cy Grant calypso number. The lyrics poke fun at Macmillan's close relationship with America, making reference to the recent agreement that America would station Intermediate Range Ballistic Missiles on British soil.

> For Uncle Sam is sending us some Guided Missiles,
> Said a shipyard worker laughing fit to bust,
> You won't see my heels for Atom Dust.

The juxtaposition of the article and the lyrics illustrated a key aspect of nuclear culture by 1957. The *Daily Express* promoted the British possession and continued testing of the H-bomb, while also implicitly demonstrating an awareness of public anxiety over the existence of thermonuclear weapons. Printing a parody that reinforces the presumed popular response to the threat of nuclear annihilation – fatalism laced with humour – illustrates the extent to which journalistic culture confirmed pre-existing assumptions over nuclear bombs. While reinforcing 'official' nuclear vocabulary, newspapers also contained 'counter-narratives' that reflected popular attitudes on nuclear technology, helping to explain any failures to emotionally manage British citizens through civil defence initiatives.

Daily Express coverage of the H-Bomb test in May 1957 was celebratory and patriotic, under the headline 'Bang Goes Ours'.[69] In June, an article penned by Cassandra appeared in the *Mirror*. Headlined 'Like an Oil Painting from Hell', the piece describes the second British H-bomb test. Cassandra appeals to religious sentiment, placing the H-bomb at the centre of wider human concerns and firmly in the foreground of an uncertain and unknowable future. The piece reinforces the idea that nuclear weapons will, in some way, shape or dictate a future over which the individual has no power.

> [...] on the 31st day of May in the Year of Our Lord 1957 [near] Christmas Island, [...] the British people exploded their second hydrogen

bomb. IT WAS A DRESS REHEARSAL FOR THE DEATH OF THE WORLD [...] we, the observers, looked like grotesque mourners [...] We were thirty-five miles from where The Beast was due to explode after being spewed out from the bomber – quite near enough in view of the fact that the power of the bomb was equal to several million tons of TNT [...] Through closed eyes, through dark glasses and with my hands still covering my face, I saw the flash. Brighter than the sun, hotter than the sun, and ripped out of the secrets of the heart of the Universe [...] AND THERE IT HUNG BEFORE US, A BOILING RED AND YELLOW SUN LOW ABOVE THE HORIZON. IT WAS AN OIL PAINTING PROM HELL, BEAUTIFUL AND DREADFUL, MAGNIFICENT AND EVIL [...] We were watching something also connected with death on a prodigious scale - death, however, that does not lie in the past, but death that is waiting in the future. The vast shape, now increasing with size every moment, rose upward and turned white with a reddish glow in the interior. A thin, snakelike stem appeared at its base, as steam and water were sucked up from the sea below. The horrible pudding in the sky became a diseased cauliflower and then changed into the familiar mushroom.[70]

On many levels, this piece of writing would have confirmed and reinforced assumptions at the core of nuclear culture in the late 1950s. Death and uncertainty, military and political power, Britishness and the self, nature and religion and enormous scale all characterize the piece. The tone of the article compels readers to recognize themselves as part of a collective – the 'British people' have exploded this bomb – that is complicit in this unnatural and dangerous act that threatens the future of humanity. Yet, readers are also compelled to conceive the H-bomb as intricately linked to their own future, their own emotional core. The activation of both a nauseous self-image and a vivid conception of the future are apparent.

Two articles from the *Daily Express* in March 1958 offer another layer of understanding to the development of nuclear assumptions. Over two days, Donald Edgar presented a series of brief interviews from members of the public. Oxford undergraduates comprised the first group to be interviewed, and workers from car factories surrounding the city were approached for the second set of interviews. The immediate context was the proposed referendum on nuclear disarmament at Oxford University amid anxiety over continuing atomic bomb tests worldwide. The coverage of nuclear issues in the *Daily Express* was clear-cut, offering negative thoughts on anti-nuclear protests, anti-nuclear plays and anti-nuclear personalities.[71]

Much of the damnation lay in stressing the centrality of emotion to the anti-nuclear argument. In both articles, readers were told of the emotional, even 'hysterical' pleas of the anti-nuclear activists. In response to such emotion, apparent calmness and rationality pervaded the undergraduate community at Oxford,[72] where 'instinctive common sense' was displayed by the workers in their approach to nuclear politics.[73] Edgar continued the narrative to its logical conclusion and argued there were acceptable ways to deal with the psychological pressures created by nuclear anxiety, and these should be articulated in particular ways in public discourse. Strangely, this narrative sat uneasily with the ideas expressed by the female interviewees. Family, children and the future were constant themes across the articles. One young lady interviewed in a 'works canteen' said, 'when I read the effects of radiation on children I feel that it's no longer worth having a family' but, she continued, 'it's no use being cowardly and allowing the Russians to have their own way'. Another young lady in the canteen said, 'I think the tests should be stopped for the sake of the children. There is too much radiation already.'[74] One female undergraduate was quoted as saying, 'sometimes when I think about the bomb and realize that I shall probably have a family I feel like cutting and running to some island.' Another female undergraduate stated, 'I feel deeply about the bomb. It is not a political issue. Mine is a feminine point of view. There are worries for a woman – genetic worries – misshapen children.'[75]

While Edgar denied that there was an overwhelming sense of anxiety, the fragments of interviews he chose to include speak of a sense of powerlessness, resignation and a surprisingly unified understanding of nuclear danger. The biological self-image of these young women was shaped by knowledge of the alternative directions their lives could take in the event of nuclear war or nuclear contamination. The women implicitly acknowledged that they had no control over this process, and profound anxieties were projected into the future. Edgar did not present these responses as 'emotional', yet they were framed with a profound sense of resignation, powerlessness and fatalism. For Edgar, there was nothing noteworthy or unusual with the fact that women – *in separate contexts* – were framing their future with reference to an imagined set of nuclear consequences on their unborn children. Anxiety over the radioactive contamination of future generations seemed to be an anxiety that straddled classes and defined individual responses to nuclear weapons.

A year earlier, in 1957, the Windscale fire gave another reason for families to worry about the health and future of their children. National symbolism was prominent in the coverage of the accident in the *Mirror*. The front-page article, headlined 'Threat to Children?' in reference to the contaminated Cumbrian milk, was placed below a piece on the Queen's state visit to Canada.[76] The *Daily Mirror, Daily Express* and *Times* carried front-page reports of the atomic leak, citing the existence of 'atomic dust'. As the reasons behind the fire became apparent, it was clear that luck and uncertainty underlay the industrial use of nuclear energy, although a façade of certainty was necessary to offer legitimacy for and public trust towards nuclear science. In an ITV *Late Evening News* interview, a Dr Kemp discussed the effects of atomic radiation, and the need to 'ease the hysteria […] and the uninformed public mind'. Asked about the danger to children born in the next ten years, Dr Kemp answered 'some 50,000 children are expected to be congenital idiots within the next ten years'.[77] On the ITV *Late Evening News* on 13 October 1957, a Dr Maclean answered questions about placing restrictions on milk supplies contaminated with radioactive iodine following the Windscale fire stating 'you can't explain radioactivity to a cow [...] with atoms you can't be too careful'.[78]

Just as the royal opening of Calder Hall a year earlier was presented as an event of national significance, the *national* failure that the fire represented is reinforced by the article's proximity to an image of the head of state. The journalistic representation of the silent and invisible danger of radiation from the reactor accident led to another layer of anxiety for British households. Although scholarly work has suggested that the incident did have a powerful and lasting impact on the local community,[79] the accident did not lead to significant panic or anxiety about the role of nuclear energy in British society. The discursive power of the vocabulary employed by journalists, with discussion of atom dust, radioactive milk and near-catastrophe, may have had more impact in its implicit reinforcement of central aspects of nuclear anxiety than anxiety over the incident itself.

The incident shows that understandings of nuclear danger developed in a number of ways. The relative passivity shown by the national public may indicate not only the level of trust still existent towards official explanations of the fire, but also acts as part of the foundation for broader anti-nuclear sentiment by reinforcing the idea of nuclear science on a knife-edge. The Penney Enquiry of 1957 seemed to confirm that a certain amount of luck and uncertainty defined the way in which the technicians dealt with the crisis.[80] Also, it is clear that if a filter, 'Cockcroft's Folly', had not been belatedly added to the huge cooling chimney during the construction of the power station, the radioactive leakage could have been disastrous. The fire at Windscale generated a nuclear assumption that would become increasingly powerful: that nuclear science was unpredictable and uncontrollable. Not only did powerlessness in the face of nuclear attack become an existential and political issue for many Britons, but powerlessness felt in the face of state-controlled use of nuclear fuel also led to an implicit understanding that the individual had little democratic voice in response to government policy on energy. This aspect of nuclear culture can be viewed as a set of understandings defined by the limits of democracy and the fragility of the modern project.

Everyday life

It was in this decade that nuclear culture began to have a significant impact on everyday life. Nuclear anxiety was echoed in the national press, and the range and variety of nuclear reportage increased. Accompanying these narratives of nuclear anxiety in the 1950s were debates on mental illness more generally. For instance, in the *Daily Mail* on 13 August 1957, a report entitled 'The Mentally Sick' gives the reader the 'facts' about mental illness, stating, 'this morning there are 250,000 people in our midst who are "certified" mental patients. Another 50,000 are voluntarily taking treatment for mental disorders but are not certified as mentally unsound.' The report does not discuss whether these figures are increasing but creates the impression of an acute social problem, as the article begins with 'Another murder. Another "maniac" sought' in reference to the murder of seven-year-old Allan Warren in East London.[81] Nuclear anxiety joined a number of other social anxieties in British national culture.

Aspects of British nuclear culture in the late 1950s were commercialized. In 1957, Kelloggs gave away 'atomic submarines' to British households, in packs of Cornflakes.[82] Advertising such toys to children and parents in the national press suggests that popular discourse was already dependent on a range of assumptions over the excitement and awe surrounding nuclear technology. Elsewhere, households were asked to 'Fit [an] Atomic weather-strip and banish draught forever.'[83] On Wednesday 11 September 1957, a horse named 'Atomic Test' ran in the 4.40 at the Doncaster St Leger.[84] Seemingly small-scale, these nuclear referents contribute to an understanding of how nuclear culture textured day-to-day life in a variety of ways. A travel piece from the *Daily Express* dwells on the memory of August 1945, when a journalist visiting Japan wrote, 'at a children's party a photographer nearly blinded us all trying to take a group photo with a home-made flash bulb. Afterwards, still rubbing my eyes, I overheard one nine-year-old boy say to another: "That was just like the pikadon". A friend explained: "That is our word for the atom bomb. Literally it means brightness-noise." I realized how deep an impression Hiroshima had made on Japan'.[85]

On occasion, the rural idyll was mobilized as a way to push away anxiety around nuclear attack. A piece in *The Listener* from May 1954 mentioned, 'when a Leicestershire man wishes to forget for a time his income tax, and politicians of all brands, and the hydrogen bomb, and the onward march of science in general, he goes for a walk along a few of the hundreds of miles of paths which in that part of England are so numerous'.[86] Scottish actor Bill Paterson recalls preoccupations with the nuclear age in his autobiography, writing

> and this is where the icon of that year [1955] came into focus. You'll have heard of it of course. It was 'the bomb'. Britain was joining the H-bomb club. We had moved on from that simple old atomic thing and we had become one of the Big Three. The world was moving to the brink. [...] And we knew quite a bit about mushroom clouds. They could be found again and again in our comics, Scottish Movietone News, bubble-gum cards – everywhere! It was the dominant image of the day rivalled only by that rounded oblong of the TV screen which framed it so well.[87]

Paterson recollects how, as a boy, he would join other children in throwing dust from the top of high-rise tower-blocks in Glasgow to create an inverted mushroom cloud: harmless play, in the nuclear age.

Interviews carried out by Sarah Hewitt suggest that knowledge of nuclear development created, for some, real anxiety. Hewitt interviewed men and women who had children in the 1950s and 1960s. One respondent, Lily, remarked on the nature of nuclear anxiety, when she said, 'it was always in the back of your mind that this was going on, it wasn't a very nice thing to be aware of'.[88] Similarly, asked to dwell on the prospect of a nuclear attack on the family, another respondent, Barbara, said,

> I always used to worry about it [...] oh. do you think the children are ever going to grow up you know. Our parents had the worry of the war but that was like a different kind of thing than a bomb, because people used to say sometimes, I know now it wasn't true, but people used to say oh they only have to drop one on England and the whole lot would go, you know, the whole lot of us would go.[89]

When asked about nuclear anxiety, another respondent, Vera, said 'Oh yes. I know other people used to feel like that because we used to talk about it with friends you know and they all felt the same, all women felt the same as me.'[90] Here, there is certainty in this memory of shared understanding of nuclear anxiety. One fascinating recollection from Barbara confirms this sense of a shared experience of nuclear anxiety and recalls a situation that occurred in the mid-1950s:

> at the time, you know, I was very frightened and I think everybody was really, if you spoke to anyone at the time they always had that underlying fear [...] I took my daughter to the clinic, she was only about six weeks old and she had a little milk rash on her face and you know being my first baby, the least little thing of course you worried sick over it don't you? So I went to the clinic, the doctor's clinic, and I went in and said to the nurse, oh, look at my babies face, she has got a milk rash all over her face. I was absolutely stunned because she said to me 'you mothers make me sick', she said, 'in six weeks we might all be getting blown to bits and your worried about a rash on your babies face'. Well you can imagine how I felt, I was absolutely horrified, I thought 'oh God does she know something?'[91]

Talking in more general terms about nuclear threat, Vera said,

> It made me very frightened and very fearful for the future and worried about my son [...] Do you know what my husband used to do? He used to hide all the papers from me because I was so worried about it [...] especially the Sunday papers because I'd sit there all day reading them up.

He'd say 'look you're worrying for nothing. What's worrying? Don't be worrying about it. Just forget about it'. But you couldn't forget about it [...] I would look at John playing in the garden with his little friends and you'd think are they going to grow up and have a future? [...] At times it made me feel very depressed as though not worth living if that's how everything is going to end up. It's an awful thing to say but you know all your loved ones and all your family and all what you have worked for and everything wouldn't mean a thing, would it?[92]

The interviews support the idea that British identity, the sense of self and nation and the biological self-image of women were shaped, to some extent, by nuclear culture in the post-war era. The recollections of people who lived as young adults through the 1940s and 1950s seem to speak of a shared understanding of the negative consequences of nuclear technology, a shared cynicism of British political culture and a tarnished view of the Allied victory. The experience and memory of war pervaded the majority of the interviews. The memories are very powerful, evoked strong emotions in the participants, and have brought to light obscure, unpleasant and unexpected stories. The specific nature of these stories and the recollection of the emotional experience of living through a period of tension in the Cold War suggest that, for some, life was punctuated by moments of real nuclear anxiety. Clearly, knowledge of nuclear danger was a consistent influence on everyday life. It is also tempting to make parallels with Edgar's *Daily Express* interviews, in terms of the shared assumptions, anxieties and powerlessness that pervade these narratives.

The family that feared tomorrow

In an upsetting incident from August 1957, a married couple, Elsie Marshall, a nurse, and Andrew Marshall, a felt weaver from Langho, near Blackburn in northwest England, gassed their three children then jumped into the sea after tying themselves together with a cord 'as thick as a window sash'.[93] Their bodies were washed up on the beach at Blackpool. The coroner's report reached a conclusive verdict of manslaughter and death by suicide pact. There are no more details about the mental state of the couple, but the story was reported in the regional and national press.[94] An article published in the *Daily Mirror* on 16 August 1957 entitled 'The Family That Feared Tomorrow' (Figure 4.4) is of particular interest because of the focus on the suicide note left by the couple. According to the *Mirror*, part of the suicide note read, 'in view of all the things that are happening in the world and the talk of new wars which will mean extermination of masses of people and especially children we decided we could not allow this to happen to our children'.[95]

FIGURE 4.4 *'The Family That Feared Tomorrow'*, Daily Mirror, *Friday 16 August 1957. Image published with permission of Mirrorpix.*

The note was a calm and resolute explanation for their decision. Although the note made no direct mention of nuclear war the report, along with an accompanying commentary by resident 'agony aunt' Mary Brown, made the assumption that the Marshalls had succumbed to the pressures of nuclear fear. The narrative constructed by the *Mirror* hinges on the tragic juxtaposition of quaint domestic concerns and fear of global nuclear war, appearing at once familiar and understandable to the contemporary reader.

The treatment of this story by the *Mirror* offers a peculiarly British vision of life in 1957. The event and its representation is one more illustration of the way in which knowledge of nuclear danger shaped domestic, social and political narratives in the late 1950s.[96] The reference in the suicide note to the fear of 'extermination of masses of people and especially children' is an articulation of a self-image where no bearable future existed. For the Marshalls, the assumption that a nuclear war would represent the end of existence itself was informed by conventional assumptions at the core of nuclear culture. That the nuclear threat appears both imminent and inevitable is itself a familiar Cold War motif.

Rather than over-privileging the role of nuclear anxiety in the Marshall's own lives, it is more fruitful to turn to the presentation of the story in the *Mirror* because this is the unofficial narrative that contributes to our understanding of nuclear culture. In an accompanying piece, Mary Brown dwelt on the fact that the Marshalls 'couldn't face bringing up their children in a world they thought threatened by war [...] a father and mother feared the nuclear bomb – not for themselves, but for their children'.[97] The tone of the piece became subtly condemnatory in tone, expressing the wish that Elsie had come to her with her anxieties. She says, 'they saw the future as a dark abyss, and this vision blotted out all the small endearing day-to-day compensations for living'. Brown went on to say, 'only last week I talked to a young mother, who said: "I wish I hadn't had my children. What future is there for them?"'[98] Brown concluded on a hopeful note, stating, 'love is stronger than fear'. Domestic tranquillity was mobilized against the dark abyss, and simple, honest, common-sense reassurances were designed to resist the perceived threat of the nuclear bomb.

This vocabulary evoked not only a threatened way of life, but threatened morality and spirituality as well. The individual was told to stand firm. While Brown acknowledged the 'weight' and power of nuclear anxiety, she told her readers that they must consciously choose love over fear to ensure the survival of the family unit and the domestic idyll. An idealized vision of Britain was offered, as a place populated by reflective moral citizens who shunned fear and anxiety by falling back on Christian doctrine and common sense. The reaction of Mr and Mrs Marshall was presented as understandable, yet futile and somewhat pathetic. The *Mirror* was happy to construct a direct link between nuclear anxiety and the suicide pact, and Brown suggested that high levels of anxiety were natural, yet *manageable and survivable* by citizens who followed a simplistic doctrine of 'how to live'. Yet again, a form of emotional management was taking place as a response to the implicit acknowledgement of the reality of nuclear anxiety. Brown did not explain or elaborate upon this anxiety. Instead, it was assumed that the reader had an implicit understanding of the negative aspects of nuclear culture. This suggests that the negative intellectual and emotional characteristics of the British nuclear state had become a normalized component of British individual experience by the late 1950s.

Furthermore, the representation of the Langho suicides suggests that departures from idyllic or conventional forms of British family life were uneasily received in the post-war era. Similarly to Edgar, Brown presented the dark heart of nuclear culture as part of the Cold War that could be defeated in the home. In his work on Englishness and landscape, Matless explored how images of the family unit produced in the post-war era contributed to a particular, idealized sense of domestic tranquillity.[99] Aspects of nuclear culture that emerged in the 1950s contributed to the disruption of this idealized sense of Britishness. Writing in 1968, Jeff Nuttall suggested that the advent of the bomb had led to pervasive and powerful social forces in British society:

> the people who had passed puberty at the time of the bomb [1945] found that they were incapable of conceiving life *without* a future. Their patterns of habit had formed, the steady job, the pension, the mortgage [...] all the paraphernalia of constructive, secure family life [...] To acknowledge the truth of their predicament would be to abandon the whole pattern of their lives. There would therefore have to pretend [...] In any case, to look the danger in the eye might wreck the chances of that ultimate total security their deepest selves had contrived, death by H-bomb [...] The people who had not yet reached puberty at the time of the bomb were incapable of conceiving life *with* a future. They might not have had any direct preoccupation with the bomb. [...] But they never knew a sense of future. [...] They pretended too, but they did not enter the pretence at all cheerfully. In fact they entered the pretence reluctantly, in pain and confusion, in hostility which they increasingly showed.[100]

If Nuttall is accurate in his analysis, he points to individual experience and selfhood in the 1950s being shaped by the realization of possible nuclear annihilation. Maybe it became *impossible* for certain people in certain circumstances to 'pretend'? In the *Mirror*, Mary Brown asked people to pretend, and it seems the women Edgar interviewed for the *Daily Express* were in the habit of pretending. The Langho incident shows us how imagined annihilation, with its assumed imminence and inevitability, became discursively linked to extreme forms of human behaviour, including suicide, in the British press. Viewed as a mental breakdown from one or both parents that led to private and then public expressions of confusion and violence, the public representation and rationalization of the act itself points towards deep-rooted and powerful assumptions on nuclear danger. This impression generated in the British press of society 'on a knife-edge' dovetails with the Langho case, where mental distress was linked with nuclear fear. The narrative of annihilation is re-emphasized a month later, with an article on a broadcast made by Sandys in Sydney, Australia, where he said that if a war started it would 'inevitably result in the wholesale destruction of her cities and the annihilation of a large part of her population'. Sandys argued for the continued policy of deterrence, commenting,

I do not believe there is any real likelihood of a direct large-scale military attack upon the free world as long as we all of us, according to our capacity, continue to maintain together an effective system of collective defence [...] the fact that we enjoy peace and freedom today is due largely to the nuclear strength of America, to whom we are all profoundly grateful [...] we are now in a position to make a limited contribution to the nuclear deterrent, either from bases in Britain or from overseas bases.[101]

So, less than a month after the dramatic Langho story, readers of the *Daily Mail* learn about ongoing nuclear geopolitics, where fears over annihilation are confirmed by the official use of the term.[102] A few days later, the *Daily Mail* ran a piece on the dangers of atomic bomb tests. The article refers to comments made by Dr Thomas Carter (a member of the Medical Research Council's team at Harwell) when asked about the danger of bomb testing. He said, 'you must accept it as a firmly established genetic fact that any radiation exposure will produce mutations [...] and therefore it is no good saying when it will become dangerous. It is already dangerous. You have to make a social and political judgement of how much genetic damage you are going to accept for whatever you conceive to be the advantages.'[103]

Actual and imagined encounters with nuclear weapons were made sense of through recognition of underlying assumptions on nuclear danger. This helps us to understand the ways in which British nuclear policy was both collectively and individually experienced.[104] Nuclear culture shaped the British self-image in many different ways. Unravelling the emotional consequences of nuclear anxiety helps us understand how individuals were reacting or conforming to, shaping or rejecting the nuclear state. The nuclear state came to represent violence and power and, for some Britons, the meaning of existence came to be informed by a deep-rooted understanding of the potential violence, unnaturalness or imminent impact of nuclear technologies. So, it is in this regard that explorations of nuclear culture can help historians understand more fully the ways in which individuals in the post-war era conceived the world, life, selfhood and nation.

Cathy Caruth wrote on traumas that can be considered to be 'deeply tied to our own historical realities'.[105] While nuclear anxiety was purely imaginary for many, it could also be linked to direct experience or indirectly shaped by the recent experience of war and the recollection of fear.[106] Nuclear anxiety could be localized for city-dwelling Britons who realized that 'the present survival and flourishing of the city were simultaneously underwritten and radically threatened by its identity as a nuclear target'.[107] Imaginary projections of nuclear attack were based on the rational realization of the *possibility* of future annihilation. Some intellectuals proved less willing to acknowledge nuclear anxiety as uniquely modern but saw it as aligned with categories of fear somehow 'inherent' to mankind. In 1966, literary critic Frank Kermode wrote, 'the paradigms of apocalypse continue to lie under our ways of making sense of the world'.[108] Even though he was clearly preoccupied with the threat of nuclear weapons, he wrote, 'it would be childish to argue, in a discussion of how people behave under eschatological threat, that nuclear bombs are more real and make one experience more authentic crisis-feelings than armies in the sky'.[109] Arguing that nuclear anxiety was just another form of fear inherent in humankind, Kermode seemed to deny the uniquely modern predicament at the heart of nuclear danger and instead insisted on 'hard-wired' responses to external threat. On the contrary, nuclear anxiety is uniquely modern in that it is a human response to a manmade threat of unprecedented magnitude. The perspective of Anthony Giddens illuminates the ways in which large-scale developments in the 'military industrial complex' can shape the self-image of citizens:

> Modernity reduces the overall riskiness of certain areas and modes of life, yet at the same time introduces new risk parameters largely or completely unknown to previous eras [...] the late modern world is apocalyptic, not because it is inevitably heading towards calamity, but because it introduces risks which previous generations have not had to face [...] In high modernity, the influence of distant happenings on proximate events, and on intimacies of the self, becomes more and more commonplace.[110]

Modernity created dangerous possibilities for mankind. Nuclear anxiety was new, unique and defined partly by the failure of the modern project.[111] In the post-war period, the British people experienced a 'changed imagination of infinitude'[112] as the structure of their present and future was altered by the shadow of the bomb. Examples of tense human experience in the 1950s speak of the incapability of some Britons to come to terms with the impact of nuclear anxiety.

Yet, some British people responded with humour. A cartoon drawn by Giles, and published in *The Sunday Express* on 2 July 1950, demonstrated the fatalism and common-sense approach to the threat of the H-bomb, acting as a cynical comment on the absurdity of the arms race. Giles had picked up on a peculiarly British sensibility, with the homely atmosphere of the cartoon highlighting the ways in which the norms of home-life and domestic activity had been overturned in the nuclear age. The destruction of the garden is calmly watched over, presented alongside a wish to preserve the family unit in the future. The cartoon was an expression of a new reality, at once inescapable but endurable. This quirky response to the atomic threat was reflected in another cartoon from Giles.[113] The appearance of the 'atom dress' was a comment on the absurdity of the atomic arms race. The sympathy of the reader would have been activated by the realization that the wearer of the asbestos suit may be the only rational person in the image. Yet, the cartoon is also an opportunity for Giles to comment on irrational overreactions to the atomic threat. Another cartoon from Giles offers a glimpse into the perceived levels of nuclear anxiety that existed in 1950. Published in the *Daily Express* on 6 December 1950, the cartoon captioned 'It's all right – 't were only boy Fred's motor-bike backfiring', demonstrated the strength of feeling around international atomic policy. The men were depicted as newspaper readers 'in the know' about nuclear world affairs, seemingly on the brink of panic over potential nuclear attack. The everyday noise of a back-firing motor is presented for comic effect. Yet, the representation of hysteria stemming from the noise signifies the potency of nuclear anxiety in day-to-day life, also reflected in the assumption that readers of the *Express* would identify with an ever-present atomic threat. One last cartoon by Giles from 1955 shows a family struggling through a snow blizzard accompanied by 'a letter from Giles', which reads,

> This family, like thousands of others who live not so very far from the great cities, where the first tiny puff of wind blows the whole electric supply out of action, wishes to register a protest. Stumbling through the darkness of a recent long-spell breakdown, banging our shins on redundant electric washing machines, silent radios, fireless electric fires, out into the blizzard. We reached our shed where we keep our faithful emergency candle. And there lay a copy of your last week's paper announcing that the Electricity Boards were going to start monkeying around with Atomic Power Stations. Many bitter neighbours who have been tempted into buying expensive items such as electric milking machines, electric poultry breeding equipment and so forth feel that the local powers-that-be should learn a little more about the power they have before they inflict us with another [...] 'No, my boy, you CANNOT have another candle to see to read *Nuclear Ned – Space Rider* in your horror comic.'[114]

The existence of these themes in popular national newspapers indicates how nuclear culture influenced the work of Giles and demonstrates how a particular type of nuclear knowledge was disseminated into everyday life in the Cold War era. Through case studies such as the Langho suicide pact, we have seen the importance of local and global lenses of analysis. British nuclear culture in the 1950s was characterized by a fusion of ambiguous attitudes towards the nuclear bomb and nuclear power. The Langho case study helps us understand the ways in which this fusion of ideas was discursively transmitted to a variety of audiences through cultural and political means. There were some similarities in the responses to perceived nuclear threat and, in the 1950s, there was the emergence of an uneasy British identity that was formed in response to common nuclear assumptions.

AIRSPACE IN THE NUCLEAR AGE

In August 1952, an Avro Vulcan (named after the Roman god of fire and destruction) took off on its first test flight. The aircraft was developed as a high-speed bomber capable of carrying a nuclear payload. This aeroplane was one of three British 'V' bombers developed for the delivery of nuclear missiles. The development of new, iconic, modern jet bombers meant that the British public was now aware of a further spatial dimension of the Cold War – the air. Airspace was populated, militarized, dangerous and defined by these new machines simultaneously representative of military defence and the deepest of psychosocial fears: the falling of the nuclear bomb, emerging silently from the clouds.

Could this be the period where the changing nature of airspace became integral to the nuclear imagination? By the end of the 1950s, it was possible to fire nuclear warheads via aeroplanes and intercontinental missiles. Airspace itself had become part of the nuclear imaginary: a normalized, occupied and militarized space, created through repetitious military routine, made real for British citizens by the visual and aural reminders in everyday life, but also through film, fiction and journalistic narratives. These nuclear objects held some control over airspace and the senses, holding material and symbolic power.

Alongside those other narratives that transformed notions of British landscape, nuclear bombers flying through the airspace of democratic Britain denote the legitimacy of deterrence, the visibility of the nuclear state and, for some, the apex of British identity and standing in world affairs. The high-tech machine as object simultaneously does the work of national strength and national vulnerability. Operating in airspace in peacetime, these machines were at once symbolically reassuring, aesthetically impressive and technologically advanced. Implicitly, they reinforced the reality of the nuclear arms race and the threat of nuclear attack. They were presented as peaceful icons of deterrence, yet were the machines that could be piloted towards Moscow, ready to initiate nuclear war.

Popular culture

Nuclear-themed films, TV dramas and fictional texts entered the mainstream as the 1950s progressed. These unofficial narratives were important articulations of nuclear opinion and prove to be excellent social commentaries for historians to analyse. They served to reinforce social anxieties over nuclear technology, radioactive contamination and the future. The visual politics elucidated by various forms of popular culture offered nuclear resistance in the form of subtle anti-nuclear ideas and implicit political statements. *The Quatermass Experiment*, broadcast on TV in 1953, then adapted to film in 1955, had expressed contamination and mutation as key anxieties, stressing the domestic setting beset by mysterious, unseen forces. *Quatermass 2*, broadcast on TV in 1955, and put to film in 1957, again with Val Guest as director, included atomic science as a central theme. Other nuclear-themed stories that circulated in British culture included the novel *On the Beach* (1957), the British film *X The Unknown* (1956) and the US film *The Day the World Ended* (1955). Other films of note included *Creature with the Atom Brain* (1955) and the French romantic drama *Hiroshima Mon Amour* (1959). Screened in 1951, *The Man in the White Suit* was an Ealing comedy revolving around the creation of an indestructible suit containing radioactive thorium.

J. B. Priestley's play *Doomsday for Dyson* was adapted for TV and broadcast on ITV in March 1958. The TV play dealt with the aftermath of nuclear war and included some distressingly violent scenes, culminating in a plea for nuclear disarmament. The overall message was that feelings of powerlessness could be overcome by political action. A televised debate on disarmament followed the transmission and, the following day, the *Daily Express* sneered at the conclusion of the play, where 'Dyson woke up to potter towards the kind of anti-bomb meeting Mr Priestley has been organising lately. It was clear that Mr Priestley was still dreaming himself.'[115] Other papers proved more sympathetic to the disarmament movement, but the *Daily Express* took a hostile line on anti-nuclear sentiment. In his analysis of *The New Men* (1954), a novel by C. P. Snow, Sinfield argues that 'cold war paranoia permeates and confuses C. P. Snow's novel about British scientists working to develop an atomic bomb'. In the book, the morality of using the bomb on Hiroshima and Nagasaki is explored alongside a spy mystery and a general crisis of liberal humanism where 'events may get too big for men'. Sinfield believes that *The New Men* reveals a 'servile adoption of the US interpretation of the Cold War and a consequent collapse of any serious political ethics'.[116]

April 1959 saw the TV adaptation of Marghanita Laski's 1954 play *The Offshore Island*, a play that again dwelt on the consequences of nuclear war, more specifically nuclear fallout, playing on fears of sterilization and mutation. The play emphasized the direct physical consequences on the human body of radiation and, again, a sense of powerlessness pervades the story.[117] Published in 1954, a character in *Secret Pilot* by George E. Rochester flies with the aid of an atomic-powered flying suit, and as a cadet in the Royal Air Force he finds himself on a dangerous mission. Children's books also reflected the preoccupation with the nuclear age, with Geoffrey Willans and Ronald Searle publishing *Whizz for Atomms* in 1956.[118] David Campton's three plays from 1960, including *Out of the Flying Pan* and *A View from the Brink*, were performed on the Aldermaston CND march in 1960. On the Aldermaston march, Alan Brien from *The Spectator* stated it was 'a tremendous stimulation of ideas and arguments and witticisms and friendships and love affairs. Perhaps it would be more tactful to keep this

X THE UNKNOWN (1956), DIRECTED BY LESLIE NORMAN/JOSEPH LOSEY

A Hammer Film Productions creation, *X The Unknown* was one of the first films to graphically depict the injuries radiation could cause on humans. Filmed in the perpetual darkness of the Scottish countryside, the threat of radiation is reinforced from the very first scene of the film, when the audience is introduced to soldiers learning to use Geiger counters on a training exercise near Lochmouth Atomic Energy Laboratory. The plot involved a series of mysterious deaths, ranging from radiation poisoning to the complete melting of human victims. The film shows this in gruesome detail: the human body powerless against the nuclear aura. As the casualties increase, the authorities, who now include Inspector McGill from the UK Atomic Energy Commission, are led by physicist Dr Adam Royston. Royston believes an ancient form of life – which resembles a huge ball of tar in the film – has been awakened from the depths of the earth. This new species is in search of radioactive substances as a source of sustenance.

The new species is highly radioactive and is endowed with glowing, dangerous and mysterious properties. It is uncontrollable, and humans are powerless if caught in its relentless path. Alongside the rural setting, the muddy plains and woodland, the creature is a force of nature, dominating and suffocating everything in its path. The film tapped into fears inherent to the nuclear age and familiar to the audience.

Although scepticism towards the role of the atomic scientist is expressed by the father of a child who has died of radiation exposure ('you should be locked up, with others like you, letting off bombs you can't control'), the film is not critical of the atomic establishment or the military. Instead, the experts are faced with a problem to solve, and they do so with calm resolve and good character. This is not a moral or political fable, and the only emotions are shown by the few female characters in the film, or men rendered weak or terrified by radiation. A highly masculinized plotline culminates in various acts of heroism in order for the authorities to regain control of the natural order of things. Royston invents a ray machine that neutralizes radiation, but once the creature has been destroyed, the film stops abruptly before it is clear what the implications of this discovery may be. It could be argued that this is a narrative that resists closure by suggesting the ambiguity of the nuclear age and the unpredictable new technologies that exist.

As an unofficial narrative, we can view *X The Unknown* as a film that reinforces anxieties over the mysteries of radioactivity and the dire realities that may be emerging in the nuclear age. Inescapability and powerlessness are ideas that are promoted in the face of nuclear danger. In the end though, the authorities of the nuclear state are able to understand and then control this powerful new danger. The film simultaneously played on contemporary fears and allayed them.

revelation a secret – but the Aldermaston March is the rare phenomenon of a physical and social pleasure which yet has an intellectual and moral justification.'[119] In this period, unofficial fictional narratives seeped into anti-nuclear protest, shaped nuclear culture and informed British culture more widely.

These brief examples show the divergent forms nuclear culture took and hint at the ambiguous messages that the public received. Fictional narratives contributed to nuclear culture by placing anxiety and powerlessness at the emotional core of assumed responses to nuclear threat. Autobiographies that dwell on this period can also help us understand the extent of nuclear anxiety and the ways in which different nuclear narratives overlapped in everyday life. In his autobiography, Richard Hoggart remembered the impact Nevil Shute's novel *On the Beach* (1957)[120] had on some of the people he knew:

> [...] it seems to have captured something in the mood of many people, especially families, whether normally middlebrow readers or not, of that first generation to be haunted by the thought that their children might have no future at all. A neighbour [...] once told us she had regular nightmares in which the bomb had been dropped and she could find neither her husband nor the children. We all have such nightmares, but it was very much of the time that such a woman, the wife of an academic and mother of four, should have these dreams; and should have read Shute. Middlebrow or not, he had touched a nerve, caught the sense of a moment.[121]

Similarly to the Langho story, this brief but powerful description suggests that individuals, in different regional, social and domestic contexts, interacted in powerful and complex ways with the imagined threat of nuclear war. These interactions were shaped by national 'real-world' events and fictional narratives and created a range of physical and emotional consequences. This combination of real and imagined threat takes on particular significance in the 1950s, a decade already defined by the trauma and memory of war.[122]

Art and design were also influenced by nuclear culture. Catherine Jolivette has been one of the first to research British art in the nuclear age. One article explores 'both the fascination and the fear that coexisted in the 1950s and 1960s, and looks not only to celebrations of technology, but also to protest art, visions of mutant hybrids, and apocalyptic landscapes'.[123] Jolivette has also edited a collection of essays that examine a range of aspects of art in the nuclear age demonstrating the extent to which art and artists were bound to the hopes and anxieties of the nuclear age.[124] *Fear and Fashion* details a major exhibition at the Victoria and Albert Museum, as does *Cold War Modern: Design 1945–1975*.[125] One way to understand the divergent responses to nuclear technology in the 1950s is to identify similarities at the heart of such responses. By analysing journalistic discourse, it emerges that British citizens had an implicit understanding of the negative aspects of nuclear technology. In turn, evidence suggests that these negative intellectual and emotional characteristics became a normalized aspect of individual experience in late 1950s Britain.

Conclusion

This chapter has examined the way in which unofficial nuclear narratives proliferated in the 1950s. The nuclear state had become public, which generated a complex range of responses and examples of resistance from the British people. Nuclear culture had now become a significant aspect of British life. On the official side, the nuclear state had become mobilized in a way that would remain persistent into the twenty-first century. As we have seen, this was a decade which saw the dramatic development of nuclear weaponry alongside the civil nuclear programme. Knowledge over the danger of fallout became widespread, publicized through the printed press. Significant trends emerged in the decade which would continue in the years after, including the institutionalization of the nuclear establishment as part of the state system. Increased awareness of nuclear danger in the 1950s generated new forms of resistance, anxiety and politics. Anti-nuclear ideas became gradually more prominent as a response to global nuclear testing and civil defence initiatives, and popular culture reflected these more mature nuclear ideas. Articulations of the nuclear age in films such as *On the Beach* marked a real shift in the representation of nuclear realities.

Central to the decade was the articulation of a larger range of responses to the nuclear age. As historians, we can explore these responses by looking at official and unofficial narratives. We have seen how newspapers not only offered both reportage on government policy and decision-making, but also offered counter-narratives which give us an insight into the lives of British people. The 1950s was the decade where unofficial anti-nuclear sentiments rose in prominence, leading to a distinct cultural politics which allowed for the emergence of new forms of expression, resistance and subjectivity. By the end of the 1950s, every adult in Britain had some knowledge of atomic bombs. Individuals understood the instantaneous and lasting damage that atomic and thermonuclear weapons could inflict on themselves and their loved ones, and they knew they had no control over this possibility. Britons watched nuclear nightmares unfurl on film in the knowledge that the British government was an active participant in the global nuclear arms race.[126] Worldwide nuclear tests conducted throughout the 1950s were well publicized and created anxiety in Britain, leading to the test ban debate. In British newspapers, it was not unusual to see familiar Cold War motifs, such as concentric circles over urban centres and mushroom clouds. Reinforcing the omnipotence of nuclear danger, journalistic narratives also stressed the importance of nuclear science and civil defence. Nuclear anxiety was reinforced by the detailed reporting of specific nuclear dangers such as the 'unnatural' and hideous consequences of nuclear fallout. These ambiguous nuclear narratives were normalized as both apocalyptic and everyday.

CHAPTER FIVE

Radicalized and Realist Nuclear Culture, 1959–1975

The 1960s is often interpreted as a decade that represented a series of turning points for British culture, culminating in a social and cultural revolution and a transformation of political and sexual rights.[1] Internationally, the decade began with the ongoing Berlin Crisis, and the most infamous moment of the Cold War, the Cuban Missile Crisis, occurring in 1962. The decade ended with the signing of the nuclear non-proliferation treaty in 1968, one of the signs of relaxed Cold War tensions. Yet, 1968 was also the year Britain launched its first medium-range nuclear missile, Polaris. In 1974, Chevaline, the Polaris improvement programme, was initiated in secret.[2] Therefore, we see a tension emerging that characterizes nuclear culture to the present day. Even in times of peace, and apparent moves towards nuclear non-proliferation, the British nuclear state sustained its policy of deterrence, which meant maintaining large numbers of cutting-edge nuclear weapons and delivery systems at huge expense. From 1973 until 1982, Britain maintained 500 nuclear warheads, its highest number in the whole nuclear century.[3] Through the long 1960s, deterrence policy did not face serious challenge, even with powerful international treaties including the Limited Test Ban Treaty of 1963 and the sustained anti-nuclear activism of the CND. The nuclear state went from strength to strength, almost completely hidden from democratic oversight.

This chapter will examine the ways in which nuclear culture fits into this political and cultural landscape. While unofficial narratives became more radicalized and vocal, it is questionable what direct impact they had on political policy. It is clear that unofficial narratives in this period increasingly challenged the nuclear state and reflected broader attitudes of cynicism and distrust towards nuclear policy. We see new forms of nuclear resistance emerging, but the nuclear state remained a persistent and committed presence in British life, as spending on nuclear defence remained high. Through their realistic visualization of nuclear war, some unofficial narratives in this era proved to be highly effective and radical statements on the nuclear present. We have seen that the diversification of responses to nuclear technology witnessed in the 1950s led to new expressions of nuclear subjectivity. The emergence of the anti-nuclear protest movements was the most visible and obviously radical reaction to nuclear danger, but a diverse set of cultural responses and individual stories offer a window onto a more complex, often understated, type of British radicalism. As the Cold War moved into a period of 'detente' in the 1970s, reporting around nuclear weapons diminished in the British press, but issues around nuclear power in Britain continued to be a frequent issue of discussion. Also, persistent public awareness of nuclear threat meant that nuclear anxiety re-emerged powerfully in the late 1970s. Silence around nuclear issues also indicates the extent to which the nuclear state had become a permanent aspect of British life.

The pattern we have already seen emerging in the 1950s, namely the clash of official and unofficial narratives, remained strong in the long 1960s. It can be argued that unofficial narratives became increasingly radicalized in this period. If nuclear counter-narratives were emerging in the 1950s, it was in the 1960s that counter-narratives flourished. Viewed alongside official sources, this chapter will argue that radical unofficial narratives in the 1960s normalized more radical anti-nuclear sentiment. The decade demonstrated the high levels of knowledge that British people had on nuclear issues and also highlighted more powerfully than ever before the many possible ways of responding meaningfully to the existence of nuclear anxiety.

Context and historiographical overview

Wider debates on 'the 1960s' are useful to acknowledge, as they help explain the cultural conditions that were in place to allow the radicalization of unofficial nuclear narratives in this period.[4] The backdrop of the social reforms of the Wilson government, increasing engagement with perceived foreign policy failings and the increased prominence and legitimacy of youth culture meant that the conditions were in place for a wider range of cultural responses to the nuclear arms race. In April 1960, 33 per cent of British people believed nuclear weapons should be given up. In the years that followed, British people demonstrated remarkably stable levels of opposition to nuclear weapons, with around one in three people voicing their wish for Britain to disarm.[5] In domestic politics, broadly bipartisan support for the nuclear deterrent continued. For analysis of British nuclear politics in the 1960s, see Epstein's article on the nuclear deterrent and the British election of 1964, Len Scott on 'Labour and the Bomb' and Kristan Stoddart's recent work which has looked at the 'technical working level' of strategy, policy and decision-making in Britain between 1964 and 1970.[6] Andrew Priest has traced the diplomatic and military relationship between Britain and the United States from 1962, including analysis of the Nassau Agreement and the launch of Britain's first medium-range nuclear missile, Polaris, in 1968.[7] In June 1959, the United States launched its first nuclear-powered submarine equipped with the Polaris missile and, in February 1960, France conducted its first nuclear test in Algeria. The Committee of 100 conducted major civil disobedience at the Ministry of Defence in February 1961, and in March, the first US nuclear submarine arrived at Holy Loch Scotland.

October 1962 is well known for the series of events that became known as the Cuban Missile Crisis. In April 1963, the Polaris sales agreement was reached.[8] The official history of the British nuclear state in this period can now be traced in some detail. A selection of government publications is freely available through the National Archives, and a considerable range of declassified government files is also available, some online.[9] These include the Home Defence Policy from 1960, *Bahamas Meetings December 1962: Texts of Joint Communiqués* (1962), *Statement on Defence 1964* (1964), the 1962 and 1963 Defence White Papers and *Statement on Defence 1964* (1964).[10] As Baylis and Stoddart state, 'in 1960 the potential vulnerability of Britain's nuclear delivery systems, the V-Bomber and the proposed Blue Streak missile system, led to the decision to purchase the air-launched Skybolt system from the United States.'[11] Furthermore, 'the 1958 MDA and 1963 PSA fundamentally altered the entire basis of British nuclear weapons policy. No longer was there a truly independent British nuclear deterrent in all its aspects as had existed prior to 1958. Instead there was a co-operative nuclear alliance with the Americans.'[12] However, 'by the mid-1960s, the fraternal association between the two Anglo-Saxon powers described by Winston Churchill was showing signs of strain.'[13]

It was in this decade that a major effort to create nuclear defence bunkers developed as part of secret 'policy to provide an alternative system of government within Britain'.[14] This had the effect of nuclearizing the British landscape and demonstrating the permanence of the nuclear state. Matthew Grant's *After the Bomb* is a very useful guide to the reasons civil defence became redundant by 1968. Owing to economic pressures, and public cynicism towards civil defence more generally, civil defence was not considered a 'necessary façade' by the end of the 1960s. First discredited, then attacked, civil defence now appeared an unnecessary burden on a stretched economy.[15] Anxieties around specific nuclear incidents were also apparent, for instance, 'Hazards of Nuclear Defence' from *The Guardian* in 1964 reported an explosion at a missile silo in Searcy, Arkansas. The article was used to open a brief discussion on the recent safety record of US and British military bases. The reader is assured that 'with aircraft only twice has a nuclear bomb been dropped accidentally, and neither went off'.[16] The piece ends with a tribute to the fact that no major accidents have befallen the British military. In this sense, the period was defined by a continuation of a range of nuclear anxieties stemming from the continuation of the nuclear state and the unpredictability of nuclear politics. This unpredictability reached potentially catastrophic levels during the Cuban Missile Crisis. In response to the Soviet attempt to station nuclear weapons in Cuba in October 1962, America created a blockade, preventing Soviet ships from delivering the weapons to Cuba. After negotiations, the crisis ended, with an agreement that the Soviets would remove nuclear missile sites from Cuba if America promised not to invade the island. A further secret deal saw America pledge to remove nuclear weapons from Turkey. On 23 October, during the crisis, British Foreign Secretary Alec Douglas-Home gave a speech which unequivocally called for a peaceful resolution to the stalemate, citing the 'choice' that faced humanity:

> By putting medium range and intermediate range ballistic missiles into Cuba Russia is deliberately placing her own power in a position to do three things – to threaten the United States, to threaten the Caribbean, and beyond those two, to threaten South America. We must recognize that this is plainly an act of power. At a time when the non-dissemination of nuclear weapons to non-nuclear countries is on the agenda at Geneva, Russia introduces these weapons into new places. I hope the Russians will see in time where their policy is leading. I can promise them this: immediately she settles down to negotiate, Russia will find the most ready response from our government [...] Meanwhile, I can only say to our own countrymen that the Prime Minister and myself, upon whom the main burden decision must fall, will, once we have checked the present fever, play our full part in an attempt to end the cold war and do everything we possibly can to cooperate with all countries, and the Russians if they will come in, in the creative tasks of peace. One other alternative is there for us. As I ventured to say to the United Nations only a few weeks ago: 'Man is now at the point of choice and the choice is this: whether we blow ourselves to bits or whether we sit down round the table and negotiate and negotiate again, however long that process lasts. That is the choice we have before us today'.[17]

Again, we have an official narrative which replicates the familiar motif of 'the choice' in the nuclear age. Humanity as a whole is implicated in the decisions of a small group of political elites, and uncertainty pervades the tone of the speech. Historical interpretation stresses the political uncertainty surrounding the situation, although Scott argues that the crisis was not as dangerous as is often claimed.[18] On 10 October the following year, the Limited Test Ban Treaty came into force, which banned above-ground nuclear testing. Seen in the light of the post-Cuba mood of reconciliation and the Anglo-US sales agreement over Polaris in April

1963, the treaty was a timely and sensible acknowledgement of the real dangers of nuclear testing. The Kennedy assassination in November, and the Stephen Ward and Christine Keeler scandal, meant that the British tabloid press quickly moved on from any discussions over the importance of the treaty, although the broadsheets dwelt on the meaning of nuclear test ban a little longer.

Commenting on the treaty in his 1963 Nobel Prize lecture, American scientist and peace activist Linus Pauling said, 'I believe that the historians of the future may well describe the making of this treaty as the most important action ever taken by the governments of nations, in that it is the first of a series of treaties that will lead to the new world from which war has been abolished forever.'[19] His speech was certainly indicative of a level of optimism at the time, with the *Daily Mirror* claiming 'tomorrow could become a turning point in the history of mankind' the day before the Treaty was signed on the anniversary of the Hiroshima atomic bombing, [20] and then a few days later stating, 'after yesterday's signing of the nuclear test ban treaty there is a spirit of self-congratulatory joy in Moscow'. American officials were reported as saying the treaty would increase security and decrease risk of war.[21] That optimism was not shared everywhere, by everyone. After the signing of the treaty, CND made a hesitant and cautious assessment of the impact of the treaty. *The Guardian* proclaimed 'last week's partial test ban may mark the beginning of the end of one cold war and the beginning of another', arguing that the treaty would not stop the manufacture of nuclear arms, only somewhat impede proliferation.[22] Additionally, the treaty did not threaten sanctions if countries violated the treaty. Letters to editors of the newspaper are also unconvinced about the importance and solidity of the treaty.[23] Details over the continuing problems related to global fallout were reported in the national press in the days after the signing of the treaty. *The Guardian* offered a stark appraisal, stating,

> there will remain, however, the fallout that is already with us – in the soil or in our bodies. Some of it, falling on grass, has been eaten by cows and has found its way into their milk, and thence into bone or tissue of people drinking it. Some, falling on the earth, is taken up by the roots and the cycle is repeated [...] it will be 20 to 30 years before the deposited fallout ceases to require careful study.[24]

Readers were asked to stretch their imagination '20 to 30 years' into the future and contemplate the extent of the unpredictable and immeasurable contamination inflicted on the world. These narratives stress the extent to which all readers are part of this new reality, in some way responsible for critiquing the long-term effects of the nuclear state. Immediate responses to the treaty, as represented in the national press, were ambiguous. There was an air of celebration on one hand, and advised caution on the other. In broader historical perspective, the treaty was hugely significant in human and wider ecological terms. To comment on Pauling once again, Masco has argued that:

> Pauling portrayed each above-ground nuclear detonation not as a sign of American technology and military strength but rather as a large scale genetic experimentation on the human species, already involving tens of thousands of victims. The scientific critique of atmospheric fallout expanded the definition of nuclear disaster from war – a thing that could be deferred into the future – to an everyday life already contaminated with the cumulative global effects of nuclear explosions.[25]

Humanity had turned away from one means of polluting the earth, its ecology and living organisms, but it did not rule out other ways to contaminate. Masco has made the point that 'the move to underground testing contained more than simply the nuclear device, it also redefined how Los Alamos scientists could experience the power of a nuclear explosion, fundamentally changing the technoaesthetic potential, and thus the politics, of the bomb'.[26] Masco argues that nuclear weapons became characterized in more banal terms due to the lack of visible effects. Also, 'nuclear fear became more mobile as the invisibility of nuclear contamination engaged new psychic and cultural registers in a global, cold war nuclear complex.'[27] If we engage with these different perspectives on the broader meaning of the Limited Test Ban Treaty, the Treaty can perhaps be considered the moment that signalled the slow disappearance of the British nuclear state from public view.

Yet, it is clear that the British glorification of military hardware was common in this era, as evidenced in films such as *Delta 8–3* (1960), directed by Harold Baim.[28] The film shows three bright white Vulcan nuclear bombers slicing through the blue sky in perfect formation. The narrator, accompanied by stirring music, reminds viewers of the skill and dedication of the pilots and the fact that the squadron is 'dedicated to peace'. By having these high-powered nuclear bombers, 'Britain can play her part' in world affairs, helping to deter nuclear conflict. Simultaneously, the nuclear referent is hidden and only implicitly stated throughout the film. At one point in the film, the audience is pointed towards contrails in the air: a new product of the jet age. At once other-worldly yet familiar, these material reminders of the nuclear age confirmed fears inherent in the nuclear imagination.

Organized anti-nuclear activism

There was significant diversity and growth of organized anti-nuclear activity in this period and, more generally, an increase in cynicism towards nuclear policy. CND continued to be a powerful presence in British life in the early 1960s, with a number of prominent personalities coming into public view in this period and membership numbers remaining healthy.[29] By the end of

1959, polls showed that 30 per cent of people agreed that nuclear weapons should be banned, and there were over 300 local CND groups in towns and cities across Britain.[30] The annual Aldermaston marches were well publicized and were a source of rich anti-nuclear expression. In terms of political policy, Labour came close to adopting a policy of nuclear disarmament, but their leader Hugh Gaitskell refused to commit to nuclear disarmament after a push for this at the Labour Party Conference in 1960. By now, Labour had split into 'nuclear warrior and nuclear abolitionist' groups, where 'the perennial battle between the Left and Right' of the Labour party saw the disarmament commitment of the 1960 conference reversed in 1961.[31] The CND archives at LSE contain details of the discussion over Bertrand Russell's decision to join and publicly support the Committee of 100, a group of anti-nuclear activists who believed direct action to be the strongest way to advance the cause. He wrote many letters to the press and caused 'regrettable' publicity because of this. A letter by Russell dated 31 October 1960, going over the controversy, explained why Russell wanted to adopt the tactic of non-violent civil disobedience. This triggered a spiralling chain of letters and alleged 'mis-reporting' in the press.[32] The archival documents certainly demonstrate the extent to which internal strife was commonplace within CND, and how conflict in the Labour Party damaged anti-nuclear solidarity between 1958 and 1962. Russell was himself imprisoned in 1961 for being part of a meeting in Trafalgar Square, which had not been granted official permission. This was considered an act of civil disobedience, even for a ninety-year-old man.

For the rest of the 1960s, the CND developed a series of initiatives in an attempt to educate the public on the dangers of nuclear war. For instance, the 'Fallex' campaigns were created to highlight the absurdity of the NATO high-security classification exercise in September 1962 to test NATO mobilization and command. 'Fallex 63', a direct pun on the official Fallex 62 exercise, was a CND publicity campaign that pointed out the contradictions inherent to the whole idea of 'peaceful nuclear deterrence'. Another campaign, 'Spies For Peace',[33] was part of a wider strategy from CND to put the government under sustained pressure regarding nuclear civil defence planning. Cynicism towards civil defence initiatives was also evident in the press. A cartoon from *The Guardian* in 1962 reads ' "Good heavens, darling, how silly of me. That was no ordinary bang. For I can hear the merry peal of the Special Issue Civil Defence Handbells. It must have been a nuclear bomb exploding". And off they trip to the Family Fallout Shelter.'[34] This parody of chirpy British responses to nuclear threat signifies the normalization in some sections of British society of anti-nuclear sentiment.

CND produced anti-nuclear literature such as 'Nuclear Inferno: Way In' by Tony McCarthy which can be found in the CND archives at the London School of Economics, a leading repository of anti-nuclear source materials.[35] A *Peace News* pamphlet written by Adam Roberts entitled

'Nuclear Testing and the Arms Race' is a useful survey of journalistic responses to atomic policy, discussing democratic deficit and the problem of newspapers bowing to 'anonymous experts'. Roberts asks, 'who are these "experts" and "scientists" who represent us?'[36] This was a period that saw deeper questions being asked of authorities and institutions. The Fabian Society published NATO or Neutrality: The Defence Debate in May 1961. Harold Davies MP published Why NATO? in March 1960 analysing the policy and future direction of NATO. Stuart Hall offered a strong opinion in 'N.A.T.O. and the Alliances' when he wrote:

> Aldermaston 1960 marked the end of the great apathy of the 1950s. The Campaign began as a movement from fear: a slow disengagement from the Cold War, accelerated by the menace of the weapons themselves and the memory of Hiroshima, and propelled by the British government, in alliance with other Western powers, to use nuclear weapons in the event of an attack.[37]

Reporting on anti-nuclear issues was common in the period and included a piece by Leonard Beaton, 'Would Labour give up the Bomb?', from August 1964.[38] Beaton was defence correspondent of The Guardian from 1957 to 1963, authored 'The Spread of Nuclear Weapons', and then became research associate at the Institute for Strategic Studies. The May 1963 issue of Sanity contained an article entitled 'Broadening our Concerns'. A previous issue refers to Punch magazine where, in the last year, 177 jokes had appeared about nuclear testing and eighty-three referred to the protest movement.[39] In July 1962, a story in the Guardian describes how 'the CND's "campaign caravan" had a rowdier send-off on its departure from London on a 1,000 mile tour of the country that perhaps it had bargained for'. There was a brief 'struggle' between CND campaigners and members of the League of Empire Loyalists. The campaign caravan was led by George Clark and toured the country, with Shelagh Delaney joining the campaign in Manchester.[40] In the April 1967 edition of Sanity, The Guardian was accused of being anti-CND.

One CND initiative from 1962 was entitled 'Operation Peanuts'. This was a 'nationally coordinated, regionally organized campaign to take our arguments and the case for our policy to the man in the street and to people in their homes'.[41] The name was a reference to Gaitskell's comment that CND was 'peanuts who don't count'. Student canvassing activity was part of Operation Peanuts in Easter 1962. Three hundred people were involved, and the constituencies of Hammersmith North and Acton were comprehensively covered. Around 4,000 items were sold, including 1,500 issues of Sanity magazine and 1,000 copies of YATB. Additionally, a list of 1,000 new supporters was drawn up.[42] In East Grinstead, 500 houses were canvassed over a week. One hundred and three people signed support for the aims of the campaign, and 42 of the 103, when visited for a second time, agreed to subscribe to Sanity magazine.[43] Organizing secretary Peggy Duff's response to the campaign in 24 September 1962 was mixed, and she said, 'the first operations have been an amazing success [...] and an amazing failure. They failed because far too few people came out. There may be many reasons for this.' She strikes a more positive note by saying, 'if Regions, Groups, and Campaigners are really serious about nuclear disarmament, this is the sort of result we can get all over the country. People are waiting for you to call [...] you will be encouraged by the number of supporters you find, by the ease with which you can sell *Sanity* and pamphlets, by the friendly attitude of many ordinary people to CND.'[44] Clearly, Duff believed that grass-roots support for CND was significant, and that greater energy from the regions would garner results.

Other documents in the CND archives relate to regional groups, for instance the work of Birkenhead and North-West CND in organizing a meeting over Polaris in Birkenhead, Liverpool on 14 March 1968. The organization of the events was evidently quite chaotic, with lots of people at crossed purposes. One letter remarking on the outcomes was sent from CND London Region, claiming that 'very few people of the local area were able to hear the speakers' and 'the environment could only serve to demoralize the supporters present. We hope you will see, if possible, that this does not occur again'.[45] These kinds of sources demonstrate the difficulty in assessing the impact of nuclear culture. They signify the levels of engagement from committed individuals, yet they cannot sum up the impact of the British nuclear state more widely. Yet, as we will see in Chapter 6, a focus on regional activity, or even a focus on individual cities, can help us think about the ways in which different types of nuclear resistance emerged in response to the nuclear state. Historians have interpreted CND activity through a variety of lenses. Jodi Burkett has considered the ways in which British identity can be read through the activities of CND, and Lawrence Wittner has shown that gender roles within CND is an important area of research.[46] Wittner has argued that:

> in the years from 1954 to 1965, the unprecedented danger of the Bomb began to disturb gender norms, turning increasing numbers of women into political activists and of men into concerned parents. This development, in turn, reflected the fact that the looming menace of nuclear annihilation undermined the justifications for traditional gender roles. Women could no longer protect children by caring for them at home and men could no longer guarantee their safety by soldiering.[47]

Wittner hints towards the fact that the nuclear age was influencing the emotional lives of individuals in profound ways. Anti-nuclear activism is one way to identify responses to this, and the transnational character of anti-nuclear thought has been studied by Holger Nehring, among others. Although the nuclear threat was, in part, about turning protectively inwards to the home and family, anti-nuclear protestors also created international networks of activism. In 1968, the national press reported on a peace tour conducted by 47-year-old Masashi Nii. Nii, a Japanese electrical engineer born in June 1921

> was 1,400 metres from the epicentre when the atomic bomb dropped on Hiroshima in 1945. In the basement of a Japanese Army barracks, he and 13 other technicians in their twenties felt a strong wind. They reached the surface to find many people burned to death and of a charcoal colour. Having never heard of radioactivity, the 16 [sic] spent the next week helping survivors. By 1968 the 16 had become four; the rest having died of leukaemia, the disease Mr. Nii has.[48]

When Nii discovered he had cancer of the blood, he 'sold his electrical goods factory for $20,000 in August, 1966. He left his family, using his money to send himself on a lecture tour around the world which he hopes will bring about "disarmament by all nations."' He bought a car, which he drove from country to country (Figure 5.1). *AJR Information* reported that his world tour was planned to be four years long.[49] Nii toured Britain in 1968 and was invited to attend the annual Aldermaston march. *The Times* reported that 'the Aldermaston March this Easter is to be led by Mr. Masashi Nii, a survivor of Hiroshima who is on a four-year peace mission

FIGURE 5.1 *Photograph of Masashi Nii and car. Library of the London School of Economics and Political Science, CND/2008/8/5/5. Photographer unknown. Image published with kind permission of LSE.*

around the world', thus continuing a CND tradition. In 1962, Hiroshima survivors Miyoko Matsubara and Hirosama Hanebusa attended the march. According to the *Morning Star*, Nii addressed the crowd, stating 'today, 100 people die every year as a result of the Hiroshima Bomb'.[50] His visit was also the subject of an article by Anthony Arblaster in the *Tribune*.[51] His tour of Britain was well attended and included talks, civic receptions and a screening of *The War Game* in Walthamstow. The narrative surrounding Masashi Nii in the British press indicates the extent to which the memory of the atomic bombing of Japan served to divide opinion within nuclear debates. The compelling story of Nii, who had survived the initial bombing but who was now succumbing to illness relating to the bomb, represented the reality of atomic victimhood. His contaminated body raised disturbing questions over the morality of the atomic bombings and the morality of the continued existence of the weapons.

Yet, Britain did not embrace atomic victimhood as thoroughly as America, where the 'Hiroshima Maidens' made a famous visit in the mid-1950s. Perhaps due to the need for public redemption for the use of the bombs by the American military, television footage survives of the moment when *Enola Gay* co-pilot Captain Robert Lewis met Reverend Kiyoshi Tanimoto from Hiroshima on *This Is Your Life* (1955). In an almost unwatchable surprise meeting, the Reverend was left consoling the pilot after a tearful recollection of the realization of the vast destruction the bomb had inflicted. This incident is featured in Steven Okazaki's documentary *White Light/ Black Rain: The Destruction of Hiroshima and Nagasaki*.[52] In contrast, the visit of Masashi Nii and other Japanese peace activists to Britain was met in a rather more muted manner, where the need for redemption was largely played out away from national public discourse. As a powerful unofficial narrative, the story of Masashi Nii highlights the nuclear subjectivity of atomic bomb survivors, and the way in which their political activism, in some small way, asked questions of the morality of the deterrence posture.

Journalism

As well as discussion over anti-nuclear debates, Chapter 4 touched upon increasing public concern surrounding fallout levels in the atmosphere due to the huge number of thermonuclear tests conducted worldwide in the 1950s. The British press followed the scientific debates on this issue and reported thoroughly on the main issues. There are instances of strongly worded reports, for instance in March 1960 where readers of the *Daily Mirror* are told that 'there has been a big increase in the level of "death-dust" found in the bones of Britain's babies [...] the highest concentration discovered in the survey was 6.9 Strontium units – found in the bones of a fourteen month Lancashire baby'.[53] Readers of *The Guardian* in October 1963 were told of 'an increase of the amount of radio-strontium found in the bones of young children towards the end of 1962'.[54] By January 1960, British citizens could also be sure that in the event of a nuclear attack, neither their bodies nor possessions would be insured. The extra layer of powerlessness guaranteed to British citizens is encapsulated in the paragraph from 'Insurance Policies and Atomic Energy Risks [...] The Committee does not, however, provide insurance against damage or injury caused by radioactive fall-out from the explosion of nuclear bombs or similar nuclear devices'.[55] Naturally, this is a reminder that acts of war would not be insured against, but elsewhere in the document it seems clear that one effect of the Nuclear Installations (Licensing and Insurance) Act (1959) was a lack of clarity over the position of the citizen in the event of nuclear contamination of any kind.

Nuclear narratives in the press continued to prove ambiguous in the 1960s. The language of danger and potential nuclear attack continued as a significant theme. On 18 April 1960, Cassandra, as part of a regular column in the *Daily Mirror*, argued that 'People, it seems, don't want to be wiped out in a trice, flayed, fried, crushed, blinded, decapitated, mutilated, suffocated or evaporated by complete strangers living in concrete emplacements on the other side of the Urals.'[56] In the *Daily Mirror* on 18 October 1961, readers were offered reports on the H-bomb on the front page and were told about Khrushchev discussing 'the big H-bomb'.[57] Naturally, nuclear politics figured highly in the press, including explicit articulations of journalistic positions in articles such as 'Labour, the *Mirror* and the Bomb'.[58] 'Ban the bomb' articles were common in the early 1960s, for example with pieces on the H-bomb being accompanied by a cartoon with a CND logo.[59] Anti-nuclear activity was sometimes linked with criminality, with a Beatnik murder in 1962 linked in with ban-the-bomb imagery,[60] or 'Ban-the-bomb women' going to jail in 1963.[61] In May 1963, readers were told about school kids prepared to 'spread the word' about the ban-the-bomb message.[62] In May 1965, the front pages of the *Daily Mirror* and the *Daily Express* carried the story of the 'ten held in CND siege of No. 10'.[63] Gaitskell hit out at anti-nuclear dissidents in 1962, and a protest by YCND at Castle Martin, Wales, was reported in the *Guardian*.[64] Space was also given to discuss new personalities within CND, such as Olive Gibbs.[65] In this period, the tone of journalism altered to reflect the range and rise of protest and covered nuclear issues in an increasing level of detail. For instance, ITV *Late Evening News* discussed whether atomic testing can cause bad weather,[66] and anxiety over the place of religion in the nuclear age was reflected in the press.[67] A letter to *The Guardian* on 11 April 1964 from Paul Oestreicher, a priest of the Church of England, reads: 'moral theology makes little distinction between sinning and being prepared for sin, should the occasion arise. Men with the finger on the nuclear trigger, however good their motives, are committing mass murder "in their hearts".'[68] Local and universal concerns were expressed and explored in journalistic narratives, as anxieties over world peace and nuclear war reminded readers about the fragility of family life.

Evidence from this era suggests that the emotional lives of individuals continued to be heavily influenced by the nuclear age, and a range of unofficial narratives helps us understand everyday life in the nuclear age. In July 1962, Suzanna Eaton made front-page news in the *Daily Mirror* by giving up her 'Miss Britain 1962' title, reportedly commenting 'I'd rather go to Russia as a nuclear disarmament supporter than to America as a beauty queen' on winning the competition.[69] Contrasting images of Eaton show her as the triumphant beauty queen, and in 1958 with 'sore feet during the Aldermaston March.' In October 1962, it was reported that the landlord of the Tickell Arms, in the Cambridgeshire village of Whittlesford, had banned members of the Campaign for Nuclear Disarmament from drinking in his public house, because

> there are more and more of these young rowdies going up to the university these days [...] they are being disloyal to the Crown and despise law and order, and I just will not have them in my place. With their jeans and dirty looks they give the place a bad name. I've got my other customers to think about. The local factory and farm workers complain about them. After all they wash their working dirt off before they come out in their cars for an evening drink. Many of the CND people never do.[70]

Although this is a dismissal of the ideals of anti-nuclear activists on the grounds of cleanliness and etiquette, high ideals do surface elsewhere in responses to CND protesters. An article from the *Brighton Evening Argus* reported how Brighton's civil defence officer Major General C. M. F. White had accused the CND of attempting to undermine national security and 'slammed them for "undermining morale [...] ignorantly jeopardising democracy [and] undermining the British will to resist"'. He continued, 'CND talk so glibly of upholding democracy, but in their ignorance, real or assumed, are jeopardising all we normal British people put so much pride and store in.'[71]

In more general terms, the tone of reporting on the CND tended to be one that equated the organization squarely with 'leftism' and the danger of 'foreignness', implying that the idea of protest clashed with a particular British conservative sensibility. The *Times* is a useful place to look for such opinion. A piece from 1958 commented on how the 'leftward ideological slant of the campaign made an immediate impression on bystanders'. In the piece, the crowd was not given prominence, yet one man is cited as saying 'they are all communists', to which another person states, 'Pro-Russian, anyhow'. 'They don't look English to me', added a third, as 'a group of foreign students went by'. The atmosphere of the protest itself was criticized for its 'oddly inappropriate air of high holiday. Nobody looked at all haggard or careworn about nuclear war or any other dangers'. Furthermore, 'untidily' dressed women are accompanied by 'bearded men', and older women were described as 'spinsterly'. The impression is one that reinforces negative perceptions of a particular type of protestor, often with reference to appearance. In the case of the women protestors in particular, the image is negative and dismissive. The report ends with a comment attributed to a bystander, but paraphrased for the reader, stating, 'they said those things that suggest that the more they know about the campaign the less likely they are to join it'. The speech from Canon Collins that mentioned the 'supreme moral issue' was mentioned only in passing.

In 1959, the *Times* made reference to the possibility that involvement with CND protests would have a negative impact on family life. In a section of the report, the middle-class make-up of the protest is highlighted, as a lady who is interviewed states that even if she has neglected her family, at least her children have the pony to keep them occupied. On the middle-class make-up of CND, the same lady says that it is disappointing that most of the participants are 'professional people' but, the reader was told, 'this confirmed her experience at home, where she has had some difficulty in even explaining the campaign case to working-class wives. "The new detergent?" they will say when she talks of the nuclear deterrent.'[72] Although much of the reporting around the Aldermaston marches was positive, an underlying narrative also argued that the CND potentially contributed to the erosion of stable British family life, while dismissing the movement as a middle-class luxury. Focus on the broader issues that were being protested about was often rejected in favour of comments from bystanders. Separate from sensible working-class concerns, the protest movement was presented as one that is liable to be shouted at, distrusted and ridiculed by those who either see their mission as futile or ridiculous. There is evidence of conflicting emotions and allegiances surrounding Britain's part in the nuclear arms race away from national journalism. An army sergeant's wife, based in RAF Marham, who had 'heard there is to be a march to RAF Marham in May', sent a letter to CND magazine *Sanity* in May 1963. She begins,

I wonder if there are many other service wives like myself, who hate the very things that their husbands stand for […] can you imagine what it feels like, with children of your own, to see and hear every single day the things you hate and fear? Any person who is not affected must in my view have very little imagination, or perhaps I have too much. Many times I look at my babies and apologize to them silently for having given life to them, with such a ghastly shadow hanging over them.[73]

Another letter from the same issue of *Sanity* reads:

I didn't go on the Aldermaston march. I have three children and the baby is still being nursed. But my husband joined the march on the Monday. I felt depressed and found it difficult to keep my temper. When the boys, aged three and two, asked me where Daddy was, the full depression of my life came upon me. And there is no rationalising away such feelings.

I tried to explain to the boys what Daddy was doing; but I couldn't. How to explain the possibility, even the probability, of absolute horror to innocence. As I answered throughout the day the thousands of questions about the world around them, I became more and more bewildered and depressed. 'What's an apple made of?' 'Mostly water, I suppose'. I didn't add 'radiation'. 'How does it grow?' 'On a tree in the sunshine', I said, and thought of other suns and burnt earth.[74]

These letters, in very different ways, speak of complex shared anxieties over nuclear war and the potential impact this may have on future generations. Although published in an avowedly anti-nuclear publication, they echo concerns shown by mothers since the world learned about the existence of atomic weaponry in August 1945 and recall those anxieties over the future of children examined in Chapter 4 of this book. There is plenty of evidence that helps bring into focus the profound ways in which individuals responded to the Cuban crisis, an event which could have ended in nuclear war. Liz Lochhead, the national poet for Scotland since 2011, remembers

the first time I fell in love with poetry – Mr Valentine was reading Keats 'La Belle Dame Sans Merci' out loud to us. We were in our third year, none of us 15 yet, and we were 'walking in the valley of the shadow of death'; I remember thinking just that, in just those words out of the psalm on the way to the school that morning. It was the time of the Cuba crisis and everybody was scared, even the grown-ups. No-one on the bus talked much, but those who did talked about nothing else and everyone's face was grim. On a placard outside the newsagents, black block capitals spelled WAR INEVITABLE. Even the newsreaders on television looked scared when they talked about 'the grave international situation'. As Mr Valentine read to us about [...] the lake where no birds sang – out of the flat normal November sky behind his head we really expected that death. And the bombs might come falling. The poem hurt us. Everyone in the class felt it, even the science boys and the maths geniuses who hated English, and the sporty class captain and Mr Valentine himself. You could feel it in the silence and the shared held breath when the voice stopped.[75]

Everyday life in the 1960s was suffused with anxieties and preoccupations over the possibility of nuclear war. Lochhead communicates a sense of collective anxiety, where silence and nervy facial expressions are recollected as those signs of individualized dread. Narratives of 'inevitable' war heightened and rationalized these fears, as they created and shaped daydreams, and made real the imaginary threat beyond the classroom. Even members of the scientific elite succumbed to Cold War anxiety. After the death of former Director of Jodrell Bank observatory Sir Bernard Lovell in 2012, the release of his diaries uncovered his belief that during a trip to the

Soviet Union in the 1960s, he was brainwashed by radiation. It is intriguing how one of the foremost scientists in Britain, surely the embodiment of rationality, should hold such irrational fears.[76]

In 1962, the ITV early evening news reported on Oxford cellars being turned into a nuclear bunker, where there would be room for 250 for one to two weeks. One interviewee on the Oxford streets stated, 'the people who have suggested this fallout shelter have neither visualized the chaos that would result from a hydrogen bomb nor have they realized that the more one resigns oneself to something, the more likely it is to happen'.[77] Here is an example of an attitude that resists the permanence of the nuclear state and the conformist attitudes that can stem from it. Another newsreel from March 1962 presented the fallout shelter as a space where fun and family life could flourish and constructions that 'guaranteed approval of the juveniles' with the commentator remarking, 'what a marvellous place to play in'.[78] In 1962, American President John F. Kennedy famously called for all good American citizens to build a fallout shelter in preparation for a possible nuclear attack.[79] No British politician ever went this far, but some British citizens felt enough emotional pressure to invest in a shelter (Figure 5.2). *The Guardian* published a curious story as a part of its regular 'Northern

FIGURE 5.2 *The prototype of Britain's first nuclear shelter at Kingsdown, Kent in 1962.* ©*TopFoto.*

Accent' column on 30 November 1963, a week after the assassination of President Kennedy. In it, the reader is told that the journalist spoke to a man who, days earlier, had dreamed telling his mother, '"they have shot the President. They have dropped the atom bomb".[...] He laughed, but I saw by his face that his reason had driven him to believe that even the personal and unthinkable was not impossible'.[80] This fragment reminds us of the real fears experienced in the Cold War era and the way in which narratives of nuclear anxiety found their way into newspapers. In general terms, as the 1960s progressed print journalism expressed less anxiety around the possibility of nuclear war.

Popular culture

Nuclear references in film, music and literature suffused the long 1960s as never before. From mainstream film, such as the James Bond series of films, to more obscure literature and screenwriting, nuclear narratives reflected anxieties in new and bold ways. Similarly to the narratives we saw in the 1950s, it can be argued that nuclear narratives in the 1960s also resisted closure, as the world outside the cinema, or away from the page, made possible imagined apocalyptic scenarios. Nuclear-themed popular culture in the late 1950s demonstrated a maturing set of ideas on the nuclear threat, which led to work in the 1960s that offered detailed critiques of the nuclear arms race. New forms of cultural expression attempted to undermine Cold War assumptions on the necessity of nuclear deterrence, pointing out the absurdity and inhumanity of the continuing threat of nuclear war.

This series of radical and self-confident reappraisals of the nuclear threat meant that by 1970, British television, radio and cinema audiences, readers of fiction and the national press were used to hearing about nuclear threat as an absurd, permanent and inescapable everyday reality. A range of popular nuclear texts such as Stonier's *Nuclear Disaster* (1964) appeared in this period, allowing the British people more exposure to alternative forms of nuclear knowledge.[81] The cinematic release of *The Day The Earth Caught Fire* in 1961 marked a certain maturity in British cultural responses to the threat of atomic warfare with its realistic and emotionally fraught depiction of nuclear-induced global warming.[82] At the same time, the James Bond films represented the threat of nuclear war as an earth-bound possibility, where the suave British protector would help a pro-deterrence government keep the peace. In this sense, while the readership of the British press received contradictory information on the safety of their families in the face of nuclear threat, fictive treatments of the nuclear threat offered new levels of realism and radicalism, conveniently represented by the shift from the cinematic version of *On the Beach* compared with the fictional documentary *The War Game* (1965) and Roger Lister's film *The Bed Sitting Room* (1969). In music and art too, the nuclear threat was being articulated in ways that faced the threat head-on.

Combined, these cultural moments certainly suggest that the 1960s represents a shift in how the British people were thinking about nuclear weapons. Perhaps Nuttall was right, and there was a generational element to how people were responding to nuclear threat. There are many instances of nuclear realities acting as a backdrop to British cultural expression. Robert Bolt's *The Tiger and the Horse* (1960) was a play representing the preoccupation with radioactive mutations in babies. One of the central characters states, 'nothing will stop humanity from using that thing'. The daughter then says, 'When we've done what we can do, then's the time to worry about what we can't do.'[83] This displays both feelings of powerlessness and a desire to 'do what we can do' to prevent humanity from using nuclear weapons. David Mercer's TV play *A Climate of Fear* from 1962 is a domestic drama in which the mother develops strong feelings over the nature of nuclear anxiety. In the words of Carpenter, 'young people, she says, are caught in the "emotional trap" of beliefs that are futile because the older generations "accept the possibility of annihilation already" '.[84] Another play, Elaine Morgan's *Licence to Murder* from 1963, was 'a suspenseful, intelligent courtroom drama about a fallout-shelter owner who killed an intruder during a practice for a nuclear attack'.[85] The comedians who made up 'Beyond the Fringe' said, in response to the 'four-minute warning' of nuclear attack on Britain, 'well I could remind those doubters that some people in this great country of ours can run a mile in four minutes'.[86] Randy Newman's song 'Political Science' (1972) was a plainly satirical song about nuclear war, and the American songwriter performed the piece on the popular British TV programme, *The Old Grey Whistle Test*.

The popular series *Dr. Who*, which was first aired in 1963, contained many references to radiation and nuclear science, as did the American series *Star Trek*, first broadcast on the BBC in 1969. Both series also reinforced notions of perpetual struggle against foes, where universal values or national interests were at stake. The 1960s is also remembered for the success of James Bond films, and Ian Fleming's bestsellers, *Goldfinger* (1959), *Thunderball* (1961) and *You Only Live Twice* (1964), were adapted into highly successful films in 1964, 1965 and 1967, respectively. Other nuclear-themed films in this era included *Dimension 5* (1966) and *Planet of the Apes* (1968), with the latter set 2,000 years in the future, introducing an age after thermonuclear war had obliterated human life.

Published in 1960, American author Walter M. Miller's *A Canticle for Leibowitz* is also based in a world after nuclear war. A post-apocalyptic scenario is the setting for a new stage of humanity, where fallout shelters are found to hold 'blue-prints' that are declared saintly relics. Miller dwells on changes in linguistic convention, where characters refer to 'a fallout', or the 'Flame Deluge', indicating their lack of understanding of the nuclear war that preceded them. Yet, 'versicles from the Litany of the Saints' revolve around the words 'tempest', 'earthquake', 'war', 'ground zero', 'cobalt', 'strontium', 'caesium', 'Fallout', 'monsters', 'Misborn'[87] This, for the reader, indicates the extent to which nuclear war and its aftermath have restructured spiritual life, through the destruction of cultural and scientific knowledge.

In *Take a Girl Like You* by Kingsley Amis, also from 1960, nuclear and cold war motifs help set the scene for Patrick's desperate and aggressive attempts to seduce Jenny. Amis used these contemporary references to suggest a new context for Patrick's frantic sexual frustration, creating an extra layer of tension and uncertainty. The text hinted towards the way in which the imagination of nuclear attack had altered sexual politics more broadly.[88] In a similar vein, Roger McGough's poem 'At Lunchtime A Story of Love' (1967) imagined a bus full of strangers making love because they heard the world was coming to an end around lunchtime. In the existentialist *Christie Malry's Own Double-Entry* by B. S. Johnson (1973), the central character mentions the 'certainty' of nuclear war a number of times as the backdrop to an anarchic scheme where he quantifies how society and various personalities have harmed him, and how he has clawed back this harm through harming others.[89] Johnson uses the steady threat of nuclear war to accentuate the psychological tension behind Malry's actions. *Penda's Fen*, written by David Rudkin, was a BBC play broadcast in March 1974. Although the play was predominantly focused upon a young man's psychosexual coming of age, a number of nuclear references contribute to a broader backdrop of anxiety and vulnerability. Kit Pedler and Gerry Davis's *Brainrack* (1974) was a spin-off from the popular BBC TV series *Doomwatch*, and dramatized the links between government, scientists and the media in the creation of a murky nuclear future, with a nuclear power station, 'Grimness', established on the Orkney Islands.[90]

Hammer production *These Are The Damned* (1963) was set in the seaside town of Weymouth, an ostensibly idyllic and peaceful part of south England. The film quickly makes clear that a menacing Teddy boy motorcycle gang, led by the actor Oliver Reed as the aggressive and wild character King, disrupts the peaceful town through their intimidating display of sexualized masculine aggression, epitomized by the roar of motorcycle engines, with the advancing threat of the gang emphasized through the cold-hearted stare of the individual gang members. The gang symbolize nihilistic and unfocused anger, and it is unclear what is at the root of this blind rage. A character who aids Wells, an American tourist who fell victim to a mugging from the gang, says, 'the age of senseless violence has reached us'. As the plot develops, Wells becomes friends with King's sister Joan, and it soon becomes clear that there is a bigger story at the heart of the film. Bernard, a civil servant scientist, has a large-scale plan in place, which involves creating a number of school children who are resistant to radioactivity. We are constantly reminded that this plan is in place so that Bernard can be prepared 'when the time comes'. He has an assumption that nuclear war will happen, and it is presented as an inevitable signpost for the future. The audience is invited to view Bernard's secret complex as a militarized, heavily policed and mysterious space. Linked with the threat of King's gang, the film generates a sense of unease and uncertainty. Eventually, Joan and King are saved by the children. Increasingly mysterious and eerie, the children also make King feel nauseous. We see a man appear in a radiation suit, as all three in the cave suffer from radiation sickness. Slowly, they realize 'the children themselves are radioactive'.

Bernard explains that 300 mothers were exposed to radiation accidents in the last few years. Because nations are striving to find an answer to survive the inevitable nuclear attack, Bernard believes that he has found a solution, and that his children will inherit the earth, 'nine ice cold children free in the ashes of the universe'. The sculptress returns to her creative work and, in a parallel vision of the future, Joan and Wells are shown on the boat, and although suffering the symptoms of acute radiation sickness, Wells pleads, 'we can start again, Joan'. Echoing some of the themes within *On the Beach*, it is clear that *These Are The Damned* also introduces new ideas. The nuclear threat is aligned with perceived social ills of the time, symbolizing the degeneration of human goodness in the post-war era. Hopeless or angry, powerless or resentful, the film must be seen as a comment not only on the post-war generation who were faced with unique social pressures, but also on the older generation who saw it as their role to offer solutions to the impending and inevitable nuclear crisis. Like *On the Beach*, the human dimension to the story, articulated as both realistic and believable, means that the nuclear narrative resists closure. Bernard's secret plan to confront nuclear danger is based on anxieties projected into the future. This is his way of gaining control over the dangers of the nuclear present, presumably familiar to the audience. The audience is shown the impact of radiation poisoning on the bodies and minds of some of the central characters. This demonstrates the extent to which knowledge of the dangers of radioactivity was used to create sympathy for even the most extreme of characters. At the end of the film, as King suffers with radiation sickness when saving a young boy, we empathize with him in his sacrifice, and we realize that he is a good human being corrupted by pressures beyond his control.[91]

Based on *Red Alert* (1958) by Peter George, the 1964 film *Dr. Strangelove* is perhaps the best known nuclear-themed film of the decade. The film portrays the slide towards nuclear war perpetuated by incompetent, stupid and possibly insane officials. Without accountability or democratic responsibility, this small nuclear clique manages to start a nuclear confrontation. Critical responses to Stanley Kubrick's film reveal the complex social, political and psychological anxieties the film addressed. One critic believed it was 'the most devastating piece of art about the bomb I can remember'.[92] Another commentator believed the film, as a cultural statement, was more powerful than formal anti-nuclear activism when he wrote:

> nuclear war, in art as in life, has tended to produce extreme reactions –
> virulent condemnation on the one hand, an absolute refusal to face it on
> the other. But this film faces it, and faces it with an ironic humour that is

particularly mature, non-virulent and yet committed [...] more effectively than any imaginable CND speech, the film suggests that human survival must depend on the capricious and the inept as much as the well balanced and ruthlessly efficient.[93]

A flurry of correctives to the film's perceived inaccuracies appeared in the press, including a piece in February 1964 by Leonard Beaton, Director of Studies at the Institute of Strategic Studies, which was intended to show readers 'How to stop worrying – and ignore the Bomb'.[94] As an unofficial expression of the nuclear predicament, *Dr. Strangelove* was a clinical, substantial and layered critique of the military and political culture surrounding nuclear weapons. *Fail Safe* was also released in 1964, and one critic argued that 'though I relished the wit and audacity of *Dr. Strangelove*, I never felt personally threatened; *Fail Safe* makes the logic of catastrophe seem much more intimate and irrefutable. Step by plausible step we are drawn into an apocalyptic experience'.[95] The film was based on the premise that 'failsafe' systems around nuclear weapons are not reliable, and that automated systems should not be trusted over human intuition. In this context of heightened threat, anxiety and knowledge, it followed that a new form of cultural expression articulated nuclear anxiety in a more sophisticated and nuanced manner. *Dr. Strangelove* and *Fail Safe* used innovative cinematic techniques to portray twitchy vulnerability, but it was *The War Game* by Peter Watkins which proved too extreme for British audiences. The BBC had commissioned Watkins, by then a renowned up-and-coming filmmaker, to create a documentary on the likely effects of nuclear war. Watkins's involvement in CND meant that the documentary would emerge as a powerful anti-nuclear text. The film is an unflinching, believable and emotive depiction of the horrors of the nuclear aftermath. Accompanied by calm narration, the docudrama offered a sustained critique of civil defence in its depiction of post-bomb panic and chaos. Perhaps the film's most important and lasting contribution was the new style of film-making in which believability and realism were central. A lively historical debate between Tony Shaw, James Chapman and others demonstrates the lack of consensus over the reasons the film was banned.[96]

The Bed Sitting Room was a film adapted from the play written by Spike Milligan and John Antrobus, itself based on a play written by Peter Cook.[97] Directed by Richard Lester (who had worked with John Lennon on *How I Won the War* and the Beatles on *A Hard Day's Night*), the film adopts a wilfully disjointed approach to film-making. It opens with the lines 'on this the first anniversary of the Nuclear Misunderstanding which led to World War Three, I'd like to point out that under a Labour Administration, this was the shortest war on record, two minutes twenty-eight seconds precisely, including the signing of the Peace Treaty, which is now on sale at Her Majesty's Stationery Office.'[98] The film offers a series of characters struggling to survive in post-apocalyptic London, now an uninhabitable wasteland, with the dome of St Pauls, a mysteriously operational underground rail system and an underground bunker the only remnants of previous urban civilization. The audience can assume that the handful of characters in the film are suffering not only from varying degrees of insanity, but also from a kind of repressed knowledge of the atomic attack that had caused the destruction of their world. A running theme of the film is that the characters cannot bring themselves to mention the Bomb. They are driven by opaque motivations, a new primitive and illogical culture, and a sadness that they do not and perhaps cannot understand. Many important details are suspended in the film, including the absence of food and water. Overall, it is an inaccessible glimpse into the unthinkable reality of nuclear winter.

Seen in the context of the late 1960s, the film, in a similar vein to *Dr. Strangelove*, was a satirical comment on the absurdity of nuclear weapons and a thinly veiled attack on the Establishment and the certainties of deterrence policy. Similar to *Fail Safe* and *The Day the Earth Caught Fire*, the film employed elaborate cinematography and lens filters to create an impression of the world, as an entirety, altered irrevocably by nuclear onslaught. We are invited into a dislocated and familiar yet unfamiliar new world. If we place *On the Beach* and *The Bedsitting Room* side by side, both films are defined by emptiness, absence and intimate articulations of the emotional lives of characters dominated by a new and terrible nuclear reality over which they have no control. *The Bedsitting Room* was not a commercial success and was dubbed an 'honourable failure' by Derek Malcolm of *The Guardian*.[99] Lester, in an interview with *The Guardian*, stated 'what I wanted to do was remind people that the Bomb is still with us; it's become almost a period piece now, there's a feeling of early Aldermaston about the whole subject.'[100] In that sense, it is intended to be a jolting viewing experience, with a deliberately incongruous and illogical plotline.

These Are The Damned, *Dr. Strangelove*, *Fail Safe* and *The War Game* represented a shift towards a more stark and extreme visual politics, and an increased readiness to engage satire in confrontation with nuclear realities. The films signalled a shift away from acute, specific and rational 'fears' over fallout to a more generalized 'anxiety' over the possibility of nuclear war. British culture became increasingly dependent on a range of nuclear assumptions and understandings in the 1960s. Perhaps a generational interpretation can be offered here too. *The Bedsitting Room* is an impatient dismissal of the perceived stupidity of the older generation, which becomes more pronounced when we turn to the 1980s in Chapter 6. Are we seeing a trajectory of unofficial narratives representing increasingly creative, original, articulate and brave anti-nuclear responses – and then these themselves become part of mainstream understanding, thus creating a new more radical cultural politics by the 1980s? As Martin Amis said in *Einstein's Monsters*, 'we are all arguing with our fathers [...] my father regards nuclear weapons as an unbudgeable given'.[101] As we saw in Chapter 4, Jeff Nuttall, in *Bomb Culture*, viewed 'the people who had not yet reached puberty at the time of the bomb were incapable of conceiving life *with* a future [...] They pretended too, but they did not enter the pretence at all cheerfully. In fact they entered the pretence reluctantly, in pain and confusion, in hostility which they increasingly showed.'[102] The 1960s was the time when more extreme and angry forms of nuclear expression took root. As Amis also argued, writers were slowly learning to write about nuclear weapons since 1945, explaining:

> it is the highest subject, and it is the lowest subject. It is disgraceful and exalted [...] I had been writing about them all along. Our time is different. All times are different, but our time *is* different. A new fall, an infinite fall [...], the present feels narrower, the present feels straitened, discrepant, as the planet lives from day to day. It has been said that the modern situation is one of suspense: no one, no one at all, has any idea how things will turn out.[103]

E. V. Cunningham's *Phyllis* (1962) involves a plotline similar to *Seven Days to Noon*, where two physicists make threats to detonate nuclear devices if America and the Soviet Union do not disarm. The memory of Hiroshima is referred to, and the scientific basis for nuclear weapons is discussed as the authorities try to conclude whether it is possible that rogue scientists could have created the weapons themselves.[104] A letter written by one of the physicists includes the passage, 'We are now possessed of the power to destroy New York and Moscow. Forty days from the date of this communication we shall exercise that power and destroy both cities – unless before the expiration of those forty days the United Sates and the Soviet Union come to some agreement for the banning of all atomic weapons.'[105] Needless to say, the hero of the book, Tom Clancy, helps to save the world from disaster. In a thoughtful refrain, he thinks:

> I did not really know what I felt or feared or dreamed or hoped. I had been in a war where bombs were dropped on the cities and the habitations of men; but somehow or other I could not associate my memories of war and bombing and death and mass mayhem and mass murder with the effect of an atom bomb melting this city and these streets and all they contained into hot and formless insanity. The atom bomb was an abstraction; and for the first time with the help of this abstraction, man's existence had departed from all the strictures of reality.[106]

The notion of uncertainty surrounding nuclear weapons and their control was emphasized in *Fail Safe* and *Dr. Strangelove* as well. A link must also be made to the narrative examined earlier in the chapter, where it is clear that nuclear preoccupations in everyday life often revolved around an uncertain, dangerous future. As a whole, popular culture in this period underwent significant transformation. Entirely new forms of nuclear expression emerged and sometimes treated the nuclear predicament in unprecedentedly extreme and satirical ways.

Conclusion

The period 1959 to 1975 saw significant shifts in cultural politics, which led to the appearance of more extreme unofficial nuclear narratives. The rise in anti-nuclear thought led to direct and confident challenges to nuclear policy, often reflected in fiction and film. The tensions between official and unofficial narratives became starker, particularly after the Cuban Missile Crisis. The Limited Test Ban Treaty and the Non-Proliferation Treaty moved nuclear testing and the nuclear arms race away from crisis point. The period saw an increased variation of responses, more frequently centring on satire and comedy, or extreme representations of nuclear war. This served to create a culture where radical anti-nuclear thought became more normalized. Civil defence dissolved in 1968, the same year the nuclear non-proliferation treaty came into being. As we will see, following a period of 'detente', the 1980s signalled the rise of an increasingly vocal and radical anti-nuclear agenda.

CHAPTER SIX

'Abused technology': Extreme Realism, 1975–1989

In 1983, a speech was drafted for Queen Elizabeth II, to be read by her to the nation in the event of a nuclear war. The speech acknowledged the 'deadly power of abused technology', offering official recognition of the potential horror of nuclear weapons, while implicitly accepting their permanence. Without a hint of irony, the speech was a comment on the way in which the normalized nuclear weapons state had at its heart both deadly power and abused technology. The early 1980s had seen a resurgence of interest in nuclear issues in British society, due largely to international developments that led to the end of the era of 'detente'.[1] In response to the Soviet SS-20 missiles that were being deployed in Eastern Europe, in 1979 NATO decided to assign a new generation of nuclear weapons to Western Europe. The Soviet invasion of Afghanistan in 1979 coincided with the election of Margaret Thatcher as Conservative prime minister in the same year, and the election of Republican Ronald Reagan as American president in 1981. This led to a hardening of nuclear rhetoric and an assertive, unified nuclear policy between Britain and the United States, symbolized by the situating of Cruise Missiles on British soil from November 1983. A series of events from the Soviet invasion of Afghanistan to the Able Archer debacle in 1983 created a renewed sense of Cold War tension, the result of which can be seen in the increase in public engagement with nuclear politics.[2] On 26 April 1986, there was a meltdown at the Chernobyl nuclear power-plant in Ukraine, which had – and will continue to have – huge human, social, political and environmental consequences. As the 1980s drew to a close, the Cold War

Parts of this chapter are expanded upon in Jonathan Hogg, 'Cultures of Nuclear Resistance in 1980s Liverpool', *Urban History*, published online as a *FirstView* article on 3 August 2015. DOI: 10.1017/S0963926815000590. I thank Cambridge University Press for their permission to use aspects of the article in this chapter.

was winding down, but questions around the continued necessity of the nuclear deterrent and the legitimacy of nuclear energy as a power source would not be answered definitively. It was in this final decade of the Cold War where it is possible to see the sharpest contrast between official and unofficial nuclear narratives in Britain. The printed press sensationalized nuclear issues like never before, and the saturation of nuclear references through a variety of cultural means increased. The unique cultural politics of the 1980s allowed new types of expression to emerge, some of which were shocking and extreme in comparison to previous eras. It was also a decade marked by the prominence of female anti-nuclear activism and new forms of nuclear resistance.

The 1980s can be viewed as a decade where official and unofficial nuclear narratives became most visibly polarized in Britain. The nature of domestic and international nuclear policy in the early years of the decade became increasingly worrying for some and led to new forms of nuclear expression. Often mature and sophisticated articulations of nuclear war, these works were urgent and exasperated human-centred dramas. Scepticism towards nuclear policy became visibly and frequently normalized within British culture. The extent to which the 'politics of vulnerability' saturated popular culture was significant, and a normative anti-nuclear vocabulary became a common component of many pop songs, plays and other works of fiction. The nuclear referent became something normal to have rumbling in the background, appearing in many hit songs in the 1980s. Nuclear anxiety had become resurgent due to public awareness of the 'Star Wars' initiative introduced by the Reagan administration, and the renewal of Cold War hostilities. Margaret Thatcher was keen to echo Reagan's hard-line rhetoric but, by the end of the 1980s, sought to take credit for the end of the Cold War and, supposedly, the end of nuclear threat. The work of Dan Cordle will be discussed to illustrate the extent to which nuclear anxieties suffused British discourse in the 1980s. The extreme nature of some of the cultural products of the 1980s illustrates the changing nature of 'unofficial' narratives of nuclear culture in Britain and hints at the sustained emotional investment in anti-nuclear ideas in the decade.

The Pochin Inquiry, carried out in 1978, confirmed that workers at Aldermaston had been found to have high levels of plutonium in their lungs. Widespread public discussion of these issues put pressure on the nuclear state to ensure that international safety standards were met.[3] The Windscale Inquiry, and the subsequent report from 1978, added to this pressure.[4] In terms of weapons, the Duff-Mason Report of the same year summarized the findings of consultation committees led by Sir Anthony Duff from the Foreign and Commonwealth Office and Professor Sir Ronald Mason from the Ministry of Defence. The report, which remained secret until 2009, concluded that the British government should purchase the Trident system from America to replace the existing Polaris system.[5] This was confirmed in January 1979 after a meeting between Prime Minister Callaghan and US president Jimmy Carter. A year later in January 1980, during a debate in the House of Commons, Francis Pym (who was Defence Secretary at the time) confirmed the existence of the expensive Chevaline nuclear programme. While the Strategic Arms Limitations Talks of 1969 (SALT 1) between the Soviet Union and the United States had frozen the number of strategic launchers, SALT 2 (1979) introduced limitations to stockpiles and proposed to initiate reductions. But, tensions over Soviet involvement in Afghanistan meant that the United States never ratified agreements that had arisen from the talks.

In terms of domestic politics, the 1983 General Election is significant because of the anti-nuclear ideas contained with the Labour Party election manifesto. Labour leader Michael Foot, a founding member of CND, had revived the stalled disarmament pledges of 1960 in the context of increased international tension in the early 1980s.[6] Indeed, 'at the TUC conference in 1981, a resolution calling for British unilateral disarmament was passed, as were resolutions calling for the removal of all nuclear bases from Britain in 1982 and 1983. By 1985, around 28 national trade unions were affiliated to CND.'[7] In the lead up to the General Election in 1983, it was not unusual to see CND linked with Communism in the national press and for CND protests to be represented negatively in favour of state authorities.[8] The Conservative Party response to Labour's anti-nuclear policy was to dismiss the defence policy as irresponsible and risky in the face of Soviet threat. This line was reaffirmed in the lead up to the 1987 General Election, when Margaret Thatcher was reported as saying 'a Labour Britain would be a neutralist Britain. It would be the greatest gain for the Soviet Union in 40 years. And they would have got it without firing a shot.' The *Daily Express* left its readers in no doubt when it reaffirmed 'the election of a ban-the-bomb Labour government would give Russia its biggest success since the war'.[9] A typical pro-deterrence line repeated throughout the decade was encapsulated by Michael Quinlan in 1981 when he wrote in *Tablet*, 'deterrence means transmitting a basically simple message: if you attack me, I will resist; I will go on resisting until you stop or until my strength fails; and, if it is the latter, my strength will not fail before I have inflicted on you damage so heavy that you will be much worse off at the end than if you had never started. So do not start.'[10]

These political and international developments were accompanied by the renewal of nuclear civil defence as a government priority in Britain, which was linked to a significant rise in formal anti-nuclear activism in the 1980s. CND membership increased, new anti-nuclear factions emerged and the Greenham Common protest camp was established as a direct, and long-lived, protest against nuclear policy.[11] A significant factor in the rise of anti-nuclear sentiment was the media storm surrounding the civil defence pamphlet *Protect and Survive* in the late 1970s (Figure 6.1).[12] Cordle has argued that *Protect and Survive* came to symbolize the 'absurdity [...] of nuclear civil defence' and 'highlight the vulnerability of ordinary citizens

FIGURE 6.1 *Anon,* Protect and Survive, *London: Central Office of Information, 1980. Crown Copyright.*

in a decade in which the threat of nuclear war came to seem much more urgent'.[13] As an icon of nuclear madness, *Protect and Survive* proved to have significant cultural impact. Books such as the provocatively titled *Protest and Survive* and *Over Our Dead Bodies: Women Against the Bomb* came to symbolize the public hostility to government civil defence plans.[14] Other popular scientific, protest and 'doomsday' literature centred on the devastating consequences of nuclear war. *Defended to Death* (1983) analysed the 'discrepancies' between official and unofficial messages, based on persuasive and detailed analysis.[15] Scepticism towards government gained legitimacy through the detailed work of scientific and political academics and commentators. Works such as *London After The Bomb* (1982), Duncan Campbell's *War Plan, UK* (1982) and *The Medical Effects of Nuclear War* (1983) were part of a surge in this type of popular nuclear educational literature.[16] This was picked up by the press at the time, with Peter Grosvenor writing a piece entitled 'The Boom in the Bomb' in the *Daily Express* in June 1982. He wrote, 'the most gruesome subject on earth – what happens if the Bomb is dropped – used to mean commercial death for publishers; books about nuclear holocaust selling only in trickles. No More. There is now suddenly a boom in "Nuke" books, a dozen or so going as quickly as anything by Barbara Cartland.' *The Fate of the Earth* by Jonathan Schell was singled out as a text advertised on television, with sales of over 80,000 in Britain in one week. Frequently, these texts deployed visual motifs such as concentric circles over urban centres to represent the potentially vast range of destruction.[17] The 'city-as-target' became a common motif, both in official and unofficial narratives. A humorous perspective on nuclear civil defence advice can be seen in the choice of front cover for the Welsh magazine *Rebecca* in November 1981 (Figure 6.2).

Echoing the concerns of the anti-nuclear activists, and the growing number of intellectual projects dismissing the usefulness of nuclear civil defence, the use of language in the press frequently articulated the likelihood and possibility of nuclear attack.[18] Trends that echo previous decades include the reporting of incidents linked to nuclear fear, such as the threat of suicide and the act of suicide linked to nuclear fear.[19] Familiar journalistic motifs were deployed, such as target maps of the country alongside narratives fearful of nuclear conflict:

the world looks a more dangerous place today than it did even a year ago. Millions of people now believe that a nuclear war one day is inevitable. The dread of it clouds the future of the young and the last years of the old. That's why thousands demonstrate against a defence policy based on the use of The Bomb. Their concern and sincerity can't be doubted. But they are wrong.[20]

Here we see intense ambiguity. This is a narrative that acknowledges and reinforces a sense of collective anxiety, while concluding that Britain needs

REBECCA

The News Magazine of Wales   November 1981   60p

A TABLE FOR FOUR
when the bomb drops

PHOTOGRAPH BY SIÂN LUCY TRENBERTH

FIGURE 6.2 Rebecca, *November 1981.* © *Sian Trenberth [www.sian-trenberth. com].*

the bomb. The threat of nuclear war and any resultant nuclear anxiety is to be accepted as the price to pay for world peace. Fears over Communist insurgence, details on nuclear bunker provision in Britain, political criticism over civil defence policy and details of US nuclear arsenal on British soil are all represented in a great amount of detail in the press.[21] Yet, the impossibility of government protection in the event of nuclear attack was also discussed in the press. For instance, a piece from the *Times* from early 1980 reads: 'the public are on their own pretty much. The government has no plans to evacuate them from big conurbations likely to be targets for Russian missiles'.[22] Here, the tension between the vulnerability of the collective and the individual can be seen in the journalistic narrative of the time. Often, the inescapable 'centrality of the individual' to the nuclear predicament was a persistently reinforced motif.

Journalism in this period contributed to a sharper popular scientific understanding of what nuclear attack on cities would mean. One extended and detailed report on the consequences of nuclear attack from 1980 shows concentric circles over north-west England (Figure 6.3). Here, and there are plentiful examples from this period, the city is reinforced as the potential target of nuclear attack. In this sense, journalistic narrative deployed the traditional visual vocabulary of the nuclear age. Images such as the concentric circle had long been deployed in journalistic and academic contexts as shorthand for the destructive potential of nuclear attack, as well

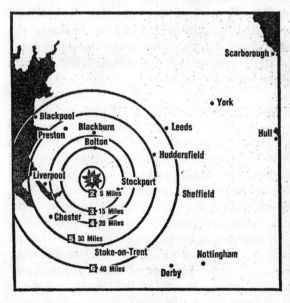

FLASHPOINT MANCHESTER

THIS, experts predict, would be the trail of death and destruction from the fireball of a Russian 5-megaton SS-19 exploding in central Manchester.

1. AT 3-4 MILES. Metals vaporise as the air temperature soars to 10 million deg. C in places such as Salford and Didsbury. Death is instantaneous.

2. AT 6 MILES. Metals melt. A bus in Sale would simply liquidise around its passengers.

3. AT 15 MILES. Rubber and plastic burst into flames. Aircraft standing at Ringway Airport explode. Car tyres in towns as far away as Stockport melt.

4. AT 20 MILES. Exposed woodwork in places as distant as Blackburn and St. Helens ignites spontaneously.

5. AT 30 MILES. Clothes flare. In Bradford, Stoke, Chester and Liverpool people caught in the open are horribly burned.

6. AT 40 MILES. People in towns like Sheffield, Leeds and Blackpool suffer second-degree burns and severe blistering.

PEOPLE IN Morecambe, Barrow, York and the North Wales resorts feel the explosion as a breath of hot air—as though they had walked past the open door of a furnace.

FIGURE 6.3 *'Flashpoint Manchester'*, Daily Mirror, 6 November 1980, p. 16. *Image published with permission of Mirrorpix.*

as underlining the imminent possibility of nuclear attack, and the reality of the city-as-target. The mushroom cloud was also a common symbol, serving a similar purpose to the concentric circle.[23] These motifs served as part of a familiar visual vocabulary that reinforced assumptions of nuclear threat: confirmation of the psychospatial nuclearization of the city. As we have already seen, the Langho suicide pact in 1957 was sensationalized in the national press. In 1983, *The Guardian* reported that 'a librarian's fear of a nuclear holocaust drove him to massacre his mother, wife and daughter before killing himself, it was said in an inquest yesterday'.[24] Thus, we can find other examples of unwell individuals citing fear of nuclear war as a justification for extreme actions. Similar to 1957, in 1983 nuclear fear is discursively linked to actions that went hand-in-hand with the unthinkability of nuclear war. Other fragments of evidence can also be found in the press that tell us about the levels of distress individuals were facing when contemplating the possibility of nuclear war.[25] Additionally, a report from 1979 reads, 'a youth who tried to commit suicide by dosing himself with radioactivity is to become a nuclear "guinea-pig" for scientists'.[26] Bel Mooney argued that culture had become saturated with nuclear references in the 1980s. In 1983, she wrote that,

> you open the pages of the *Guardian* to discover a fashion writer starting an article on home dressmaking with the cheery thought that after the big bang we will all have to learn fundamental skills like sewing again. Articles on fallout shelters appear in colour supplements. Another day you go into a restaurant for a simple hamburger, (in my case into a place called Sweeney Todd's, in Bath) to find this on the menu: The Nuclear Holocaust Kit: A Sicilian Pizza scorched with Jalapeno peppers, contaminated with hot chilis, mutated with pimentos, defoliated with pepperoni, and neutralized with a pint of bitter.[27]

This tongue-in-cheek reference to the omnipresence of nuclear discourse does seem to confirm the widespread appearance of nuclear references in everyday life. Research conducted in 1987, and presented in *British Attitudes to Nuclear Defence*, involved around 2,400 interviews with the British public. The results are interesting and seem to suggest that the British population took a calm and rational approach to nuclear politics. Some quotes from the report included, 'the public is very well aware of the dangers of nuclear weapons, but accepts them as being apparently the best option currently on offer for maintaining the peace as long as possible' and 'there are few illusions about the likely consequences of a nuclear war, and a good deal of resigned acceptance of the likelihood of ultimate catastrophe' and finally 'the survey provides very little ground for optimism for the peace movement. The overwhelming majority of the population rejects its basic premises and therefore its prescriptions, not through misunderstanding, but from reasonably informed deliberation.'[28] These conclusions are bold and are not entirely backed up by other opinion polls.[29] In a fascinating front-page from 1984, a group of mothers threatened to commit suicide if nuclear arms were not abolished (Figure 6.4).[30] The narrative surrounding this bizarre story, accompanied by a large picture of a smiling mother, was extreme but presented comparatively neutrally by the *Daily Mirror*.

FIGURE 6.4 *'Mothers in A-War Death Pact'*, Daily Mirror, *5 March 1984. Image published with permission of Mirrorpix.*

On the contrary, press attitudes towards CND's nuclear protests appear increasingly dismissive and negative from the broadly supportive tones from the late 1950s. This is, in part, because of the normalization of the annual Aldermaston march, increasingly hostile depictions of the women protestors, especially the Greenham Common protesters, and the assumption expounded in the press that CND was a futile and fanatical movement that would not hear reason. On leaving Newbury town hall in 1983, Secretary of State for Defence Michael Heseltine slipped following a crowded confrontation with CND activists, and he was reported as saying 'their minds are closed to all arguments. It would be pointless trying to have a sensible discussion with them.'[31] At the time Heseltine received criticism for refusing even to meet with CND, but it is clear that Heseltine was part of a concerted campaign to discredit anti-nuclear protestors.[32] The perceived futility of the CND is expressed in clear terms by John Haines in his Friday column in the *Daily Mirror* from 8 April 1988, entitled 'A Nuclear Waste'. Haines betrays a set of assumptions that tells us about the perceived make-up and character of CND members. He puts forward the stereotypical set of attitudes on the physical appearance of CND protesters, stating 'thousands of CND members have worn out countless numbers of sandals in the lanes of Berkshire leading to the centre of nuclear research'. The main point of the article is that CND is 'a cause without effect [...] it has been the worst of all protest movements'.[33]

This type of reporting defines a central motif of press reporting of CND protests. Rather than concentrating on the message coming from the protest, the reader is drawn to the image of the protestors. The labelling of the women as 'untidy' or 'spinsterly' places the female CND protestor outside the mainstream, away from conceptions of 'normal' femininity that classically revolve around tidiness and cleanliness. The issue of cleanliness is one that defines the impression of a 1958 vigil at Aldermaston. Again in the *Times* we are told that the 'caravans [are] parked on rubbish', and the protestors only encountered 'a few jeers and cat calls'.[34] This places the protestors and their lifestyle at the forefront of the story rather than the bigger protest issue. The focus on individual protestors becomes judgemental when the concept of conventional family life is challenged. This becomes hugely important in relation to the Greenham Common women, and it is interesting to see a fairly consistent tone in journalistic discourse. The labelling of women as 'types' is striking, especially the frequent accusations of lesbianism and irresponsibility in the reporting in the *Sun* and the *Daily Express*. The focus of reporting is often on the perceived war of rationality versus emotion. Words such as 'fanatical' or 'wild' are attributed to them, and they are described as the opposite of 'sensible' or 'reasonable'. The issue of family and children is constant, and the lack of sympathy for the Greenham Women compared to the A-Bomb suicide threat women is interesting and tells of the short-termism of the press and of the ready embrace of the acceptable face of protest. This is also evident in an article from 1983 in the *Daily Mirror*. On the same page as the doomsday clock, it is reported that the 'face of protest has changed' and describes how the complexion of early CND made up of 'woolly hatted feminists going through a protest phase, who now vote Tory', is vanishing. New CND chair Joan Ruddock is interviewed and describes CND as 'classless', clearly hoping to change negative perceptions of CND. The way in which Ruddock is described is of significant interest. She is sexualized and objectified in a blunt manner, with the reporter introducing her as 'a beautifully intact lady of 38, with model's legs and a great amount of femininity', later describing how Ruddock's 'fine dark eyebrows arched with passion' as she spoke. Ruddock is presented as the acceptable, sexy face of protest, with the tone of the reporting suggestive of a newly found legitimacy for CND, as the protest group becomes more classless and more beautiful. It is clear that because Ruddock symbolizes something nearer the classical idea of femininity, the image of CND is implicitly more positive, more accessible, healthier and more vital.[35]

On the one hand, we have explicit opinions offered by the press on CND. There is a sense of a habitual structure to the discourse, and this in part shaped public perceptions of CND. Alison Young offered a compelling thesis in *Femininity in Dissent*. Taking an explicitly Foucauldian approach, her argument was that the British national press constructed a set of ideas about Greenham women, labelling them as deviant, unclean, irresponsible and unpatriotic. Focusing closely on the language used in the *Daily Express, Sun* and the *Daily Mirror*, a strong argument is put forward that the women were consistently presented as abnormal and therefore illegitimate as members of a thriving democracy. Dominant, patriarchal notions of legitimate protest and the legitimate role of women is discursively bolstered by the repetition of prejudicial and unbalanced reporting practices.[36] Young detailed the different ways in which the female protesters were systematically de-legitimized through their representation in the popular press. She discussed the derisive language used to label women, for instance calling them 'thugettes'.[37] An article from the *Sunday Express* in June 1982 accused CND of traitorous intent, asking 'whose side are they on?'[38] It was not uncommon to see CND charged with communist sympathies. Headlines included, 'Storm erupts as CND priest praises Reds' or 'This Unholy Alliance' in a piece by Lord Chalfont.[39] Young attacked the media for their insistent and sustained attack on the Greenham women in a persuasive but polemic account. Newspapers imprinted complex sets of political, moral and sexual assumptions into the reporting of CND in the 1980s. Part of this prejudicial language emanated from a distrust of protest, distrust of new types of mass protest, especially new types of protest that – directly or indirectly – challenged gender stereotypes. Responses to this perceived challenge to norms took on an accusatory and aggressive tone in the *Sun* and *Daily Express* particularly but were also detectable through wider discourse. It is clear that the press treated 'official' nuclear issues, government representatives and personal nuclear stories such as 'Mothers in

A-War Death Pact' in one way, and then consistently produced a narrative that served to marginalize the concerns of members of CND. In the 1980s, newspapers proved sympathetic to nuclear anxiety and offered occasional condemnation of nuclear policy, yet habitually reinforced negative attitudes towards CND.

In the later period of the Cold War, the British press used increasingly sensationalist language when discussing nuclear politics. In the *Daily Mirror* on 6 November 1980, the readers were told 'no-one, neutral or not, will escape the horrors of nuclear war if one breaks out. No one. There is no hiding place.'[40] Many articles in the popular press presented in stark detail the likely consequences of nuclear attack. The 'touchdown' of the first Cruise Missiles at Greenham Common was front-page news on 2 November 1983. Some articles strengthened the unpredictability of nuclear danger. For example, following Chernobyl, the headlines 'Don't drink the rainwater!',[41] and 'Did radiation kill this boy?'[42] or 'British lamb and radiation'[43] brought the disaster into British homes. Visual references included a cartoon of a skeleton being rained on with radioactive rain.[44] Stories followed which spoke of the 'menace of the weekend rambos', where 'thousands are buying crossbows, knives and guns and learning to live off the land as insurance against Doomsday'.[45] These reports, serious in their prediction of impending nuclear doom, presented complex nuclear nightmares to their readership. Yet, readers were also told not to overreact, for example 'Housewives were urged not to panic last night after the Government slapped a shock ban on the sale of radioactive lamb from two big farming areas.'[46] For the British population, the psychological and toxic impact of Chernobyl proved lasting.[47] Recent research by Jon Agar uncovered the fact that ageing nuclear experts were asked to volunteer to sacrifice themselves in the event of a nuclear disaster.[48] Chernobyl did not prevent people from ruminating on the potential for nuclear weapons to be misused. Prince Philip, on the front page of the *Daily Mirror*, was reported as saying 'nuclear weapons are not going to go off by themselves. Some idiot has to order it to happen. Although there are idiots about – there's one in Libya – I think even the biggest must know the dangers.'[49] Officials were also using emotive language in relation to nuclear tension. In parliament, there were discussions of the certainty of 'fail-safe' systems, for example with Francis Pym defending military technologies in 1980.[50]

The Guardian was active in the debate around the Windscale Inquiry in 1977. One report offers a lot of detail and mentions the National Council for Civil Liberties at the court case surrounding the Inquiry.[51] In the same paper, a column by Dennis Barker is interesting for the variety of public opinion mentioned. Some are frustrated at the 'lethargy of the public', with a young mother commenting, 'as far as the future of my children is concerned, progress has to be seen to be made'. The report goes on to mention another 'member of the public', who remarked, 'I don't worry about living near to Windscale. When you've got to go, you have to go'.[52] The overall tone of the piece is wry sensitivity to the anxieties of people over the expansion of 'Doomsdale', undershot with the knowing assumption that those who disagree with the plans will have little chance of changing a thing. Again, the implicit message is one of powerlessness, of a nuclear subjectivity unable to resist and protest in a meaningful manner. A piece written after 100 days of the Windscale Inquiry by Malcolm Pithers is useful,[53] and we are told 'Anthony Tucker says we are marching into the nuclear era under a blanket of ignorance'.[54] A major nuclear accident occurred in Pennsylvania, United States in 1979 when the power plant at Three Mile Island experienced a partial meltdown. This led to reaction in the British press, with headlines such as 'So how safe is safe' turning the focus on the safety of British nuclear power stations.[55] A *Daily Express* article entitled 'Doomsday on the doorstep' described the situation in America, interviewing people around the nuclear power station. One interviewee grew up in Liverpool and related the nuclear scare to fear of bombing in the Second World War: 'as a schoolgirl in England during the last war she would hide under the dining room table when the Germans bombed Liverpool. "That was different", she explained, as the birds sung outside, "you could hear the planes coming."'[56] In one of the more obvious links to real-world nuclear events, *The China Syndrome* was released twelve days before the incident, with the plot in the film also echoing elements from the Karen Silkwood controversy.[57]

The 1980s also saw a surge of interest in the language around nuclear institutions and politics. Hilgartner et al. and Aubrey were publishing on 'nukespeak' in the mid-1980s, and British journalists and activists also questioned government policy with a sustained intensity not witnessed in previous decades.[58] John Pilger's documentary *The Truth Game* was a public critique of 'nuclear propaganda', which will be examined shortly. Bel Mooney also pointed out the importance of nukespeak, arguing that 'such language makes the idea of nuclear confrontation a reality. Slowly and insidiously, what was unthinkable becomes thinkable, and all the glib phrases politicians have at their command [...] are absorbed into our common language, so that the thinkable becomes acceptable.'[59] Increasingly, social commentators were questioning the language used to support and legitimize the nuclear state. In 1980, Professor Michael Pentz from the Open University was scheduled to give a lecture on the nuclear arms race, but the BBC initially stepped in to prevent the lecture. This move led to heated discussions in the national press, with one letter to *The Guardian* drawing a parallel with the banning of *The War Game* in 1965.[60]

Popular culture

Nineteen-eighties Britain generated a cultural politics that allowed politically radical nuclear art forms to find their way into 'mainstream' culture. Many of these also focused on urban destruction following an imagined nuclear attack, or presented sustained critiques of civil defence policy and government policy on nuclear issues more widely. Such examples include the TV films *Threads* and *On the Eighth Day* from 1984, the well publicized screening of the American production *The Day After* in 1983 and the first broadcast on terrestrial television of *The War Game* in 1985. The title sequence of the TV sitcom *Whoops Apocalypse* (1982) was a run-through of a city destroyed by nuclear war.[61]

Nuclear references in comedies such as *Spitting Image* (1984–1996), *Only Fools and Horses* (1981) and *The Young Ones* (1982–1984)[62] ensured there was a strong anti-nuclear satirical presence on television in this period, helping to underline and naturalize distrust of the nuclear state.[63] *The Defence Diaries of W. Morgan Petty*, published in 1984, offered a satirical perspective on nuclear anxiety with the main protagonist attempting to turn his house and garden into a nuclear-free zone.[64] Yorick Blumenfeld's imagining of life in a fallout shelter after the bomb, *Jenny: My Diary*, was the bestselling British work of fiction for eight weeks in 1984. It is through the narrative devices of these cultural works that the 'centrality of the individual' is stressed especially strongly. Readers and audiences were, more frequently than ever before, asked to contemplate themselves at the centre of nuclear devastation, in increasingly accessible, extreme and politicized forms. *Q.E.D.: A Guide to Armageddon*, broadcast by the BBC on 26 July 1982, was written and directed by Mick Jackson.[65] It was an informative, stark and unflinching production. After being told that 'most of us live in cities', viewers were shown a nuclear attack scenario where the bronze cross of St Pauls in London melted under the heat of nuclear attack. The documentary was a sustained and relentless string of nightmarish images relating to destruction and the inescapable forces involved in nuclear explosions. Repetitive images of the city and indications of the blast radius utilize that pragmatic motif of measurable destruction: the concentric circle. Zooming down onto the city streets, we are invited into the lives of a young couple who are determined to follow the advice in *Protect and Survive*. We follow them in their attempts to construct a fallout shelter in the wet mud of the back garden. The absurdity of civil defence is implicitly reinforced through dead-pan narration. Scenes in the documentary are at once familiar, yet occupy a psychological space where the viewer is invited to assume the possibility of the unthinkable on an individual and collective level. The overall impression is rendered more realistic by the innovative special effects, a novel departure for TV.[66] In this sense, 'A Guide to Armageddon' can be seen as a companion piece to the docudrama *Threads*, also directed by Jackson in 1984.[67]

John Pilger's *The Truth Game* from 1983 is a similarly unflinching assault on government policy and displays an interest in 'nukespeak'. Offering a detailed critique of 'nuclear propaganda', Pilger argues that 'by using reassuring, even soothing, language – language which allowed the politicians and us to distance ourselves from the horror of nuclear war –

this new kind of propaganda created acceptable images of war and the illusion that we could live securely with nuclear weapons'. Pilger uses the Chevaline project to demonstrate the fact that huge amounts of money were spent without democratic approval and points out the fact that from 1965 to 1980 the British parliament did not once debate nuclear weapons. He states: 'in a democracy, secrecy and propaganda ought not to control how we think, especially in matters of national survival. [Today, for many of us] the unthinkable has become the thinkable.'[68] Using 'first-person' cinematic techniques to highlight the urgency, tragedy and absurdity of the nuclear imaginary, viewers are invited to examine their own fears. It is the viewer – the modern citizen – that is placed at the centre of the nuclear predicament. Whether we examine documentaries, journalistic narrative, docudrama, film or literature, it is clear that the 'cultural politics of the nuclear' transformed in early 1980s Britain. The centrality of the (often city-bound) individual within the nuclear predicament became increasingly powerful as a motif, and the reality of the city-as-target was reinforced across many aspects of British culture. Detailed anti-government stances emerged in a way unprecedented in the nuclear century, thus undermining the legitimacy of civil defence initiatives and the nuclear state. It is in this sense that the cultural politics of the early 1980s created powerful nuclear counter-narratives which, through their informative and imaginative richness, contributed to a new set of assumptions around nuclear danger and imaginary nuclear war. In turn, this served to normalize new types of nuclear resistance in Britain and allowed new types to emerge.

Nuclear references suffused popular culture in the 1980s. A significant array of American films, viewed in Britain, utilized nuclear themes either strongly or as contextual references. *Raiders of the Lost Ark* (1981) can be read as an allegory of nuclear energy: characters who are unfortunate enough to look at the light of the 'ark' are vaporized. The ark is something to be sought, but feared. At the end of the film, the ark is put back in a box and stored away from those irresponsible enough to use it for ill means. The teenage film *WarGames* (1983) echoes a central motif of the nuclear age, namely the impenetrability of fail-safe systems. David, the main protagonist, is a young computer hacker who mistakenly initiates global nuclear conflict. The dramatic tension is diffused by the playful tone of the film, but the uncertainty surrounding nuclear weapons technology is reinforced, and nuclear war is presented as an ever-near possibility.[69]

Another film, *Short Circuit* (1986), also playful but more determinedly a comedy, has nuclear weapons culture at its core. The film features a robot created to deploy nuclear weapons, 'Number Five', which following a lightning strike gains a familiarly 'human' consciousness and becomes a pacifist. An entertaining reading of the film has been offered by anthropologist Hugh Gusterson, who wrote 'where I had read the film as a transparent (almost embarrassingly so) warning about the evils of scientific militarism [...] Ray [an engineer at the Lawrence Livermore National

Laboratory, US] had seen it as a technological fantasy mocking popular fears of technology and celebrating the possibility that machines might be alive, magical, and essentially harmless.'[70] Gusterson's analysis reminds us that readings of popular culture must remain open to alternative interpretations, and we must demonstrate awareness of the different ways in which texts can be received.

Empire of the Sun (1987) presents the atomic bombings of Hiroshima and Nagasaki as a profoundly spiritual experience for child protagonist Jim, the starved and exhausted British prisoner of war. Removed from the reality of the atomic bombings, he is intimately connected to death, as he cradles the dying Mrs Victor in his arms. The film was based on J. G. Ballard's *Empire of the Sun*, published in 1984. It was a partly autobiographical work that reflected both the trauma of war and the ability of authors to link the advent of the atomic bomb with broader themes of spirituality, childhood, nature and mortality. Lying among dying and dead Allied prisoners of war in the Japanese Olympic Stadium, and close to death himself, Jim describes how

> a flash of light filled the stadium, flaring over the stands [...] its pale sheen covered everything within the stadium, the looted furniture in the stands, the cars behind the goal posts, the prisoners on the grass. They were sitting on the floor of a furnace heated by a second sun [...] Jim smiled at the Japanese, wishing that he could tell him that the light was a premonition of his death, the sight of his small soul joining the larger soul of the dying world.[71]

It is a jarring narrative, as we are at once reminded of our permanent removal from the reality of those bombings, yet implicated in the 'larger soul of the dying world'. Less existentially profound, the highly popular James Bond franchise continued to use nuclear and global threat as themes during the late Cold War era. James Bond had to prevent a global nuclear war in *The Spy Who Loved Me* (1977), prevent global holocaust by nerve agent in *Moonraker* (1979) and protect nuclear submarines in *For Your Eyes Only* (1981). In *Octopussy* (1983), Bond defused a nuclear warhead placed in a US military base in West Germany. Just like the films from the 1960s, these films can be viewed as a pro-deterrent unofficial narrative. It is not Bond's place to question the validity or morality of nuclear weapons, but to protect the status quo, of which nuclear deterrence and state-sanctioned violence is part. Laucht argues that '007 films and stories often paralleled or even mirrored official British nuclear policy and propaganda in their attempts to portray Britain as a nuclear superpower through their constant overvaluation of the country's nuclear capability and discounting of radiation effects, in particular fallout'.[72] Other nuclear-themed films from this era include *Testament* (1983), *Red Dawn* (1984), *Star Trek IV: The Voyage Home* (1986) and the *Mad Max* films from 1979 to 1985 which are set in a barren post-nuclear world. *The Way the Wind Blows* (1986) was an animated cartoon based on a graphic novel by Raymond Briggs, which reminded viewers that even in rural Britain nuclear war was a potential threat. The film confronted the absurdity of *Protect and Survive* head-on, offering a searing attack on the logics of nuclear civil defence. *Threads* (1984), directed by Mick Jackson, also offered a critique of official civil defence advice, in what proved to be a landmark televisual moment. It was broadcast in August 1985 in the same week that *The War Game* was shown on British television for the first time as part of a series of broadcasts marking the anniversary of the atomic bombings of Japan. Set in the northern industrial town of Sheffield, *Threads* centres upon the lives of a young couple while the world heads towards nuclear war. The film is a relentless and harrowing depiction of the likely consequences of nuclear war. In the short term, civil defence is presented as ineffective, and distressing scenes present many of the main characters succumbing to violent deaths. Characters attempt to follow the official advice from *Protect and Survive*, which is presented as wholly futile. In the longer term, the characters try to survive in a chaotic and violent world. In the absence of authority and the rule of law, physical and sexual attacks become commonplace, communities collapse, language begins to dissolve, food is scarce and the terrifying results of radiation on unborn children becomes apparent. The final scenes of *Threads* are perhaps the bleakest and most extreme depictions of human life after nuclear war ever put to film and epitomize the distinctive forms of expression that the cultural politics of the 1980s produced.

Following the screening of *Threads* and *The War Game*, a formal debate on BBC's *Newsnight* sought 'to examine the political and military ideas that those programmes deliberately didn't set out to do, but were urgently raised by them'. The entirely male panel focused on three main areas of discussion, namely nuclear escalation, lessons to be drawn about civil defence programmes and what effect the nuclear winter hypothesis had on the idea of deterrence. The debate was placed in context alongside Reagan's recent speech where he talked about the need for better communication with Russia.[73] The audience were told that Michael Heseltine declined to join the debate. Robin Cook argued that the whole idea of limited nuclear war was pure fantasy, making the point that movements towards peace would be nearly impossible after a nuclear exchange. George Walden stated 'any film which is really worth its salt is not going to simply arouse people's fears'. Yet, Cook was keen that people should begin 'thinking about the unthinkable', arguing that if limited nuclear war is seen as possible or acceptable, there is a danger to think 'you could actually get away with it' or that leaders would actually 'cross the nuclear threshold'. Eric Alley believed 'we've got to do something' in terms of civil defence, and *Threads* concentrated on Sheffield, an 'unprepared city'. He argued that 'we can mitigate the effects of the attack' if Britain prepared properly. Phillip Steadman argued that civil defence attempted to deceive people by underestimating casualty rates while

Alley argued that Steadman represented 'tunnel vision, and that good civil defence planning can ease the pain' for small numbers of people. He was frustrated by 'this apocalyptic mode that we always seem to get into, where everyone dies.' Steadman then made the point that 'the title of *Protect and Survive* is intended to portray a comforting vision', while Cook made the point that most of the people in *Threads* who tried to follow advice died realizing the futility of it and concludes civil defence is 'deeply dishonest'. General Farrar-Hockley thought the films strengthen the case for deterrence and stated, 'they [nuclear weapons] are here, and they won't go away'. Gwin Prins discussed the militarization of international relations and says, 'we place a dark hand which covers whole areas of human experience [...] nuclear weapons make lousy political signals'. Overall, the broadcast of *Threads* and *The War Game* marked a significant moment in British cultural history. These two films cut to the heart of debates over nuclear armament and civil defence in their realistic depictions of the hellish aftermath of nuclear war. They served to humanize the nuclear debate by reminding British citizens that nuclear politics touched individual lives far more than male-dominated television discussions might suggest.

Nuclear literature has been recognized as a crucial aspect of 1980s nuclear culture. Dan Cordle has argued that nuclear literature, 'by exposing the vulnerability of individuals, nations and the world to nuclear devastation [...] delegitimizes a Cold War status quo predicated on nuclear peril'.[74] Russell Hoban, an American writer who settled in London, wrote *Riddley Walker* (1980), a post-apocalyptic story written in a language that is a mutated version of English. Along similar lines to both *Threads* and *A Canticle for Leibowitz*, the book explores the notion that nuclear war could mean the death or reconfiguration of language and culture in ways that are unimaginable. The children's book *Brother in the Land* by Robert Swindells was first published in 1984. The book follows the life of Danny, an adolescent who survives a nuclear war along with a scattering of his family and local community. The book hinges on the two types of response to living in a post-apocalyptic era. First, Danny is representative of a humanist, relatively selfless and loving response – the positive view of human nature. The second view is of human nature as inherently selfish, short-sighted and violent. Louse Lawrence's *Children of the Dust* (1985) created a harrowing dystopia where humanity struggles to survive in mutated form after nuclear war.

The bestselling Adrian Mole series by Sue Townsend can be considered formative texts for the youth of the 1980s. Starting with *The Secret Diary of Adrian Mole Aged 13¾*, the series is composed of the fictional diary entries of an adolescent boy pre-occupied with girls, spots, current affairs and nuclear war. The books were extremely popular. The first instalment sold over five million copies in 1982, was adapted for radio and TV, and turned into a West End musical. In 1984, an *Observer* article branded the Adrian Mole series a 'phenomenon', citing 'record-breaking sales'. On meeting Townsend, the journalist makes a point of saying 'my first impression was that she was equipped as if heading off to Greenham Common, since she wore a long, heavy, dark coat, red boots, with a thick scarf wound round her neck'. In the interview, Townsend is adamant that Adrian Mole is about class.[75] One fictional diary entry from *The Secret Diary of Adrian Mole Aged 13¾*, reads, 'Wednesday, January 6th: I keep having nightmares about the bomb. I hope it isn't dropped before I get my GCE results in August 1982. I wouldn't like to die an unqualified virgin.'[76] This quote cleverly combines Adrian's sustained fear of nuclear war with anxieties over his sexual and scholarly status. Townsend places 'the bomb' at the heart of Adrian's teenage crisis, alongside those things that all middle-class British adolescents worry about. With this, the nuclear threat diminishes, partly through the humorous juxtaposition of anxieties. The persistence of the nuclear theme is emphasized when it is referenced as an explanation for failing family relationships, when Adrian says 'interpersonal relationships in our family have gone completely to pot. This is what living with the shadow of the bomb does to you.'[77]

After Adrian runs away from home for a spell in 1983, a consultant psychologist meets with him. Adrian explains, 'Dr. Donaldson has just left my bedside after listening to my worries with grave attention. When I'd sunk back into my pillows he said, "We'll take them one by one." 1. Nuclear war is a worry, but do something positive about your fear – join CND. 2. If you fail your "O" levels you can retake them next year, or never take them – like the Queen.'[78] Again, Townsend seems determined to face the nuclear threat with humour and does not introduce pro-nuclear figures of authority. Adrian's diary entry a month later, on 12 May, reads: 'I thought my parents had given up on the idea of moving house, but no! My mother struck terror into my heart and bowels at breakfast time by announcing that after the exams, we are going to sell our house and move to a desolate area of Wales! She said "I want to give us a chance of surviving a nuclear attack."' The next day, Adrian writes 'my mother has borrowed ominous books from the library: *The Treatment of Radiation Burns*; *Bee-Keeping, an Introduction* [...]'.[79]

Here is an extreme nuclear narrative, again presented with humour. Adrian's family is on the verge of moving to a remote rural location due to anxiety over possible nuclear attack, with the image of his mother consumed with nuclear anxiety. She is also presented as a constantly politicized anti-nuclear personality, as part of Adrian's entry from 15 May describes his mother 'haranguing' a Labour candidate on the household doorstep 'about nuclear disarmament'.[80] In *Adrian Mole*, nuclear war serves as part of an explanatory backdrop to various forms of neuroses: serving as part of Adrian's adolescent menu of angst, which then leads his mother to seriously contemplate living in a 'desolate area of Wales'. The political nature of these anxieties is reinforced throughout, with references to Tony Benn, Greenham Common and political debates on the doorstep emphasizing the everyday reality of nuclear danger. These themes are not articulated or justified fully in Townsend's work, indicating an implicit acknowledgement of the reality of nuclear anxiety, and how the cultural politics of the decade caused individuals to act in varying and unpredictable ways. It is in this sense that the fictional narratives of the era bolstered the pre-existing knowledge gleaned from journalistic narratives, again 'exposing the vulnerability of individuals'.

In *Einstein's Monsters*, Martin Amis presents five short stories, with nuclear war having varying degrees of influence on the characters and context of the stories. The first stories look back at the psychological and spiritual fallout from Hiroshima and Nagasaki, tending to see the texture of life forever altered by the impact of the use of atomic devices in anger. Later stories explore dystopian futures, describing horrific mutational and psychological possibilities. Amis, in his polemic introduction to the collection of stories, admits to being powerfully influenced by Jonathan Schell's *The Fate of the Earth*, illustrating the impact of powerful anti-nuclear ideas on the cultural politics of the 1980s.

As if to demonstrate this, popular music referenced nuclear war with increased regularity during the late Cold War period. Even when nuclear politics and the nuclear threat were referenced indirectly, there are clear indications that nuclear culture was one of the more significant influences on creative expression in the 1980s. Dorian Lynskey dedicates a chapter in his book *33 Revolutions Per Minute* to the surge in nuclear-themed music in the 1980s.[81] He mentions the fact that the Glastonbury festival became the biggest fundraiser for CND in the early 1980s. In an interview in *Sanity*, Liverpool band The Beat were asked whether they'd ever thought about writing a song on the danger of nuclear war. In response, they said 'I think everything we write has an ominous cloud of nuclear threat hanging over it.'[82]

German band Kraftwerk released the album 'Radioactivity' in 1976, while Ultravox released 'Hiroshima Mon Amour' in 1977, based on the film of the same name. Gill Scott-Heron's song 'We Almost Lost Detroit' appeared in the same year. Orchestral Manoeuvres in the Dark (OMD) released 'Enola Gay' in 1980, a bittersweet song which makes sarcastic references to the pride felt over the *Enola Gay* mission, reflecting on the broader meanings of the atomic attack. Duran Duran released the song 'You're About as Easy as Nuclear War' in 1983, and Jefferson Starship released 'Rose Goes to Yale', one of several nuclear themed songs on their album 'Nuclear Furniture' from 1984. In the same year, Alphaville's single 'Forever Young' dwelt on the uncertainty of the nuclear stalemate, and German band Nena's anti-nuclear song '99 Red Balloons' was released in Britain in 1984, making it to the top of the charts. Another successful song from this year was 'Dancing With Tears In My Eyes' by Ultravox, which imagined how people might respond to an imminent nuclear power station 'explosion'.

'Everyday is Like Sunday', written by Morrissey and Stephen Street, was released in May 1988 and reached number nine in the UK singles charts. The lyrics of the song match the melancholic tune itself, a bittersweet ode to crumbling British seaside towns. The lyrics speak of an attempt to disrupt the traditional conception of the British beach resort by suggesting there is nothing of interest here to the younger generation. The use of the nuclear weapon is invited on these resorts, we assume ironically. The use of nuclear imagery here is stark and is not only a self-consciously flippant comment on British life, but also an existential reflection on the post-war predicament, a gentle and articulate rebellion. In a similar manner to 'Enola Gay' and 'Forever Young', 'Everyday is Like Sunday' juxtaposes striking nuclear lyricism with an unexpectedly emotive melody, which highlighted the ways in which British culture was bound up with the emotional realities of the nuclear age.

It is important to recognise that musicians became directly involved in anti-nuclear activism in this period. For instance, Graham Nash was involved in the US 'No-Nukes' event in 1980 and George Harrison supported CND's 'Nuclear Freeze' campaign in 1986. As well as British-produced music, there was a huge amount of American and European popular music that dwelt on nuclear themes that emerged in British popular culture. Bruce Springsteen organized the 'No-Nukes' event in 1980 with around thirty major recording artists, including his own song 'Roulette', which imagined the aftermath of a nuclear meltdown at Three Mile Island. In December 1980, Jona Lewie reached number three in the UK charts with 'Stop the Cavalry', with the lyrics citing a fictional character waiting in a fallout zone, juxtaposed with the narrator's wish to be dancing with the girl he loves. In the same year, Hazel O'Connor released 'Eighth Day', which overlay a dystopian nuclear scenario on a biblical narrative. In 1978, The Clash released 'Stop the World', which also sketched a dystopian scene, describing a destroyed city on fire, where only the rich are safe in their nuclear bunkers. Through creating dark dystopias through their lyrics, these artists were implicitly reminding their audiences that such a future could become a reality.

Bob Marley's 'Redemption Song' from 1980 contained lyrics that explicitly referred to the fear of atomic energy, while Oi Polloi's 'No Filthy Nuclear Power' was explicitly anti-nuclear. In the same year, The Jam released 'Going Underground', which placed 'atomic crimes' alongside frustration with a militarized and untrustworthy government, while despairing at the state of contemporary British life. In 1982, Flux of Pink Indians released 'They Lie We Die', again displaying anger towards the motivation of government, with specific reference to their mendacious schemes, and the dubious ways the nuclear bomb was financed. There is clear evidence of emotional and angry connections with nuclear politics and the perceived nuclear stalemate in the world. For this reason, Frankie Goes to Hollywood's 'Two Tribes' is perhaps the archetypical popular representation of nuclear paranoia, a notion strengthened by the fact it was number one for nine weeks in the spring of 1984. The frenetic tempo of the song, mixed with samples of political journalism, induces the feeling of a real countdown to nuclear war. The music video featured two elder politicians fighting in a sandpit, with the lyrics pointing to the futility of nuclear conflict: this was a war that could not be won.

Other musicians faced the nuclear situation directly. In 1980, The Specials released 'Man At C&A' which peaked at number five in the

UK charts. The song begins with a warning of imminent nuclear attack shouted through a loud-hailer, reminding listeners that nuclear war was a real possibility. Queen's 'Hammer to Fall' from 1984 displayed frustration with the lack of political power the individual had in the face of the ever-present nuclear threat. The Dubliners released 'Protect and Survive' in 1987, which served as a scathing comment on the pointlessness of civil defence initiatives.

Thus, we see some of the most popular bands of the era referencing the nuclear realities around them, offering a glimpse of the preoccupations that can also be seen in journalistic and cinematic narratives. It is in this sense that we can see British culture becoming saturated with unofficial nuclear narratives. The majority of popular music containing nuclear references was unified in highlighting the absurdity of atomic diplomacy and often expressed vivid frustration with the continuing threat of nuclear war. The 1980s, then, can be viewed as the decade where nuclear armageddon seemed a possibility once more, yet the cultural response was significantly stronger than any time in the twentieth century. To explain this, analysis must be given to the increasing centrality of popular culture in the lives of individuals, a freer culture of censorship, a vibrant satirical and comedic culture, and the renewed activity of CND. Much of the popular culture in the 1980s took it as self-evident that the existence of nuclear threat was both absurd and morally outrageous. The most skilful musical articulations of the nuclear present gave voice to the emotional strain of the era, and through their concise encapsulations of the mood of the 1980s, perhaps best translated and reiterated the 'politics of vulnerability' for the British population. Nuclear-themed film, literature, satire and music of the 1980s had at its heart the absurdity of the global nuclear situation. It is in this sense that popular culture in this decade spoke more directly to British citizens, compelling them to join in a broader critique of nuclear policy and recognizing the absurdity of civil defence policy.

Everyday life

Changes in cultural politics in the 1980s influenced everyday life, and to end this chapter, we will take one angle of interpretation to explore this further. By taking localized historical perspectives of Cold War cities, we can bring into sharper focus the impact of national nuclear policy on cultures of local government. In a recently published article focusing on the city of Liverpool in the 1980s, I argue that 'nuclear cultures that existed in the city were shaped by ideas and assumptions discursively reinforced at both a national and local level'.[83] This book has shown that, by the early 1980s, imagining the effects of a nuclear attack on urban centres had become a normalized aspect of British culture. As just one example, an article on contemporary nuclear policy published in the *Liverpool Echo* in 1980 shows one of the many ways British citizens were reminded of the possibility of nuclear attack on their immediate surroundings:

> Thousands of people throughout North Wales, North Lancashire and as far south as Derbyshire intuitively turned their heads towards Liverpool as a one-tenth of a second flash flitted across the city [...] in the ten seconds that followed, a fireball, measuring almost 1.5 miles in diameter, flashed across the inner city, reaching out across the Mersey to Birkenhead and Wirral waterfront [...] human beings vanished like they were never there [...] below the fireball where once had stood offices, factories, churches, schools, houses and the greater part of the city's dock complex appeared a crater of massive proportions. A depression 100 feet deep and three-quarters of a mile across [...] a mushroom cloud stood 15 miles high over Liverpool.[84]

This type of narrative contributed to deeply embedded nuclear anxieties that were both local and global in character. Through this imaginary scenario, readers are reminded of the potential devastation of human life, city infrastructure and the cityscape that exists as a reality for them. The 'unthinkable' had become a familiar imaginary, as individual citizens were reminded of their own vulnerability and centrality to the nuclear predicament, while the city itself was a constant, vulnerable, immovable nuclear target. As I argue in *Urban History*, 'people's lives and minds, like their cities, had become nuclearized'.[85] The city itself was, like all British cities, uniquely involved in the nuclear age. Its physical infrastructure, scientific and military traditions, as well as its prevailing cultural politics ensured this.[86] The city became 'nuclear free' in June 1981, and Liverpool MPs, including Eric Heffer and Allan Roberts, were part of 'CND 120', which was a group of MPs who openly declared their CND membership.[87] The nuclear controversy surrounding the gaseous diffusion plant at Capenhurst prompted the creation of a peace camp on the site.[88] Evidence from the local press, and anti-nuclear archives, suggests that broader anti-nuclear activism thrived in Liverpool in the early 1980s.[89]

Through an exploration of a selection of Liverpool and Merseyside council archives and private papers, a picture emerges of 'local officials displaying apathy and frustration towards nationally defined civil defence exercises'. This manifested itself with a reluctance to partake in national civil defence exercises.[90] Yet, there is also evidence that these local officials 'attempted to empower themselves, their citizens and, it could be argued, democratize the nuclear state by taking control of local nuclear narratives by constructing alternative and open visions of the nuclear present, and future. They resisted, or reshaped, the nuclearization of their city'.[91] One example of this is the production of alternative forms of civil defence advice in the booklet *Merseyside and the Bomb*, which was co-produced with Merseyside Campaign for Nuclear Disarmament, and influenced on information provided by Scientists Against Nuclear Arms (SANA). This became the 'official' council pamphlet, and its front cover was a collage of the CND peace symbol, the nuclear mushroom cloud and a skull (Figure 6.5). This imagery opposed the sterile and reassuring visual vocabulary of *Protect and Survive*. On the last pages of *Merseyside and the Bomb*, the reader is advised to 'compare what the Home Office says in its publication with what the United States government and British scientists have published'. It is clear that 'Merseyside residents are being urged to make their own minds up about nuclear policy [and] the booklet is an implicit rejection of national nuclear civil defence policy'.[92] The booklet becomes explicit in this regard when, on the very last page of the pamphlet, the council pledges 'not to be party to civil defence exercises designed to mislead the public into believing that adequate protection is available in the event of such an attack'.[93] There is plenty of evidence that helps explain the specific emergence of this resistance to national nuclear policy.[94] Focusing on one city alone suggests that individuals interacted in powerful, diverse and *locally specific* ways to the imagined threat of nuclear war. This complicates how we might choose to interpret the nuclear century. In a broader sense, it can be argued that historicizing cities in the Cold War era influences how we interpret nuclear subjectivity and nuclear resistance as concepts.

While these localized and unique forms of nuclear resistance echo familiar types of nuclear activism displayed by citizens throughout the nuclear age, I argue that their specific nature must be interpreted alongside the cultural politics of the 1980s. Then, what emerges is a 'historically and locally specific picture of the intersections between city-dwelling individuals and their perceptions of nuclear policy, and nuclear danger' that allows us to evaluate one possible way nuclear culture shaped everyday life.

Conclusion

Analysis of 1980s British nuclear culture suggests that the cultural politics of the era gave rise to more extreme forms of unofficial nuclear expression. It became the norm for artistic responses to be avowedly anti-nuclear, sometimes in direct response to the public relations disaster *Protect and Survive*, which confirmed for many the ludicrous logic sustained by government towards nuclear war preparation. The renewed activity of organized anti-nuclear groups, and the creation of the Greenham Common protests, meant that journalistic narrative became newly politicized, especially as nuclear policy once more became an election issue. The 1980s was the decade where popular culture reflected preoccupations with nuclear conflict most frequently. It would be just as common to hear fierce anti-nuclear voices, as it would be to hear passing references to nuclear war in a top-ten hit. The cultural logic at play meant that it became normal for anti-nuclear sentiment to be part of the cultural backdrop of British culture,

FIGURE 6.5 *Merseyside CND*, Merseyside and the Bomb, *1983. Image published with kind permission of Merseyside CND.*

suffusing many cultural forms in a way that could not have happened in the 1950s. We have seen how types of nuclear resistance could also exist in local government. Sometimes viewed as engendering conformity and obedience within government, nuclear civil defence initiatives also created pockets of resistance. While Grant has argued that up to 1968 civil defence was considered a 'rational and understandable sham' or a 'necessary facade' by government officials, by the 1980s it was far more common to find examples of local nuclear resistance to civil defence.[95]

Unique to the 1980s was the emergence of sustained nuclear criticism involved in 'historicising the production and accommodation of nuclear hegemony, exposing its ambiguities and contradictions, restoring to public consciousness what it has repressed, providing alternative narratives of the nuclear future, and energising democratic participation in nuclear policy-making'.[96] We saw in the introduction to this book that Taylor's own work analysing nuclear photography introduced the concept of 'nuclear subjectivity', understood as those reminders of the physical and psychological impact the nuclear state can have on individual lives, as seen through unofficial narratives. Taylor argued that these narratives could be powerful enough to compel us to 'revise official accounts of nuclear history',[97] and that official accounts of nuclear history have still, on the whole, left nuclear subjectivities hidden.[98] Yet, in the 1980s, the cultural politics of the era allowed 'alternative narratives of the nuclear future' and enabled 'democratic participation in nuclear policy-making'. In the Liverpool context, officials took control of local nuclear narratives, thereby offering alternative and open visions of the nuclear present and future. This served to both democratize and destabilize the nuclear state.

As we will see in Chapter 7, part of the cultural legacy of the 1980s that carried through into the post–Cold War period was the normalization of nuclear references in British culture. In the 1980s, these references were often politicized, but this gradually changed in the years following the end of the Cold War. The 1980s can be viewed as representative of an increase in cultural works that 'disrupt the passivity of viewers and implicated them in the evaluation of nuclear representations'.[99] Thus, it was more likely that forms of nuclear representation that emerged in the 1980s would 'destabilize the authority of official nuclear images and narratives by contrasting them with their unofficial counterparts'.[100] In the 1980s, those 'unofficial' narratives that were not institutionally produced and shaped, and often challenged political orthodoxy, rose in frequency and cultural importance. These powerful and confident nuclear narratives proved more representative of a citizenry willing to take intellectual and political ownership of nuclear threats to the family, selfhood and a peaceful life.

CHAPTER SEVEN

Rendered Invisible:
The Persistence of
Nuclear Culture, 1990–2015

We will finish this book with some reflections on nuclear Britain and representations of nuclear war in the period since the end of the Cold War. The British nuclear state in this period attracted a great deal of attention from scholars of international relations, politics, anthropology and sociology, but less so from contemporary historians. The period affirmed, for various reasons, a renewed but cautious commitment to nuclear weapons capability. After a decrease of 100 nuclear warheads in the first three years after 1989 (350–250), the number rose to 280 in 2000, before dropping to 225 from 2006 onwards. In terms of the potential yield of the stockpile, it steadily dropped from 114MT in 1989 to 22.5MT in 2014. From the standpoint of 2014, this represented 19.7 per cent of the yield level of 1989 across 64 per cent of the number of warheads.[1]

In July 2014, The Trident Commission published a report that recommended the renewal of Trident. While CND's response to the report argued that it was a 'rehash of Cold War thinking which fails to acknowledge that the world has moved on',[2] the report was an extremely lucid and sober assessment of the nuclear status quo, and after a survey of relevant historical context, it argued that 'future requirements demand a clean assessment of the changed strategic context'.[3] In terms of finance, the 'spending profile on current plans' suggests that renewal would cost around £2bn a year up to 2062, rising to almost £4bn a year between 2024 and 2027 as money is pumped into developing new nuclear submarines. The report offered a fairly nuanced assessment of the security implications of discontinuing nuclear capability, before concluding that an 'ideal world, where all states have abandoned their nuclear arsenals, where we look ahead with confidence three to four decades into the future, and where power is clearly in the hands of allies and institutions in which we can trust, will not be achievable in the foreseeable future'.[4] This pessimistic outlook legitimized the proposed plan to preserve the nuclear state, but some of the contradictions in the overall philosophy of this approach were acknowledged in the report:

> It has been suggested that the renewal of Trident is contrary to the UK's treaty obligations and international law, by committing us to possession of nuclear weapons into the second half of this century. We do not accept this argument, for while there exists a clear obligation to make progress towards these aims, there is no commitment to a timeline for their achievement [...] Some members of the Commission believe that a decision to renew the Trident submarine system on a like-for-like basis would detract from the perception of the UK as a strong contributor to the momentum towards the global reduction of nuclear weapons holdings and make it more likely that the NPT process will lose credibility, and harm prospects for the UK's national security.[5]

Perhaps unsurprisingly, the report was not discussed extensively in the national press. Even though the report legitimized and justified huge amounts of government spending on the nuclear deterrent up until 2062, there was no significant public debate on the future of British nuclear weapons capability. The nuclear state has succeeded in becoming invisible. After the storm of protest, resistance and anxiety in the Cold War era, the British nuclear state had largely disappeared from the journalistic agenda but remained at the heart of defence thinking. Perhaps most significantly, new threats to national security emerged in the twenty-first century, specifically around 'terrorism' and cyber-crime, meaning that state-sanctioned use of nuclear weapons moved lower down the hierarchy of security risks. In the American context, Joseph Masco has argued that the 'disappearance' of the nuclear state since the end of the Cold War is, of course, illusory, and the foundation of nuclear interests actually became more strongly ingrained in American life. He claims that

> the constant end game articulation of nuclear discourse has, I think, enabled two of the most profound cultural achievements of the nuclear age: the near erasure of the nuclear economy from public view, and the banalisation of U.S. nuclear weapons in everyday life. The consequence of this historical structure is that the U.S. nuclear complex is primarily visible today only in moments of crisis, when the stakes of nuclear policy are framed by heightened anxiety, and thus, subject, not to reassessment and investigation, but to increased fortification.[6]

This broad logic can equally be applied to the British nuclear state. The evidence and arguments in British Nuclear Culture suggest that it was more common for the nuclear state to become silently fortified, rather than publicly scrutinized and reassessed in the years after 1945. Once the threat of nuclear war lifted after 1989, it is perhaps unsurprising that public nuclear weapons discourse fell into the background. On the other hand, debates over climate change and energy production ensured that discussions over the efficacy of nuclear power remained prominent in the post–Cold War era. With the advent of new technologies, some groups promoted nuclear energy as the best 'carbon-free' solution to the energy crisis.[7] The debates and anxieties that emerged in Britain in 2011, after the disastrous events at Fukushima Daiichi nuclear power plant following the earthquake and resulting tsunami in Japan, demonstrated the importance of identifying and analysing 'official' narratives of the disaster in an attempt to uncover the damage inflicted by the triple meltdown. Only then can evaluations of the broader social and political consequences begin. The way in which these 'official' narratives clashed with unofficial narratives is one way of understanding the impact of the disaster, and one way to restart public debate on the future role of nuclear technology worldwide. The disaster was also a reminder of the global character of nuclear power production and its ever-present dangers. Just as fallout from Cold War nuclear testing altered the atmosphere of the entire world, fallout from nuclear power station accidents wrought significant environmental and human consequences across thousands of square miles. Among the most thought-provoking reflections on Fukushima was Jacob Hamblin's article on the recurrence of the nuclear motifs of 'risk society', the 'nuclear watchdog' and 'fear' in the journalistic narrative.[8] Hamblin argued that Fukushima highlighted the vacuum of accountability that historically defined the aftermath of nuclear disasters.

Within this final chapter, it will be argued that nuclear culture has remained a powerful aspect of British life both in terms of its physical legacies and its forms of representation. While official nuclear narratives fell further into the background in this period, unofficial narratives within popular culture, and more specifically computer gaming culture, came to represent the increasingly depoliticized and stable assumptions around the dangers of the nuclear state. While new types of nuclear threat emerged, older motifs such as the nuclear mushroom cloud dissolved into a harmless and kitsch icon of popular culture. As well as examining new forms of nuclear representation, the chapter will offer commentary on issues surrounding nuclear power, state-based nuclear proliferation and the threat of non-state groups using nuclear explosives or incorporating radioactive materials within conventional explosions.[9] As Paul Boyer and Eric Idsvoog argued about the post–Cold War era, nuclear 'menace now unfolded in a destabilised, decentred world [...] the prospect of a future in which nuclear weapons and nuclear know-how form a constant of the human condition is hardly reassuring'.[10] Like Masco, a note of pessimism is sounded about the nuclear future.

Context

As the Cold War was ending, there was excitement about the new opportunities offered by a future uncontaminated by nuclear anxiety. One reporter in the *Express* wrote 'these are exhilarating, uncertain times. They should be enjoyed. It is too soon to regret the passing of those old grey days when we worried about a single atrocious thing: The Bomb'.[11] All of a sudden, nuclear weapons were seen as something that did not actively merit concern. Yet, the years following 1989 saw the proliferation of nuclear weapons, as India and Pakistan conducted an exchange of nuclear tests in 1998, and North Korea began testing nuclear weapons in 2006. From the 1990s onwards, uncertainty over Iraqi and Iranian nuclear weapons programmes led to armed conflict and diplomatic tension in the region. South Africa proved to be the exception to the rule when the country started to dismantle its nuclear weapons arsenal in 1991. The new START treaty between America and Russia was signed in 2011, signalling a pledge to reduce the nuclear arsenal of both countries to 1,550 warheads by 2018.[12] Although a series of nuclear treaties led to the steady reduction of weapons stockpiles, the best information suggests that 16,300 nuclear warheads still remained in the world in 2014.[13] Peter Hennessy points to the correspondence between British prime minister Tony Blair and American president George W. Bush between 2006 and 2007 which 'should ensure that the UK will have a nuclear weapon with a "bloody Union Jack on top of it" [...] for at least a century from the date of the first atomic test in October 1952'.[14] It could be argued that this determination to sustain the nuclear weapons complex is echoed in the continued support and promotion of nuclear power generation.

In 2014, there were 440 nuclear reactors worldwide, producing nearly a quarter of global energy output. In Britain, a series of controversial government energy reviews and White Papers since 2002 led to renewed commitment to build new nuclear reactors on five sites by 2020. In the years following 1945, nuclear power stations have been over three times more expensive to build in comparison to coal-fuelled power stations. Each new nuclear power station requires around £2bn in government subsidies. Nuclear waste needs to be securely stored for years after, so long-term planning and investment is needed to deal with this.[15] Nuclear waste disposal is an uncertain legacy for the future of the earth, its oceans and its living inhabitants. In the short term, it has proved difficult to find safe ways to dispose of nuclear waste while keeping communities happy, while in the longer term, the safety of disposal techniques is inherently uncertain.[16] With Christoph Laucht, I argued 'that the 2006 and 2008 White Papers on the renewal of Britain's nuclear deterrent and the construction of new nuclear power stations demonstrate the extent to which nuclear "sociotechnical imaginaries" are embedded in official government thinking up to the present day.'[17] Nuclear decision-making requires uniquely long-term thinking on a range of issues that have the capacity to transform the lived environment for decades.

In the years after 1989, the print media understandably concentrated on movements towards global nuclear disarmament in a new international context where the necessity of nuclear deterrence decreased. Sections of the press, most notably *The Guardian*, called for substantial stockpile reductions.[18] It is clear that nuclear weapons remained a key aspect of British security policy, and the years after the attacks against America on 11 September 2001 proved that nation states would still regard nuclear capability as a cornerstone to any adapted security strategy. In this new international atmosphere of vulnerability and uncertainty, particular countries were singled out as dangerous or extreme and possible nuclear threats.[19] North Korea and Iran were used to justify 'plans for a new generation of Trident nuclear missile submarines' in 2007.[20] Additionally, the press reflected and reinforced widespread feelings of vulnerability in British culture with a series of reports on the possibility of nuclear terrorism, lax security around nuclear power stations and nuclear waste disposal.[21] This included the *Mirror* staging the sabotage of a nuclear waste disposal train in 2004.[22] In November 2006, Alexander Litvinenko, a Russian ex-secret service operative, was poisoned by ingested polonium-210 in London and died later that month. Partly due to the gruesome nature of his alleged assassination, the story was front-page news in the British press, with close-up photographs of Litvinenko on his deathbed.[23] Once again, this was a reminder of the deadly characteristics of radioactive substances and proved to be a dramatic and tragic personal narrative played out in public. Sensationalist headlines such as 'Nuked by a Cuppa', 'From Russia With Loath' and 'Irradiated' fuelled public anxiety over possible contamination in the places he visited on the day he became ill.[24] Such headlines are evidence of the continued dramatic potential of nuclear culture, while also demonstrating a lack of empathy for the destructive human consequences when highly radioactive materials cause harm. The headlines, and the story itself as it is represented, have an air of unreality which becomes a hallmark of nuclear culture in the twenty-first century.

Popular culture: Nuclear representations

Trends in popular culture after 1989 signified a wider tendency to emphasize not only the banal and permanent qualities of the nuclear state, but also the postmodern turn towards alternative forms of expression, defined by a depoliticization of nuclear references. Journalistic reports about massive spending on nuclear infrastructure, weapons and submarines, often hidden deep within newspapers, did not result in public outcry. This was mainly due to the fact that the perceived danger of nuclear conflict had diminished greatly. The growth of the internet, in terms of breadth of content and increase in use, led to deeper and yet more scattered knowledge and increasingly diffuse forms of community, and political activism proved more inclined to fight for economic issues not tied directly to the nuclear state. After a decade of extreme representations of nuclear war, and the cataclysmic event at Chernobyl, the relaxation of tensions in the post–Cold War era led to new types of nuclear representation in popular culture, which tended to offer nostalgic, politically passive or kitsch visions of nuclear war.[25] As nuclear danger receded, iconic motifs such as the nuclear mushroom cloud served mainly as static, depoliticized representations of the nuclear past. Unofficial narratives in this period became repetitious shorthand for a number of simplistic ideas around nuclear threat. The brief examination of nuclear references in popular culture that follows should not be thought of as exhaustive, but indicative of a number of trends.

Paul Boyer and Eric Idsvoog argued that by the mid-1990s, 'the language and the imagery of nuclear war so permeated U.S. culture that one hardly noticed them'.[26] Many American TV shows and films were hugely popular in Britain. These images extended to ironic depictions of the nuclear power industry. The long-running animated sitcom *The Simpsons* was first broadcast in 1989 and attracted large audiences in the United States and the UK well into the twenty-first century. Homer Simpson, as the loveable but inept father of the family, works as a hapless nuclear technician in the town's nuclear power station. In many episodes, nuclear energy is depicted as problematic and dangerous, represented continuously by a three-eyed fish in the opening credits. Episodes create humour in the supposed irresponsibility of Mr Burns, the miserly nuclear power station owner, and the persistent incompetence and laziness of nuclear technicians like Homer.[27] With deliberate echoes of *The China Syndrome*, the depiction of nuclear power in *The Simpsons* is a depoliticized comment on the inevitability of an imperfect nuclear power industry. By stressing irony, absurdity and a repetitious, comfortable familiarity, *The Simpsons* served as the dominant cultural mode at the beginning of the twenty-first century: depoliticized in its postmodern irony, in the end nothing was serious, and everything could return to normal.

It is in this sense that *The Simpsons* perhaps epitomizes the depoliticization of nuclear representation, influencing cultural perceptions of nuclear power through the repetitious use of the three-eyed fish, perhaps the postmodern icon of popular nuclear perceptions. While the imperfect nature of the nuclear power industry is acknowledged, it is never seriously critiqued, nor its permanence challenged. Beyond irony, imperfect nuclear technologies become an object of a self-conscious comedy. It is perhaps in this way that the influential motifs displayed in *The Simpsons* did a great deal to change the tone from the politicization of the 1980s to the rendering invisible of the nuclear state by allowing it to be legitimate to replace critique with irony and humour.

It was common for nuclear references to be used for comic effect in Hollywood blockbusters, for example in *Austin Powers: International Man of Mystery* (1997), where Dr Evil holds the planet to ransom under the threat of nuclear annihilation. The plot of *Hot Shots!* (1991) was based around a mission to destroy all of Saddam Hussein's nuclear facilities. British popular culture was suffused with nuclear references being mentioned in passing for comic effect, for example in the sitcoms *I'm Alan Partridge* (2002) and *The Inbetweeners* (2008), with the throwaway lines 'going nuclear' and reference to a 'dirty bomb', respectively. *Toast of London* (2014) had the lead character Stephen Toast recording voice-overs for nuclear submarines, including the dramatic phrase 'fire the nuclear weapons!'[28] The ITV sitcom *Cockroaches* (2015) was set ten years in the future following a nuclear attack on contemporary London. The opening credits included imagery directly inspired by *Protect and Survive* and the programme followed the main characters through their daily quest for survival. Scenarios are constructed primarily for comedy, and the most negative aspects of nuclear survivor fiction – namely death, psychological trauma, radioactive contamination or genetic mutation – are either ignored, downplayed or played for laughs.

The central difference between these most recent unofficial narratives in comparison to the satire of the 1960s and 1980s is that the humour stems, in part, from the unreality and depoliticization of the nuclear weapons state. The humour of *Cockroaches* does not stem from a political swipe at the nuclear weapons state, but from how young, trendy adults react to the restriction of everyday luxuries and warped normality. The survivors camp resembles a rock festival, and the overall assumption is that nuclear war is not really so bad. Echoing the humour offered in *The Simpsons*, the humour derives, in part, from the assumption that nuclear war could never happen. Revisiting Cordle's concept of the 'politics of vulnerability' discussed earlier in the book, the cultural politics of the post–Cold War era became the politics of nuclear invisibility and irony. Of course, the fragmentary examples given above are brief and obscure, but they have in common a set of assumptions on audience response that reflects a broader shift in nuclear perceptions.

It is common for nuclear references to appear in a variety of films, television programmes and music. Like the brief examples above, many of these references are incidental, but central to communicating instant, large-scale danger. For instance, the nuclear threat in *The Dark Knight Rises* (2012) demonstrates the extent to which cinema audiences have instant understanding of what nuclear danger can mean. There are many other films which fall into this category, and they include *True Lies* (1994), *Crimson Tide* (1995), *Broken Arrow* (1996), *The Peacemaker* (1997), *The World is Not Enough* (1999), *The Sum of All Fears* (2002), *The Hills Have Eyes* (2006) and the cinematic adaptation of *Watchmen* (2009).

Graphic depictions of nuclear war appeared in *Terminator 2: Judgement Day* (1991) and *Terminator 3* (2003), with new types of nuclear war being imagined, carried out by as yet unknown and uncontrollable machines. Sarah Connor's nightmare sequence in *Terminator 2* is particularly evocative of the extreme unofficial narratives of the 1980s, graphically depicting a nuclear weapon hitting an urban centre, destroying a children's playground. Films that made various nuclear or post-nuclear scenarios the central focus include *By Dawn's Early Light* (1990), *Thirteen Days* (2000), *Fail Safe* (remake, 2001), BBC TV film *Dirty War* (2004), the adaptation of Cormac McCarthy's *The Road* (2009), *The Book of Eli* (2011), *The Divide* (2012) and the rather curious *The Hot Potato* (2011) which, 'based on real events', tells the story of two characters who attempt to sell a block of uranium they stumbled across. There continue to be more artistic responses to the nuclear century, increasingly reflecting upon the legacy and meaning of the actions of nuclear states. Thoughtful reflections on the meaning of the atomic bombings of Japan include Akira Kurosawa's *Rhapsody in August* (1991) and Shohei Imamura's cinematic portrayal of *Black Rain* (1989). References to specific historical events featured in numerous plays and films, including Michael Frayn's *Copenhagen* (1998), the opera *Doctor Atomic* (2007) and the American TV series *Manhattan* (2014). Dramas that focused on nuclear intrigue included the remake of the 1980s television series the film *Edge of Darkness* in 2010 and nuclear terrorism in *24* (2001–2010). A significant number of popular TV dramas used the nuclear referent as an important contextual backdrop. Television dramas such as *The Hour* (2011) and the US series *Mad Men* (2007–2015) have successfully articulated everyday life in the Cold War era, evoking nuclear anxiety as a constant backdrop to life. US drama *Breaking Bad* (2008–2013) was set in Albuquerque, New Mexico, and contained many deliberate references to nuclear history. Apart from Albuquerque's geographical proximity to Los Alamos, the main site of the Manhattan Project, references to atomic history include scenes shot in the old National Atomic Museum in Albuquerque and main character Walter White's nickname 'Heisenberg'. In terms of literature, *Devices and Desires* by P. D. James (1991), *The Crow Road* by Iain Banks (1992), Clare George's *The Cloud Chamber* (2006), Stephen Baxter's *The H-Bomb Girl* (2007) and Will Self's *Shark* (2014) all contain references to nuclear history.

The American TV series *Jericho* which was first broadcast in Britain in 2009 hinges on the dramatic idea of a rural community under threat after nuclear war. The nuclear mushroom cloud that appears on the Kansas horizon shapes the lives of all residents of the small town of Jericho, but many of the themes that were developed in TV dramas such as *Threads*, for instance the detonation of a nuclear device over an urban centre and the depiction of panic, death, contamination and mutation, are downplayed in favour of in-depth development of characters and their complex life stories. In this sense, the nuclear mushroom cloud and nuclear danger appear incidental and distant rather than central and immediate. The physical distance of the known blast means that the element of mystery and the unknown are used to create tension – from the outset, knowledge of the nuclear event is partial, both in terms of the motives of the perpetrators and the extent of the perceived attack on America. There is no panic in Jericho, apart from flashpoints surrounding food or crime. Shared humanity and purpose are an ongoing part of the story, with national and local markers of traditional civic identity pitched against the aggressive behaviour of those whose motivations have been changed due to the realities of post-apocalyptic survival.

In terms of art and design, nuclear imagery continues to inspire, and intellectual movements have developed that reflect more consciously on the problematic links between the nuclear state and artistic expression. Recent work curated by Ele Carpenter explored the ways in which artists can contribute to the decommissioning of nuclear submarines.[29] Nuclear references have continued to suffuse popular culture in the twenty-first century, and they most commonly represent the unreality and depoliticization of the nuclear weapons state. Joseph Masco has argued that nuclear-themed film in the 1980s and beyond fed into patriotic notions of national identity in post–Cold War America. In the British context, nuclear references in post–Cold War popular culture were sanitized, and rarely critically examined. It could be argued that British popular culture helped render the nuclear state invisible, reinforcing the nostalgic appeal, harmlessness, or purely dramatic potential of nuclear weapons culture.

Computer games

Computer game culture is an under-researched area of British cultural history, yet the significance of gaming to the generation that was born after 1989 should not be underestimated. Like any other cultural artefact, computer games generate and reinforce certain political attitudes but offer particularly seductive and powerful visual interpretations of the world. Nuclear imaginaries are used in a high percentage of computer games. Recalling some of the ideas explored earlier in this book, the drama, exoticism and mystery of radioactive substances are played upon by computer game designers. The invisible danger of radiation is presented as an 'ultimate' danger to life and environment and, in a similar way to cinema, used as an emotive and militaristic shorthand for threat. Radioactive zombies, post-apocalyptic urban spaces and contaminated buildings are all rendered to signify the decline of humanity and the establishment of a new virtual imaginary, perhaps best exemplified in *Half-Life* (1998) and *Half-Life 2* (2004). In a recent article, Campbell notes, 'resistance to serious consideration of the videogame is based on not only the specific content of contemporary products and their situated cultural role, but also the nature of the form itself'.[30] Nuclear-themed computer games were introduced in the 1980s, with *Missile Command* (1980) based around the idea of defending national territory against nuclear attack.[31]

In a similar way to popular culture more generally, it could be argued that nuclear scenarios in computer games depoliticize nuclear realities, as the sanitized effect of one more nuclear blast is at once glorified and then disappears from view. The player can walk away from the game. It could be argued that particular games hold an anti-nuclear dimension, but other games tread close to the line of decency, for instance *S.T.A.L.K.E.R: Shadow of Chernobyl* (2007). The *Fallout* series includes levels resembling nuclear test towns, with the original *Fallout* (1997) featuring the atomic bomb 'Fat Man', and *Fallout 3* (2008) containing a scenario where your character has to decide whether to detonate the device. This may represent a consignment of nuclear danger to the past, nuclear nostalgia which was also represented in the film *Indiana Jones and the Kingdom of the Crystal Skull* (2008), where Indiana Jones somehow escapes an atomic test site in a flying fridge.

Campbell thinks about the 'historical videogame', those games that deliberately try to invoke the past for the purpose of entertainment. He states, 'the historical videogame [...] through digital-virtual referential mimesis, brings "the past-*as*-history" to narrative life by asking and allowing us to experience and explore its sounds, sights and processes and requiring us to make decisions about and within that constructed past-as-history'.[32] Through their 'aesthetics of historical description',[33] computer games immerse and incorporate the user into their peculiar dynamic. They tend to be politically conformist and deal with 'recognisable metonymic narrative devices'.[34] In terms of the entertainment element, 'the sights and sounds of the past-as-history, as well as the algorithms that represent its processes and allow play to occur, together create a resonant narrative, both constructed *and* referential, and thus undeniably historical'.[35] Computer games serve as powerful, popular and interactive unofficial narratives, also offering subtle historical interpretations. They will remodel familiar motifs in the existing culture, as well as create wholly new immersive worlds. The overlaps with film and literary culture are clear, and computer games have become the primary space where the nuclear mushroom cloud appears as a normalized part of young people's leisure activity, and 'nukes' are merely an ultimate weapon to help you win the game. Nuclear wastelands are instantly recognizable through the use of bright radiation symbols, yet remote and threatening enough to act as a stage for mutated humans, animals, aliens or other radioactive scenarios.

From an early stage, nuclear representations in computer games were effective evocations of existing understandings of the nuclear state. In his analysis of *Pong* (1972), Peter Bacon Hales reflects that 'in some ways, its sonic oddity and its visual screen called up the imagery of atomic apocalypse: radar screens, nuclear sub sonar pings, the hush of the nuclear war room'.[36] The computer game here serves as an aesthetic and sensory reminder of nuclear realities. If we move away from thinking about nuclear representations in video games in terms of historical accuracy, we can see how these unofficial narratives reinforce elements within the pre-existing visual politics of the nuclear. There are obvious conclusions to be made over the weapon used as a recognizable representation of ultimate destruction, but it has also been normalized as a depoliticized icon of entertainment or emblematic of a lost world. In *Call of Duty 4* (2007), nuclear weapons form part of a cinematic scenario where the device causes helicopters to lose power. The game presents nuclear weapons in a familiar manner: militarily sophisticated, spectacular, aesthetically impressive. These characteristics are very common in other computer games, such as *Mercenaries 2* (2008) and *Call of Duty: Modern Warfare 2* (2009) which feature a nuclear explosion seen from space, emphasizing the global scale of the weapons. In *Wolfenstein: The New Order* (2014), the storyline revolves around alternative historical scenarios, including Nazi development of nuclear weapons. Many other computer games either contain nuclear references or use nuclear danger as a key aspect of gameplay.[37]

Nuclear representations in computer games signal the normalization of a sanitized nuclear politics. Echoing the visual politics defined by Hollywood, the motifs are normally instantly recognizable, yet can offer dystopian visions of post-nuclear life. Nuclear stories acknowledged as historical 'realities' are introduced to provide notions of authenticity. If 'believability' within the computer games is enhanced, the nature and experience of the immersive act will be much more effective. Thus, historical accuracy or authenticity is secondary to player satisfaction. In this sense, computer game designers will often present historical 'realities' that are both recognizable and unproblematic to the gamer. To create a sense of dislocation or alienation from familiar landscapes, the inclusion of familiar and instantly recognizable threats is also necessary. Nuclear weapons top the list of instantly recognizable, vast threats, but rarely appear as historicised or politically problematic objects.

Computer gaming significantly reinforces the depoliticization of the nuclear present. Bolstering well-developed assumptions around key nuclear motifs, the politics of the nuclear is relegated to the background.[38] The depiction of nuclear weapons in computer games reinforces nostalgic ideas of nuclear weapons as a lost historical object or as a fantastic and futuristic weapon to help accomplish a mission. While some games do problematize the use of nuclear weapons, the majority of games reinforce the legitimacy of military use of nuclear force. Highly sophisticated cinematic depictions will rarely offer ethical, moral or political perspectives on their use, while implicitly reinforcing a particular politics of the nuclear as permanent, spectacular and invisible. While nuclear explosions are repeatedly rendered visible in this way, they acquire harmless qualities. As Frederic Jameson wrote in 1991, 'we are condemned to seek History by way of our own pop images and simulacra of that history, which itself remains forever out of reach'.[39] Through assembling simplistic motifs and assumptions about the nuclear past, the nuclear present is rendered invisible.

Nuclear legacies

Away from nuclear representations within popular culture, this book ends with some reflections on the very real nuclear legacies that remain in the twenty-first century. British atomic veterans are still fighting for their right to compensation for alleged contamination they received while on active duty. British and Australian military personnel were ordered to stand in the vicinity of nuclear tests in the 1950s, did not wear protective clothing and some became ill immediately afterwards. It is alleged that congenital abnormalities have been passed on to the children of atomic veterans.[40] British atomic veterans were told in March 2012 that they would be unable to sue the Ministry of Defence because of the amount of time that has elapsed since the tests were conducted in the 1950s.[41] Although other nations, most notably the United States during the Clinton administration, did award compensation to atomic veterans, the lawyer representing the British veterans stated, 'the approach that this government takes is to waste resources on fighting veterans rather than co-operating with them [...] every other single nuclear power has established ways to recognise and compensate veterans'. The Ministry of Defence stated, 'all the [supreme court] justices recognised that the veterans would face great difficulty proving a causal link between illnesses suffered and attendance at the tests. The supreme court described the claims as having no reasonable prospect of success and that they were doomed to fail'.[42] A documentary on British atomic veterans, *Nobody Told Us Anything*, is set to be released in 2015. Add to this the issues around British atomic contamination of Aboriginal communities and Australian military personnel, and it is understandable why there is a global *Hibakusha* justice campaign.[43]

An important part of how we conceive British nuclear culture is now defined by our relationship with the material remnants of Cold War infrastructure. Hack Green 'Secret Nuclear Bunker' in Cheshire tempts visitors to view its 'Awesome Weapons of Mass Destruction' on the site of a former Regional Government Headquarters.[44] There are other nuclear bunkers that are opened up to the public around Britain, including Scotland's Secret Bunker near St Andrews and Kelvedon Hatch in Essex (Figure 7.1).[45] Orford Ness, a nuclear test facility in Suffolk, is now owned by the National Trust and kept as a nature reserve. These architectural legacies of the nuclear Cold War are etched into rural and urban spaces, with huge installations such as Fylingdales and HMNB Clyde dominating, demarcating and forever altering the existing landscape. It remains to be seen what the future of these Cold War constructions will be, but while some render visible the continuation of the nuclear state, the Cold War bunker as visitor attraction can offer the misleading suggestion that the nuclear weapons complex is consigned to history. Nuclear power stations are a permanent reminder of the nuclear state, and their future seems secure for decades to come.

FIGURE 7.1 *End of the Cold War: the underground nuclear bunker at Kelvedon Hatch, Essex on decommissioning, 1992.* © *Imperial War Museums (MH 33659).*

One final legacy of the nuclear era is the continued existence of anti-nuclear pressure groups. A report in the *Independent* in 2006 reported that CND membership had risen in response to Trident renewal plans, with a rise 'by 300%' of new members. The paper reported membership numbers of 32,000 in 2005 compared with 110,000 in 1983.[46] While anti-nuclear activism declined in the years following 1989, new forms of activism have emerged, made more visible by their online presence.[47] Debates over nuclear disarmament in Scotland played a significant part in the 2014 Scottish independence referendum. If the vote for an independent Scottish government had been successful, the Scottish National Party had 'pledged to safely remove and permanently ban nuclear weapons from Scottish territory within the first term of a newly independent parliament'.[48] It would have been some legacy indeed if a democratic vote had the direct consequence of eliminating nuclear weapons from Scottish territory.

Conclusion

On the face of it, the period 1990–2015 was one defined by a reduction and recalibration of nuclear threat and active movements towards nuclear non-proliferation. The end of the Cold War signalled an end to the public and aggressive nuclear arms race, but nuclear weapons development did not end. In the years after 9/11, nuclear threat was re-imagined as emanating from random or unpredictable 'terrorist' attacks. This at once continued the immediacy of the nuclear threat experienced in the Cold War era but became spatially different as civilian suspicion focused on the city streets rather than the skies. In this sense, the nature of nuclear threat proliferated, as new perceptions of threat came into existence. Political commitment towards non-proliferation and disarmament is, for some, an understandably slow process, yet nation states continue to pursue the development of nuclear technologies, and the risk of nuclear war, theoretically at least, still exists.

Nuclear representation has reached a depoliticized, sanitized stage, where the nuclear state is rendered invisible by the familiar and repetitive iconography of the mushroom cloud, where victimhood or nuclear legacies are rarely explored. Rather, nuclear kitsch is mobilized to recreate a lost and harmless past, doing the work of depoliticization in its absence of critical engagement with the politics of the nuclear state or its denial of after-effects and victimhood. It is here that nuclear subjectivity falls away to reveal the emptiness of nuclear iconography. Once the Cold War ended, unofficial narratives became fewer, and less politicized. As this chapter has demonstrated, British culture continued to find new ways to respond to the existence of nuclear technology, but these narratives predominantly relied on pre-existing nuclear assumptions. Perhaps this brief analysis of nuclear iconography reminds us that we need to trace the genealogy of public understandings of the British nuclear state more fully. As we acknowledge the real nuclear legacies around us, and remind ourselves of the complex realities of the nuclear present, it is important to attend to the persistent visual and textual nuclear vocabularies that suffuse contemporary culture, and to think about how and why they have emerged in their present form. This book has argued that unchallenged use of language and assumptions can have the power to construct and then reinforce a range of ideas about the nuclear state. This chapter has hinted that assumptions galvanized in a depoliticized nuclear culture can also make the reality of the nuclear state fade from view.

CHAPTER EIGHT

Conclusions: The Nuclear Century, 1898–2015

This book has surveyed British nuclear culture in the long twentieth century. It has argued that 'unofficial' narratives tell us a great deal about what it was like to live in a world increasingly shaped by nuclear technological development. Alongside consistent support and dedication to nuclear development for military and civilian uses, which official sources can tell us a lot about, we have seen that unofficial source materials can offer a series of perspectives on the overall impact nuclear technology had on many facets of British life. This book has focused on British perspectives, making an intervention into a young area of historiography. For the future, it should be acknowledged that the nuclear story is global, and the transnational elements of the nuclear age should not be downplayed.

The British people experienced nuclear culture in complex ways. The book began with a statement from J. B. Priestley, proclaiming the inescapable fact that everyone was involved in the atomic age. Through the course of this book, we have seen that some lives were shaped and defined by British nuclear culture in the long twentieth century: perhaps by their involvement in anti-nuclear activism, artistic endeavours, simply reading their choice of daily newspaper, or being involved in the production and testing of nuclear weapons. We have seen that before the invention of atomic reactors and bombs, these technologies were imagined in various ways. They symbolized the atomic crossroad, of a choice between hope and fear. For the vast majority of the British people following 1945, imagining the devastation of nuclear weapons was at the root of how they experienced British nuclear culture. We have seen how the visibility of nuclear politics, and the extent to which nuclear anxiety was widespread, fluctuated greatly since 1945. With the absence of mass anti-nuclear protest in the twenty-first century, it could be argued that by 2015, the nuclear state has been rendered largely invisible, while remaining a permanent part of political, scientific and military culture and institutions.

In the introduction to this book, I described British nuclear culture as the 'distinct corner of British culture defined by the complex and varied ways in which people controlled, responded to or represented nuclear technology'. Through the course of the book, I hope it has become clear that there are many nuclear 'cultures' to think about. We have seen how government institutions and individuals controlled and shaped, mostly in secret, 'official' nuclear knowledge closely throughout the long twentieth century. Until recently, historians were unable or unwilling to approach nuclear history in ways that challenged or problematized this control of knowledge, but it is now clear that the official nuclear narrative must be critically examined in order to better understand the wider historic significance of the nuclear state and its continuing implications for British life.

Indeed, the range of 'unofficial' narratives presented in this book demonstrates the extent to which the official narrative was challenged and resisted by individuals. These responses were varied and powerful and need to be interpreted flexibly. We have seen how these responses dovetailed with or authored unofficial representations of nuclear technology, through an examination of journalism, literature, film, TV and music. Although some of these representations supported a pro-deterrence line, we have seen the extent to which unofficial narratives served to disrupt, challenge and resist the nuclear state. Along with anti-nuclear protest, it is perhaps this dynamic which best exemplifies the political and discursive power of the unofficial nuclear narrative. This is why many of the accepted 'official' histories of the nuclear state bear no resemblance to the nuclear century as experienced by many British citizens.

British Nuclear Culture has demonstrated the variety of nuclear narratives that emerged in the twentieth century and argued that unofficial and official narratives clashed with increasing severity as the twentieth century developed, before unofficial narratives became fewer and less politicized once the Cold War ended. This book has argued that, on the whole, unofficial narratives have remained absent from the interests of historians of modern Britain. Yet, we have learned from arguments of contemporary commentators such as Joseph Masco that 'the nuclear complex *remains* a particularly potent national project, informing one way in which citizens imagine both their lives and deaths'.[1] The historical process by which this normalization occurred, and remains to the present day, has not been fully explored in nuclear historiography. There is much research to do in the future in order to better understand the psychosocial pressures at the heart of the nuclear age. With its focus on 'narratives', this book has not engaged in any great depth with the spatial and affective turns that have influenced historical scholarship in the past decade. These approaches promise to raise new questions for nuclear scholars in the next decade.

Approaching the study of nuclear culture is a difficult task, but interdisciplinary approaches that take inspiration from many subjects, such as literary and political theory, sociology, historical geography, philosophy and psychology, will be at the heart of nuclear culture studies for many years to come. Only through new and imaginative thinking around human interaction with nuclear science and technology can we properly understand what the British nuclear century meant. The unofficial narratives analysed in this book remind us that our continued use of nuclear technologies leaves us with a complex set of legacies that future generations will need to deal with. These legacies can all too easily be rendered invisible if we refuse to engage critically with the very real implications of the first nuclear century and the nuclear future.

It is familiar enough for scholars to claim that the advent of the atomic bomb had a social and psychological impact of a kind, or to speak of the advent of the 'atomic age'. However, research is only just starting to uncover how knowledge of nuclear danger became embedded in British discourse, and how this knowledge shaped the modern British subject. British people were not passive instruments of nuclear discourse but displayed emotional responses to nuclear dangers and carried out, sometimes by reflex, complex varieties of resistance. I hope this book will encourage others to uncover more of these stories which, after all, give social and cultural meaning to the British nuclear century while simultaneously challenging us to continue posing difficult questions about the condition of our nuclear future.

NOTES

Chapter 1

1 Of course, this is greatly simplifying Oppenheimer's role in the atomic bomb project and his biography. For an excellent intellectual biography that stresses the social context of his work, see Charles Thorpe, *Oppenheimer: The Tragic Intellect* (Chicago: University of Chicago Press, 2006). An interview with Oppenheimer was televised in 1965 and can be found here: <http://www .atomicarchive.com/Movies/Movie8.shtml> [accessed 10 November 2014].

2 Andrew J. Rotter, *Hiroshima: The World's Bomb* (Oxford: Oxford University Press, 2009).

3 J. B. Priestley, 'On the Stairway of the Stars', *The Listener* 13 March 1947, p. 355.

4 Ibid.

5 J. B. Priestley, 'Britain and the Nuclear Bombs', *The New Statesman*, 2 November 1957.

6 Robert S. Norris and Hans M. Kristensen, 'The British Nuclear Stockpile, 1953–2013', *Bulletin of the Atomic Scientists* 69, 4 (2013), pp. 69–75.

7 Throughout the text, 'nuclear' will be the word used to describe nuclear science and anything relating to the development and perception of thermonuclear weapons and reactors. There are technical distinctions to make between the precise meaning and use of the words 'atomic' and 'nuclear', and they can be used interchangeably, but for the purposes of clarity the term 'nuclear' will be used for the majority of the book. It is only really the period 1945–1952 (the explosion of the first 'atomic' weapon until the explosion of the first 'thermonuclear' weapon) where 'atomic' will be used.

8 Michel Foucault, *The Will to Knowledge: The History of Sexuality, Volume 1* (London: Penguin, 1998), p. 137.

9 Kirk Willis, 'The Origins of British Nuclear Culture, 1895–1939', *Journal of British Studies* 34, 1 (1995), p. 60.

10 Christoph Laucht, *Elemental Germans: Klaus Fuchs, Rudolf Peierls, and the Making of British Nuclear Culture, 1939–59* (Basingstoke: Palgrave Macmillan), p. 5.

11 Jeff Hughes, 'What Is British Nuclear Culture? Understanding Uranium, 235', *The British Journal for the History of Science* 45, 4 (December 2012), p. 496.

12 Richard Maguire, '"Never a Credible Weapon": Nuclear Cultures in Government During the Era of the H-bomb', *The British Journal for the History of Science* 45, 4 (December 2012), pp. 519–534.

13 Jonathan Hogg and Christoph Laucht, 'Introduction: British Nuclear Culture', *British Journal of the History of Science* 45, 4 (December 2012), p. 488.
14 Catherine Jolivette (ed.), *British Art in the Nuclear Age* (Surrey: Ashgate, 2014).
15 Hughes, 'What Is British Nuclear Culture?', p. 496.
16 Ibid., p. 497.
17 Ibid., p. 503.
18 Jonathan Hogg, '"The Family That Feared Tomorrow": British Nuclear Culture and Individual Experience in the Late 1950s', *The British Journal for the History of Science* 45, 4 (December 2012), p. 535.
19 Ian Welsh, *Mobilising Modernity: The Nuclear Moment* (London: Routledge, 2003), p. 3.
20 David Nye, *American Technological Sublime* (Cambridge, MA: MIT Press, 1994), p. 231.
21 David Vincent, *The Culture of Secrecy: Britain, 1832–1998* (Oxford: Oxford University Press, 1998), pp. 9–18; 194–210.
22 Hogg and Laucht, 'Introduction: British Nuclear Culture', pp. 491–492. See also, Margaret Gowing, *Independence and Deterrence: Britain and Atomic Energy, 1945–1952* (London: Macmillan, 1974), pp. 126–127; Nicholas Wilkinson, *Secrecy and the Media: The Official History of the United Kingdom's D-Notice System* (London: Routledge, 2009).
23 Ian Welsh, *Mobilising Modernity: The Nuclear Moment* (London: Routledge, 2003), p. 4.
24 Hogg, 'The Family That Feared Tomorrow', p. 535.
25 Dan Cordle, 'Protect/ Protest: British Nuclear Fiction of the 1980s', *The British Journal for the History of Science* 45, 4 (December 2012), pp. 653–669.
26 On varieties of resistance, see James C. Scott, *Weapons of the Weak: Everyday Forms of Peasant Resistance* (New Haven: Yale University Press, 1985).
27 Carole Gallagher, *American Ground Zero: The Secret Nuclear War* (Cambridge, MA: MIT Press).
28 Brian C. Taylor, 'Nuclear Pictures and Metapictures', *American Literary History* 9, 3 (Autumn 1997), pp. 567–597.
29 Ibid.
30 Ibid., p. 568.
31 Ibid., p. 593.
32 Recent movements towards empathetic approaches to the nuclear century are best encapsulated by Kate Brown, *Plutopia: Nuclear Families, Atomic Cities and the Great Soviet and American Plutonium Disasters* (Oxford: Oxford University Press, 2013); Joseph Masco, *Nuclear Borderlands: The Manhattan Project in Post-War New Mexico* (Princeton: Princeton University Press, 2006).
33 See Stephen Hilgartner, R. C. Bell and R. O'Connor, *Nukespeak: Nuclear Language, Visions and Mindset* (San Francisco: Sierra, 1982).
34 Crispin Aubrey (ed.), *Nukespeak: The Media and the Bomb* (London: Comedia, 1982).
35 Hayden White, *Tropics of Discourse: Essays in Cultural Criticism* (Baltimore, MD: The Johns Hopkins University Press, 1979), pp. 126–127.

36   Robert Jacobs, *The Dragon's Tail: Americans Face the Atomic Age* (Amherst: University of Massachusetts Press, 2010), pp. 4–5.

37   Jonathan Hogg, 'Cultures of Nuclear Resistance in 1980s Liverpool', *Urban History*, published online as a *FirstView* article on 3 August 2015. DOI: 10.1017/ S0963926815000590.

38   Hogg and Laucht, 'Introduction: British Nuclear Culture', p. 479.

39   Roger Ruston, *A Say in the End of the World: Morals and Nuclear Weapons Policy, 1941–1987* (Oxford: Oxford University Press, 1990).

40   Matthew Connelly has argued that we should back away from using the term 'cold war' as a definitive, descriptive or analytical category in Matthew Connelly, 'The Cold War in the *Longue Dureé*: Global Migration, Public Health, and Population Control', in M. P. Leffler and O. A. Westad (eds.), *The Cambridge History of the Cold War: Volume 3, Endings* (Cambridge: Cambridge University Press, 2010), pp. 466–488. Holger Nehring in *Politics of Security: British and West German Protest Movements and the Early Cold War, 1945–1970* (Oxford: Oxford University Press, 2013) has offered a new way to think about the politics of security in the 'cold war' context.

41   See Frank Biess, '"Everybody Has a Chance": Nuclear Angst, Civil Defence, and the History of Emotions in Postwar West Germany', *German History* 27, 2 (2009), pp. 215–243; Joe Moran, 'History, Memory and the Everyday', *Rethinking History* 8, 1 (2004), pp. 51–68; Joel Isaac and Duncan Bell (eds.), *Uncertain Empire: American History and the Idea of the Cold War* (Oxford: Oxford University Press, 2012).

42   For a good example of a 'social constructivist' approach to the nuclear age, see Charles Thorpe, *Oppenheimer*.

43   Margaret Gowing, *Britain and Atomic Energy 1939–1945* (London: Macmillan, 1964); Lorna Arnold, *Windscale 1957: Anatomy of a Nuclear Accident* (Basingstoke: Palgrave Macmillan, 1995); Lorna Arnold and Mark Smith, *Britain, Australia and the Bomb: The Nuclear Tests and Their Aftermath* (Basingstoke: Palgrave Macmillan, 2006).

44   Hogg and Laucht, 'Introduction: British Nuclear Culture', pp. 479–493.

45   Jeff Hughes, 'Deconstructing the Bomb: Recent Perspectives on Nuclear History', *British Journal for the History of Science* 37, 4 (2004), pp. 455–464.

46   For example, see J. Baylis and A. MacMillan, 'The British Global Strategy Paper of 1952', *Journal of Strategic Studies* 16, 2 (1993), pp. 200–226; Ian Clark, *Nuclear Diplomacy and the Special Relationship: Britain's Deterrent and America, 1957–1962* (Oxford: Clarendon, 1994); Stuart Croft, 'Continuity and Change in British Thinking about Nuclear Weapons', *Political Studies* XLII (1994), pp. 228–242; David Edgerton, *Warfare State: Britain, 1920–1970* (Cambridge: Cambridge University Press, 2006); Leon D. Epstein, 'The Nuclear Deterrent and the British Election of 1964', *The Journal of British Studies* 5, 2 (May 1966), pp. 139–163; Lawrence Freedman, *Britain and Nuclear Weapons* (London: Macmillan, 1980); Matthew Grant (ed.), *The British Way in Cold Warfare* (London: Continuum, 2008); Peter Hennessy (ed.), *Cabinets and the Bomb* (Oxford: Oxford University Press, 2007); Richard Maguire, 'Scientific Dissent Amid the United Kingdom Government's Nuclear Weapons Programme', *History Workshop Journal* 63 (2007), pp. 113–135; David Reynolds, *Britannia Overruled: British Policy & World Power in the 20th Century* (London: Longman, 1991).

47   There is a vast amount of literature on this topic. Useful histories include John Baylis, *Anglo-American Defence Relations 1939–1984: The Special Relationship* (London: Macmillan, 1984); John Baylis, *Ambiguity and Deterrence: British Nuclear Strategy, 1945–1964* (Oxford: Clarendon, 1994); Michael S. Goodman, *Spying on the Nuclear Bear: Anglo-American Intelligence and the Soviet Bomb* (Stanford: Stanford University Press, 2007); Matthew Jones, 'Great Britain, the United States, and Consultation over Use of the Atomic Bomb, 1950–1954', *Historical Journal* 54, 3 (2011), pp. 797–828; Saul Kelly, 'No Ordinary Foreign Office Official: Sir Roger Makins and Anglo-American Atomic Relations, 1945–55', *Contemporary British History* 14, 4 (2000), pp. 107–124; Jenifer Mackby and Paul Cornish, *U.S.-UK Nuclear Cooperation After 50 Years* (Washington, DC: Center for Strategic and International Studies Press, 2008); Richard Moore, *Nuclear Illusion, Nuclear Reality: Britain, the United States and Nuclear Weapons, 1958–1964* (Basingstoke: Palgrave Macmillan, 2012); Septimus H. Paul, *Nuclear Rivals: Anglo-American Atomic Relations, 1941–1952* (Columbus: Ohio State University Press, 2000); Andrew Priest, 'In American Hands: Britain, the United States and the Polaris Nuclear Project, 1962–1968', *Contemporary British History* 19, 3 (2005), pp. 353–376; S. Schrafstetter, ' "Loquacious … and Pointless as Ever?" Britain, the United States and the United Nations Negotiations on International Control of Nuclear Energy 1945–48', *Contemporary British History* 16, 4 (2002), pp. 87–108; John Simpson, *The Independent Nuclear State: The United States, Britain and the Military Atom* (London: Macmillan, 1983); Kristan Stoddart, *Losing an Empire and Finding a Role: Britain, the USA, NATO and Nuclear Weapons, 1964–1970* (Basingstoke: Palgrave Macmillan, 2012); Stephen Twigge and Len Scott, *Planning Armageddon: Britain, the United States and the Command of Western Nuclear Forces, 1945–1964* (Amsterdam: Harwood Academic, 2000); John R. Walker, *British Nuclear Weapons and the Test Ban, 1954–1973: Britain, the United States, Weapons Policies and Nuclear Testing: Tensions and Contradictions* (Farnham: Ashgate, 2010).

48   See Richard Moore, *The Royal Navy and Nuclear Weapons* (London: Cass, 2001); Michael Quinlan, *Thinking About Nuclear Weapons: Principles, Problems, Prospects* (Oxford: Oxford University Press, 2009); Duncan Redford, 'The "Hallmark of a First-Class Navy": The Nuclear-Powered Submarine in the Royal Navy 1960–1977', *Contemporary British History* 23, 2 (2009), pp. 181–197.

49   See Christopher Andrew, *The Defence of the Realm: The Authorised History of MI5* (London: Allen Lane, 2009); Michael S. Goodman, 'Who Is Trying to Keep What Secret From Whom and Why?', *Journal of Cold War Studies* 7, 3 (2005), pp. 124–146. Richard J. Aldrich, *The Hidden Hand: Britain, America and Cold War Secret Intelligence* (London: Murray, 2001); Michael S. Goodman, 'The Grandfather of the Hydrogen Bomb? Anglo-American Intelligence and Klaus Fuchs', *Historical Studies in the Physical and Biological Sciences* 34, 1 (2003), pp. 1–22.

50   Paul S. Boyer, *By the Bomb's Early Light: American Thought and Culture at the Dawn of the Atomic Age*, 2nd edn. (Chapel Hill: University of North Carolina Press, 1994).

51 Elaine Tyler-May, *Homeward Bound: American Families in the Cold War* (New York: Basic, 1988); Dee Garrison, *Bracing for Armageddon: Why Civil Defense Never Worked* (Oxford: Oxford University Press, 2006); Kenneth Rose, *One Nation Underground: A History of the Fallout Shelter* (New York: New York University Press, 2004); Spencer R. Weart, *The Rise of Nuclear Fear* (Cambridge, MA: Harvard University Press, 2012); Allan M. Winkler, *Life Under a Cloud: American Anxiety About the Atom* (New York: Oxford University Press, 1993); Margot A. Henriksen, *Dr. Strangelove's America: Society and Culture in the Atomic Age* (Berkeley: University of California Press, 1997); Scott C. Zeman and Michael A. Amundson (eds.), *Atomic Culture: How We Learned to Stop Worrying and Love the Bomb* (Boulder: University Press of Colorado, 2004); Rosemary B. Mariner and G. Kurt Piehler (eds.), *The Atomic Bomb and American Society: New Perspectives* (Knoxville: University of Tennessee Press, 2009); Bo Jacobs, *The Dragon's Tail: Americans Face the Atomic Age* (Amhurst, MA: University of Massachusetts Press, 2010).

52 Matt Houlbrook, 'Towards a Historical Geography of Sexuality', *Journal of Urban History* 274 (2001), p. 498.

53 David Monteyne, *Fallout Shelter: Designing for Civil Defense in the Cold War* (Minneapolis: University of Minneapolis, 2011), p. xv.

54 Special issue of *Urban History* on nuclear cities (forthcoming 2016); Wayne D. Cocroft and Roger J. C. Thomas, *Cold War: Building for Nuclear Confrontation 1946–1989* (Swindon: English Heritage, 2003); Peter Hennessy, *The Secret State: Preparing for the Worst 1945–2010*, 2nd edn. (London: Penguin, 2010).

55 Sophie Forgan, 'Atoms in Wonderland', *History and Technology* 19, 3 (2003), pp. 177–196.

56 Matthew Grant, *After the Bomb: Civil Defence and Nuclear War in Cold War Britain, 1945–1968* (Basingstoke: Palgrave Macmillan, 2010); Hennessy, *The Secret State*.

57 Duncan Campbell, *War Plan UK: The Truth About Civil Defence in Britain* (London: Burnett, 1982); Matthew Grant, 'Home Defence and the Sandys White Paper, 1957', *Journal of Strategic Studies* 31, 6 (2008), pp. 925–949; Matthew Grant, *After the Bomb*; Matthew Grant, '"Civil Defence Gives Meaning to Your Leisure": Citizenship, Participation, and Cultural Change in Cold War Recruitment Propaganda, 1949–1954', *Twentieth Century British History* 22, 1 (2010), pp. 52–78; Jeff Hughes, 'The Strath Report: Britain Confronts the H-Bomb, 1954–1955', *History and Technology* 19, 3 (2003), pp. 257–275; Melissa Smith, 'Architects of Armageddon: the Home Office Scientific Advisers' Branch and Civil Defence in Britain, 1945–1968', *British Journal for the History of Science* 43, 2 (2010), pp. 149–180; Melissa Smith, '"What to Do If It Happens": Planners, Pamphlets and Propaganda in the Age of the H-Bomb', *Endeavour* 33, 2 (2009), pp. 60–64.

58 Adrian Bingham, '"The Monster?" The British Popular Press and Nuclear Culture, 1945-Early 1960s', *The British Journal for the History of Science* 45, 4 (December 2012), pp. 609–624; Christoph Laucht, '"Dawn – Or Dusk?": Britain's *Picture Post* Confronts Nuclear Energy', in Dick van Lente (ed.), *The Nuclear Age in Popular Media: A Transnational History, 1945–1965* (Basingstoke: Palgrave Macmillan 2012).

59 Richard Hornsey, '"Everything Is Made of Atoms": The Reprogramming of Space and Time in Post-War London', *Journal of Historical Geography* 34

(2008), pp. 94–117; David Crowley and Jane Pavitt (eds.), *Cold War Modern: Design 1945–1970* (London: V&A Museum).

60 Tony Shaw, *British Cinema and the Cold War: The State, Propaganda and Consensus* (London: I.B. Tauris, 2001). See also, Charles A. Carpenter, *Dramatists and the Bomb: American and British Playwrights Confront the Nuclear Age, 1945–1964* (London: Greenwood Press, 1999).

61 See Linda Rosso, 'Introduction: Radio Wars: Broadcasting in the Cold War', *Cold War History* 13, 2 (2013), pp. 145–152.

62 Matthew Grant and Benjamin Ziemann, *Unthinking the Imaginary War: Intellectual Reflections of the Nuclear Age, 1945–1990* (Manchester: Manchester University Press, forthcoming).

63 Cordle, 'Protect/ Protest'.

64 Lawrence S. Wittner, *Resisting the Bomb* (Stanford: Stanford University Press, 1997); Alison Young, *Femininity in Dissent* (London: Routledge, 1990); Mark Phythian, 'CND's Cold War', *Contemporary, British History* 15, 3 (2001), pp. 133–156.

65 Jodi Burkett, 'The Campaign for Nuclear Disarmament and Changing Attitudes Towards the Earth in the Nuclear age', *British Journal for the History of Science* 45, 4 (December 2012), pp. 625–640. See also J. R. McNeill and Corinna R. Unger (eds.), *Environmental Histories of the Cold War* (Cambridge: Cambridge University Press, 2010); Lawrence Badash, *A Nuclear Winter's Tale: Science and Politics in the 1980s* (Cambridge, MA: MIT Press, 2009); Jacob D. Hamblin, *Poison in the Well: Radioactive Waste in the Oceans at the Dawn of the Nuclear Age* (New Brunswick, NJ: Rutgers University Press, 2008); Holger Nehring, 'National Internationalists: British and West German Protests Against Nuclear Weapons, the Politics of Transnational Communications and the Social History of the Cold War, 1957–1964', *Contemporary European History* 14, 4 (2005), pp. 559–582.

66 Alison Kraft, 'Atomic Medicine: The Cold War Origins of Biological Research', *History Today* 59, 11 (2009), pp. 26–33; Alison Kraft, 'Between Medicine and Industry: The Rise of the Radioisotope 1945–1965', *Contemporary British History* 20, 1 (2006), pp. 3–37.

67 Hogg and Laucht, 'Introduction: British Nuclear Culture'. For work in this area, see David James Gill, 'Ministers, Markets and Missiles: The British Government, the European Economic Community and the Nuclear Non-Proliferation Treaty, 1964–1968', *Diplomacy & Statecraft* 21, 3 (2010), pp. 451–470; Helen Parr, 'Transformation and Tradition: Anglo-French Nuclear Cooperation and Britain's Policy Towards the European Community', in Grant (ed.), *The British Way in Cold Warfare*, pp. 87–103; also see Tracy Davies, *Stages of Emergency: Cold War Nuclear Civil Defense* (Durham, NC: Duke University Press, 2007); Mark B. Smith, 'Peaceful Coexistence at All Costs: Cold War Exchanges Between Britain and the Soviet Union in 1956', *Cold War History* 12, 3 (2012), pp. 537–558.

68 Bo Jacobs, 'Nuclear Conquistadors: Military Colonialism in Nuclear Test Site Selection During the Cold War', *Asian Journal of Peacebuilding* 1, 2 (November 2013), pp. 157–177. See also Robert Milliken, *No Conceivable Injury: The Story of Britain and Australia's Atomic Cover-Up* (Ringwood, Victoria: Penguin, 1986).

69   Christine Leah, *Australia and the Bomb* (Basingstoke: Palgrave Macmillan, 2014); John Crawford, '"A Political H-Bomb": New Zealand and the British Thermonuclear Weapon Test of 1957–1958', *Journal of Imperial and Commonwealth History* 26, 1 (1998), pp. 127–150; Roger Cross, 'British Nuclear Tests and the Indigenous People of Australia', in Douglas Holdstock and Frank Barnaby (eds.), *The British Nuclear Weapons Programme 1952–2002* (London: Cass, 2003), pp. 76–90; Joan Smith, *Clouds of Deceit: The Deadly Legacy of Britain's Bomb Tests* (London: Faber, 1985); Arnold and Smith, *Britain, Australia and the Bomb*, p. 11.

70   The Sellafield Stories Oral History Project <http://www.sellafieldstories.org .uk/> [accessed 14 June 2013]; Hunter Davies (ed.), *Sellafield Stories: Life with Britain's First Nuclear Plant* (London: Constable, 2012); Derek Robinson, *Just Testing* (London: Collins Harvill, 1985).

71   Roy, 'The End of Imagination', first read as the memorable epigraph in Paul Williams, *Race, Ethnicity and Nuclear War* (Liverpool: Liverpool University Press, 2011).

72   For a list of UK nuclear test explosions, see Frederick Warner and René J. C. Kirchmann (eds.), *Nuclear Test Explosions: Environmental and Human Impacts* (Chicester: John Wiley, 2000), pp. 243–244.

73   Williams, *Race, Ethnicity and Nuclear War*.

74   Rotter, *Hiroshima*, p. 6.

75   Taylor, 'Nuclear Pictures and Metapictures', p. 571.

76   Ibid.

77   For concise and accessible texts that deal with the science behind nuclear technology (most suited to students approaching nuclear history from the perspective of the humanities), see Maxwell Irvine, *Nuclear Power: A Very Short Introduction* (Oxford: Oxford University Press, 2011) and Joseph M. Siracusa, *Nuclear Weapons: A Very Short Introduction* (Oxford: Oxford University Press, 2008).

78   Joseph Masco, '"Survival Is Your Business": Engineering Ruins and Affect in Nuclear America', *Cultural Anthropology* 23, 2 (2008), pp. 361–398.

79   Imaginative ways to think about nuclear legacies in the digital age include The Global Hibakusha Project, run by Bo Jacobs and Mick Broderick, which is involved in *Hibakusha* community projects around the world. Also, Nuclear Futures is a project that 'bears witness to the legacies of the atomic age through creative arts'. <http://nuclearfutures.org/> [accessed 2 October 2014]. Ele Carpenter's Nuclear Culture project explores the artistic or humanist responses to the legacies of the nuclear age. <http://nuclear.artscatalyst.org/> [accessed 2 October 2014].

Chapter 2

1   For a detailed survey of these developments, see Jeff Hughes, 'Radioactivity and Nuclear Physics', *The Cambridge History of Science, Volume 5* (Cambridge: Cambridge University Press, 2002), pp. 350–374; Jeff Hughes, '"Modernists With a Vengeance": Changing Culture of Theory in Nuclear Science, 1920–1930', *Studies in History and Philosophy of Modern Physics* 29 (1998), pp. 339–367.

2 Existing work addressing the advent of 'big science' and the role of the scientist in liberal democracies includes Charles Thorpe, 'Disciplining Experts: Scientific Authority and Liberal Democracy in the Oppenheimer Case', *Social Studies of Science* 32, 4 (August 2002), pp. 527–564.

3 For the German bomb project, see Paul Lawrence Rose, *Heisenberg and the Nazi Atomic Bomb Project, 1939–1945* (Berkeley: University of California Press, 1998).

4 Willis, 'The Origins of British Nuclear Culture, 1895–1939'.

5 See Michael I. Freedman, 'Frederick Soddy and the Practical Significance of Radioactive Matter', *British Journal for the History of Science* 12, 42 (1979), pp. 257–260; Richard E. Sclove, 'From Alchemy to Atomic War: Frederick Soddy's "Technology Assessment" of Atomic Energy, 1900–1915', *Science, Technology and Human Values* 14, 1 (1989), pp. 163–194; Edward Shire, *Rutherford and the Nuclear Atom* (Harlow: Longman, 1972); Thaddeus J. Trenn, *The Self-Splitting Atom: The History of the Rutherford-Soddy Collaboration* (London: Taylor and Francis, 1977); Thaddeus Trenn, 'The Central Role of Energy in Soddy's Holistic and Critical Approach to Nuclear Science, Economics, and Social Responsibility', *British Journal for the History of Science* 12, 42 (1979), pp. 261–276; Margaret Gowing, 'James Chadwick and the Atomic Bomb', *Notes and Records of the Royal Society of London* 47, 1 (1993), pp. 79–92; Andrew Brown, *The Neutron and the Bomb: A Biography of Sir James Chadwick* (Oxford: Oxford University Press, 1997); Peter Rowlands, *125 Years of Excellence: The University of Liverpool Physics Department 1881 to 2006* (Liverpool: UoL Science Communication Unit, 2003), p. 17; Charles King, 'Chadwick, Liverpool and the Bomb' (Unpublished PhD thesis, 1997); Guy Hartcup and T. E. Allibone, *Cockcroft and the Atom* (Bristol: A. Hilger, 1984).

6 Hogg and Laucht, 'Introduction: British Nuclear Culture', p. 480.

7 Richard Overy, *The Morbid Age: Britain and the Crisis of Civilisation* (London: Penguin, 2010).

8 Hughes, 'What Is British Nuclear Culture?', p. 496.

9 See Weart, *The Rise of Nuclear Fear*, also John Canaday, *The Nuclear Muse: Literature, Physics, and the First Atomic Bombs* (Madison: University of Wisconsin Press, 2000).

10 Richard Rhodes, *The Making of the Atomic Bomb* (London: Simon & Schuster, 1986).

11 Hughes, 'Radioactivity and Nuclear Physics', p. 352.

12 Hughes, 'Deconstructing the Bomb', p. 373.

13 Jeff Hughes, 'The French Connection: The Juliot-Curies and Nuclear Research in Paris, 1925–1933', *History and Technology* 13, 4 (1997), p. 326.

14 For a useful synthesis of historical interpretations, see Andrew Rotter, *Hiroshima: The World's Bomb*, pp. 7–30.

15 For instance, a brief report on a talk by Becquerel in London, where the 'magical' properties of radium is mentioned, in *The Manchester Guardian*, 8 March 1902, p. 7.

16 James Maheffey, *Atomic Awakening: A New Look at the History and Future of Nuclear Power* (New York: Pegasus, 2009), pp. 31–35.

17 Ibid., p. 33.

18 Ibid., p. 34.

19 Jon Agar, *Science in the Twentieth Century and Beyond* (Cambridge: Polity, 2012), p. 20.

20 Ibid., p. 21.
21 Ernest Rutherford, *Radioactivity* (London: Cambridge University Press, 1904).
22 Lawrence Badash, *Scientists and the Development of Nuclear Weapons: From Fission to the Limited Test Ban Treaty 1939 – 1963* (New Jersey: New Humanities Press, 1995), p. 14.
23 Ibid., p. 16.
24 Ibid., p. 15.
25 See 'The Origin of Matter', *The Manchester Guardian*, 27 February 1932, p. 11.
26 Spencer R. Weart and Gertrud Weiss Szilard (eds.), *Leo Szilard: His Version of the Facts* (Cambridge, MA: MIT Press), p. 17
27 Ernest Rutherford, *Nature* 132 (Sept 1933), pp. 432–433.
28 Arnold and Smith, *Britain, Australia and the Bomb*, p. 1.
29 Badash, *Scientists and the Development of Nuclear Weapons*, p. 29.
30 *The Sunday Express*, 30 April 1939, p. 17.
31 C. H. Viol and G. D. Kammer, 'The Application of Radium in Warfare', *Transactions of the American Electrochemical Society* 32 (1917), pp. 381–388.
32 Willis, 'The Origins of British Nuclear Culture, 1895–1939', p. 76.
33 See for instance 'Our London Correspondence', *The Manchester Guardian*, 8 March 1902, p. 7; 'Dr. H. Wilde on Radium', *The Manchester Guardian*, 7 October 1903, p. 12.
34 'Editorial', *The Manchester Guardian*, 6 March 1903, p. 6.
35 'New Radium Discovery', *The Manchester Guardian*, 4 December 1908, p. 9.
36 *Daily Mirror*, 9 December 1932, p. 7.
37 Willis, 'The Origins of British Nuclear Culture, 1895–1939', p. 67.
38 Lawrence Badash, 'Radium, Radioactivity, and the Popularity of Scientific Discovery', *Proceedings of the American Philosophical Society* 122, 3 (June 1978), p. 154.
39 'The Need for Increasing the Manchester Supply', *The Manchester Guardian*, 4 November 1910, p. 4.
40 *Daily Mirror*, 13 March 1937, p. 11.
41 For a fuller exploration of these texts, see Willis, 'The Origins of British Nuclear Culture', p. 62, and passim.
42 *Nash's Pall Mall Magazine* 89, 472 (September 1932), p. 16.
43 S. Irwin Crookes, 'Radium and Its Utility to Mankind', *Practical Teacher* 27, 2 (August 1906), p. 92.
44 David Low, 'Behind the Curtain', *Evening Standard*, 2 January 1928.
45 'Remarkable Scientific Study: Continuous Heat Without Combustion: A Mystery of Radium', *The Manchester Guardian*, 26 March 1903, p. 12.
46 'Radium and Cancer', *Daily Mail* 4 July 1903, p. 5.
47 'New Radium Discovery: Is It the Long-Looked-For Cancer Cure?', *The Manchester Guardian*, 4 December 1908, p. 9.
48 *Daily Mail*, 17 February 1904, p. 3; *Daily Mail*, 3 February 1904, p. 3.
49 'Wonders of Radium', *Daily Mail*, 20 June 1903, p. 3.
50 Bo Jacobs, *The Dragon's Tail*, p. 5
51 'The Radium Treatment', *Daily Mail*, 25 September 1903, p. 7.
52 Advertisement from *The Observer*, 19 March 1922, p. 16.

53 See the letter from Norman Ellis 'Is the Sun Made of Radium?', *Daily Mail*, 4 November 1903, p. 4 and 'Can Radium Produce Life in Dead Matter', *Illustrated London News*, 1 July 1905, p. 12.

54 'Radium vs Grey Hair', *Nash's Pall Mall*, August 1934, p. 75.

55 For example, *Daily Mirror*, 10 March 1933, p. 14.

56 *Daily Mail*, 8 February 1904, p. 5.

57 *Nash's and Pall Mall Magazine*, December 1917, p. xi.

58 See Chapter 1 in Weart, *Nuclear Fear*.

59 *The Manchester Guardian*, 20 July 1912, p. 7.

60 *Daily Mirror*, 8 January 1936, p. 21.

61 *The Manchester Guardian*, 7 July 1932, p. 8.

62 'Twin Doctors found Dead with Throats Cut', *The Manchester Guardian*, 16 January 1929, p. 11.

63 *The Manchester Guardian*, 19 January 1929, p. 9.

64 *The Manchester Guardian*, 1 July 1920, p. 7.

65 'Ordeal of X-Ray Martyr', *Daily Mirror*, 2 May 1933, p. 6.

66 Oliver Lodge, 'Sources of Power', *The Observer* 17 August 1919, p. 5.

67 Willis, 'The Origins of British Nuclear Culture, 1895–1939', p. 86.

68 Paul Brians, *Nuclear Holocausts: Atomic War in Fiction, 1895–1984* (Kent, Ohio: Kent State University Press, 1987); David Dowling, *Fictions of Nuclear Disaster* (Iowa City: University of Iowa Press, 1987).

69 Canaday, *The Nuclear Muse*, p. 24.

70 H. G. Wells, *The World Set Free* (London: Corgi, 1974 [1914]), p. 7.

71 Willis, 'The Origins of British Nuclear Culture, 1895–1939', p. 73.

72 Sclove, 'From Alchemy to Atomic War', p. 164.

73 Ibid.

74 Ibid., p. 179.

75 Civis Milesque, 'The Last Unscientific War', *English Review*, October 1919, p. 367.

76 Charles A. Carpenter, *Dramatists and the Bomb*, p. 15.

77 'The Romance of the Atom', *The Bookman* 74, 442 (July 1928), p. 234.

78 Olaf Stapledon, *Last and First Men* (1930).

79 Brians, *Nuclear Holocausts*, p. 67.

80 *The Manchester Guardian*, 3 August 1939, p. 17.

81 Arnold and Smith, *Britain, Australia and the Bomb*, p. 68.

82 For the full text, see: <http://www.atomicarchive.com/Docs/Begin/FrischPeierls .shtml> [accessed 4 November 2014]. For thorough background information, see Lorna Arnold, 'The History of Nuclear Weapons: The Frisch-Peierls Memorandum on the Possible Construction of Atomic Bombs of February 1940', *Cold War History* 3, 3 (2003), pp. 111–126.

83 Arnold, 'The History of Nuclear Weapons', pp. 3–4.

84 Ferenc M. Szasz, *British Scientists and the Manhattan Project: The Los Alamos Years* (New York: St. Martin's Press, 1992); see also Gowing, 'James Chadwick and the Atomic Bomb'; *The Listener* March 1947, p. 7.

85 Andrew Brown, *Keeper of the Nuclear Conscience: The Life and Work of Joseph Rotblat* (Oxford: Oxford University Press, 2012); Christoph Laucht, *Elemental Germans*; Lorna Arnold with Katherine Pyne, *Britain and the H-Bomb*; Frank Barnaby and Douglas Holdstock (eds.), *The British Nuclear Weapons Programme*; Brian Cathcart, *Test of Greatness: Britain's*

Struggle for the Atom Bomb (London: Murray, 1994); Ronald W. Clark, *The Birth of the Bomb: The Untold Story of Britain's Part in the Weapon That Changed the World* (London: Phoenix House, 1961); Margaret Gowing, *Britain and Atomic Energy, 1939–1945*; Lillian Hoddeson et al., *Critical Assembly* (Cambridge: Cambridge University Press, 1993); Néstor Herran, 'Spreading Nucleonics: The Isotope School at the Atomic Energy Research Establishment, 1951–1967', *British Journal of the History of Science* 39, 4 (2006), pp. 569–586; Christoph Laucht, '"Los Alamos in a Way Was a City of Foreigners": German-Speaking Émigré Scientists and the Making of the Atom Bomb at Los Alamos, New Mexico, 1943–1946', *New Mexico Historical Review* 86, 2 (2011), pp. 223–250; Graham Spinardi, 'Aldermaston and British Nuclear Weapons Development: "Testing the Zuckerman Thesis"', *Social Studies of Science* 27, 4 (1997), pp. 547–582; Ian Welsh, 'The NIMBY Syndrome: Its Significance in the History of the Nuclear Debate in Britain', *British Journal for the History of Science* 26, 1 (1993), pp. 15–32; Sabine Lee, '"In no Sense Vital and Actually Not Even Important"? Reality and Perception of Britain's Contribution to the Development of Nuclear Weapons', *Contemporary British History* 20, 2 (2006), pp. 159–185; Greta Jones, 'The Mushroom-Shaped Cloud: British Scientists' Opposition to Nuclear Weapons Policy, 1945–1957', *Annals of Science* 43, 1 (1986), pp. 1–26. On Americanization, see John Krige, *American Hegemony and the Postwar Reconstruction of Science in Europe* (Cambridge, MA: MIT Press, 2006); Christoph Laucht, 'An Extraordinary Achievement of the "American Way": Hollywood and the Americanization of the Making of the Atom Bomb in *Fat Man and Little Boy*', *European Journal of American Culture* 28, 1 (2009), pp. 41–56.

86 A full transcript of the Quebec Agreement can be found at <http://www.atomicarchive.com/Docs/ManhattanProject/Quebec.shtml> [accessed 6 September 2014].

87 For a detailed account of Churchill's perspective on the tensions in Anglo-American relations around Tube Alloys, see Martin Gilbert, *Winston S. Churchill, Volume VII, Road to Victory* (Boston, MA: Hodder Mifflin, 1986), pp. 415–419; 470–471; for agreements on atomic technology, see 'Articles of Agreement', 19 August 1943; Premier papers, 3/139/8A, folios 356–359.

88 Matthew Jones, 'Great Britain, the United States, and Consultation over Use of the Atomic Bomb, 1950–1954', p. 800. Jones cites various files from The National Archives, including the declassified pamphlet by John Ehrman, 'The Atomic Bomb: An Account of British Policy in the Second World War', CAB 101/45, TNA.

89 Hennessy, *Cabinets and the Bomb*, p. 56.

90 Winston S. Churchill, *The Second World War, Volume 6* (London: Cassell, 1955), pp. 552–554.

91 See Rotter, *Hiroshima*, p. 64.

92 For an explanation of the financial side of the atomic bomb decision, see David Edgerton, *The Shock of the Old: Technology and Global History Since 1900* (London: Profile Books, 2006), pp. 15–19.

93 Patrick M. S. Blackett, *Fear, War, and the Bomb: Military and Political Consequences of Atomic Energy* (New York: McGraw Hill, 1948).

94 See the updated articulation of Gar Alperovitz's thesis in *The Decision to use the Atomic Bomb and the Architecture of an American Myth* (London: Fontana, 1996).

95 Robert J. Maddox, 'Gar Alperovitz: Godfather of Hiroshima Revisionism', in Robert J. Maddox (ed.), *Hiroshima in History: The Myths of Revisionism* (Columbia: University of Missouri Press, 2007).

96 Zygmunt Bauman, *Modernity and the Holocaust* (Cambridge: Polity, 2000).

Chapter 3

1 For issues around commemoration in Hiroshima, see Yuki Miyamoto, *Beyond the Mushroom Cloud: Commemoration, Religion, and Responsibility After Hiroshima* (New York: Fordham University Press, 2012).

2 For Hibakusha testimony, see <http://www.hiroshima-nagasaki.com/> [accessed 10 September 2014]. See also Yuki Miyamoto, *Beyond the Mushroom Cloud*. The entry 'Hiroshima/Nagasaki' by Travis J. Hardy in *Oxford Bibliographies* is useful.

3 Accessible at: http://www.historynet.com/michie-hattori-eyewitness-to-the-nagasaki-atomic-bomb-blast.htm. Please also see, Kyoko Selden and Mark Selden (eds.), *The Atomic Bomb: Voices from Hiroshima and Nagasaki* (Armonk, NY: M.E. Sharpe, 1990).

4 United States Strategic Bombing Survey, *The Effects of the Atomic Bombs on Hiroshima and Nagasaki* (Washington, DC: US Government Printing Office, 1946).

5 Ibid.

6 Jacob Bronowski, 'Mankind at the Crossroads', *Listener*, 4 July 1946, p. 7.

7 British Information Services, 'Statements Relating to the Atomic Bomb', *Reviews of Modern Physics* 17 (1945), pp. 472–490.

8 Letter from James Chadwick to Edward Appleton, 5 September 1945. Churchill Archives Centre, Churchill College, University of Cambridge, UK. Papers of Sir James Chadwick, CHAD IV/3/13.

9 Letter to the editor from Julian Brown, 'Dropping of Atom Bombs', *The Times*, 30 January 1947, p. 5.

10 The work of Robert J. Lifton is illuminating in this regard. See the classic *Death in Life: Survivors of Hiroshima* (New York: Random House, 1968) and *Indefensible Weapons: The Political and Psychological Case Against Nuclearism* (New York: Basic Books, 1982).

11 Bo Jacobs, *The Dragon's Tail*.

12 For the system of 'D-Notices', see Nicholas Wilkinson, *Secrecy and the Media*.

13 Anne Deighton, 'Britain and the Cold War, 1945–1955', in *The Cambridge History of the Cold War* (Cambridge: Cambridge University Press, 2010), p. 117.

14 Robert Hewison, *In Anger: Culture in the Cold War, 1945–60* (London: Weidenfeld and Nicholson, 1981), pp. 14–15; George H. Gallup (ed.), *The Gallup International Public Opinion Polls: Great Britain, 1937–1975: Volume One, 1937–1964* (New York: Random House, 1976).

15 For evidence of sustained anxiety over the cost of living and housing throughout the 1950s, see sections on the 'Most Urgent Government Problem' in Gallup (ed.), *The Gallup International Public Opinion Polls, Volume 1*, pp. 217–489. The Gallup Polls are useful for gauging opinion over atomic and nuclear weapons in this era. Towards the end of the 1950s, public opinion against nuclear testing grew: the way in which questions were framed demonstrates growing public anxiety over the health effects of fallout.

16 For evidence of ambivalent public mood in the post-war era, see Gallup (ed.), *The Gallup International Public Opinion Polls, Volume 1*, pp. 103–217.

17 Boyer's *By the Bomb's Early Light*; Jacobs, *The Dragon's Tail*.

18 van Lente (ed.), *The Nuclear Age in Popular Media*.

19 Gowing, *Britain and Atomic Energy 1939–1945*; Hennessy, *The Secret State*.

20 Arthur Marwick, *Britain in the Century of Total War: War, Peace and Social Change 1900–1967* (Middlesex: Penguin, 1968), p. 262.

21 Rotter, *Hiroshima*, pp. 166–173 and Boyer, *By the Bomb's Early Light*, Chapters 1 and 16.

22 Henry De Wolf Smith, *Atomic Energy for Military Purposes: The Official Report on the Development of the Atomic Bomb Under the Auspices of the United States Government* (Princeton: Princeton University Press, 1945), which is commonly known as The Smyth Report.

23 Hennessy, *Cabinets and the Bomb*, pp. 4; 35.

24 'The Atomic bomb: Memorandum by the Prime Minister', GEN 75/1, 28 August 1945, TNA, PRO, CAB 130/3, quoted in full in Hennessy, *Cabinets and the Bomb*, p. 38.

25 TNA, GEN75, 25 October 1946, Hennessy, *Cabinets and the Bomb*, p. 44.

26 For work on the UN and atomic diplomacy, see Bourantonis and Johnson, 'Anglo-American Diplomacy and the Introduction of the Atomic Energy Issue in the United Nations', pp. 1–21.

27 See John Baylis and Kristan Stoddart, *The British Nuclear Experience: The Roles of Beliefs, Cultures and Identity* (Oxford: Oxford University Press, 2015), p. 44.

28 Jones, 'Great Britain, the United States, and Consultation over Use of the Atomic Bomb, 1950–1954', p. 802.

29 John Baylis and Kristan Stoddart, 'The British Nuclear Experience: The Role of Ideas and Beliefs (Part One)', *Diplomacy and Statecraft* 23, 2 (2012), p. 339.

30 Jones, 'Great Britain, the United States, and Consultation over Use of the Atomic Bomb, 1950–1954', p. 802.

31 Rotter, *Hiroshima*, p. 275.

32 Simon Ball, 'Military Nuclear Relations Between the United States and Great Britain Under the Terms of the McMahon Act, 1946–1958', *Historical Journal* 38, 2 (1995), pp. 439–454.

33 Baylis and Stoddart, 'The British Nuclear Experience', p. 335.

34 Ibid., p. 336.

35 Ibid., p. 334.

36 Lorna Arnold and Mark Smith, *Britain, Australia and the Bomb: the Nuclear Tests and Their Aftermath*, 2nd edn. (Basingstoke: Palgrave, 2006).

37 Hogg and Laucht, 'Introduction: British Nuclear Culture', pp. 481–482, with the quote taken from Peter Hennessy, 'Revealed, 30 Years After Our First Nuclear Explosion … How Bevin Saved Britain's Bomb', *The Times*, 30 September 1982, p. 10.

38 Gowing, *Independence and Deterrence*, p. 184.

39 Hogg and Laucht, 'Introduction: British Nuclear Culture', p. 482.
40 Hansard, quoted in Hennessy, *Cabinets and the Bomb*, p. 69.
41 Hennessy, *Cabinets and the Bomb*, p. 69. Hennessy speculates that the lack of reporting on this issue was due to the D-Notice system in place. He also quotes Michael Quinlan, who saw the British decision to pursue atomic development in the years after 1945 as inevitable.
42 John Jenks, *British Propaganda and News Media in the Cold War* (Edinburgh: Edinburgh University Press, 2006), p. 118.
43 'International Control of Atomic Energy: Memorandum by the Prime Minister', 5 November 1945. TNA, CAB 129/4/22.
44 Baylis and Stoddart, 'The British Nuclear Experience', p. 343. See also their 'The British Nuclear Experience: The Role of Ideas and Beliefs (Part Two)', *Diplomacy and Statecraft* 23, 3 (2012), pp. 493–516.
45 Hugh Beach and Nadine Gurr (eds.), *Flattering the Passions: Or, the Bomb and Britain's Bid For a World Role* (London: I.B. Tauris, 1999), p. 21.
46 Grant, *After the Bomb*, pp. 18–20.
47 Peter N. Kirstein, 'Hiroshima and Spinning the Atom: America, Britain, and Canada Proclaim the Nuclear Age, 6 August 1945', *The Historian* 71, 4 (2009), pp. 805–827.
48 Boyer, *By the Bomb's Early Light*, p. 87.
49 For a selection of British responses to the bomb, see David Kynaston, *Austerity Britain, 1945–51* (London: Bloomsbury, 2008), pp. 82–85; Simon Garfield, *Our Hidden Lives: The Everyday Diaries of a Forgotten Britain, 1945–1948* (London: Ebury, 2004), pp. 72–78. On religious responses and debate on the bomb, see 'The Shadow of the Bomb' in Michael Hughes, *Conscience and Conflict: Methodism, Peace and War in the Twentieth Century* (Peterborough: Epworth, 2008), pp. 140–180; Diane Kirby, 'The Church of England and the Cold War Nuclear Debate', *Twentieth Century British History* 4, 3 (1993), pp. 250–283; Kirk Willis, '"God and the Atom": British Churchmen and the Challenge of Nuclear Power 1945', *Albion: A Quarterly Journal Concerned with British Studies* 29, 3 (1997), pp. 422–457.
50 Bo Jacobs, *The Dragon's Tail*, p. 4.
51 Jenks, *British Propaganda and News Media in the Cold War*, p. 52.
52 Ibid., p. 85.
53 Forgan, 'Atoms in Wonderland', p. 178.
54 Jenks, *British Propaganda and News Media in the Cold War*, p. 52.
55 *Daily Mirror*, 8 August, p. 1.
56 John Langdon Davies, 'Meaning of Atomic Power: It Can Change Our World – Or Destroy It', *Daily Mail*, 7 August 1945, p. 2.
57 Ibid.
58 *Daily Mail*, 6 November 1945, p. 1.
59 *Daily Mail*, 8 August 1945, p. 1.
60 Ibid.
61 *Daily Mail*, 8 August 1945, p. 2.
62 *Daily Mail*, 9 August 1945, p. 2.
63 John Langdon Davies, 'Atomic Age', *Daily Mail*, 13 August 1945, p. 2.
64 Laucht, 'Dawn – Or Dusk?', passim.
65 *Daily Mail*, 22 August 1945, p. 3.
66 *Daily Mail*, 27 August 1945, p. 2.
67 *Daily Mail*, 19 February 1946, p. 2.

68   *Daily Mail*, 24 August 1945, p. 4.
69   David Nye, *Narratives and Space: Technology and the Construction of American Culture* (New York: Columbia University Press, 1997), pp. 81–83.
70   *Daily Mail*, 3 September 1945, p. 2.
71   'Harnessing the Atom For Industry', *The Manchester Guardian*, p. 8.
72   *Daily Express*, 20 September 1945, p. 2.
73   *Daily Mirror*, 4 October 1945, p. 1.
74   *Daily Express*, 23 September 1946, p. 4.
75   *The Manchester Guardian*, 3 September 1946, p. 4.
76   *Daily Mail*, 5 November 1945, p. 2.
77   J. B. Priestley, 'On the Stairway of the Stars', *The Listener*, 13 March 1947, p. 355.
78   Ibid.
79   Illingworth, 'Pilgrim's Progress', *Daily Mail*, 1 January 1946, p. 2.
80   *Daily Mail*, 10 November 1945, p. 4.
81   *Daily Mail*, 5 March 1946, p. 1.
82   A *Guardian* article claims that before his death in 2003, he confessed his spying activity: <http://www.theguardian.com/uk/2003/jan/27/science.internationaleducationnews> [accessed 23 June 2013].
83   *Daily Mail*, 18 February 1946, p. 1.
84   *Daily Mail*, 21 February 1946, p. 1.
85   Michael Goodman and Chapman Pincher, 'Research Note: Clement Attlee, Percy Sillitoe and the Security Aspects of the Fuchs Case', *Contemporary British History* 19, 1 (2005), pp. 66–77.
86   *Daily Mail*, 10 April 1946, p. 2.
87   M. L. E. Oliphant, 'Atomic Energy--II', *Listener*, 13 March 1947, p. 358.
88   G. L. Cheshire, 'Dropping the Bomb', *The Listener*, 13 March 1947, p. 361.
89   Sir George Thomson, 'International Control', pp. 368–370 and 'Is Defence Possible', p. 363. Jacob Bronowski, 'Assessing the Damage', pp. 361–363.
90   *The Manchester Guardian*, 25 September 1949, p. 5.
91   *Meccano Magazine*, XXX, 9 September 1945, p. 1.
92   *Daily Mirror*, 1949, p. 2.
93   Hughes, 'What Is British Nuclear Culture?'.
94   *The Garston and Woolton Weekly News*, 10 August 1945, p. 1.
95   *Bath Weekly Chronicle and Herald*, 18 May 1946, p. 2.
96   *Hull Daily Mail*, 2 February 1946, p. 2.
97   'Children will make decision on atomic age possibilities', *The Cornishman*, 21 November 1946, p. 6.
98   *The Cornishman*, 2 March 1950, p. 4.
99   *The Derby Evening Telegraph*, 12 September 1950, p. 7.
100   *The Cheltenham Chronicle and Gloucestershire Graphic*, 9 December 1950, p. 10.
101   *The Western Morning News*, 25 July 1950, p. 3.
102   *Hull Daily Mail*, 1 July 1946, p. 4.
103   *Tamworth Herald*, 14 October 1950, p. 1.
104   *Hull Daily Mail*, 24 September 1949, p. 4.
105   Richard Broad and Suzie Fleming (eds.), *Nella Last's War* (London: Profile, 2006), p. 292
106   Ibid., p. 293.
107   Diary entry from Nella Last, Barrow, 26 September 1949, Mass Observation Archives.
108   Interview with Lily, conducted by Sarah Hewitt.

109 Interview with Lily, conducted by Sarah Hewitt.
110 Interview with Barbara, conducted by Sarah Hewitt.
111 Interview with Doris, conducted by Sarah Hewitt.
112 Interview with Vera, conducted by Sarah Hewitt.
113 For the legacies of Soviet nuclear testing, see Kate Brown, *Plutopia*.
114 Diary entry from Holness, 23 September 1949, Mass Observation Archives.
115 Diary entry from Reginald C Harper, London, 24 September 1949, Mass Observation Archives.
116 Diary entry from Holness, 25 September 1949, Mass Observation Archives.
117 See Roger Luckhurst, *Science Fiction* (London: Polity, 2005).
118 George Orwell, 'You and the Atomic Bomb', *The Tribune*, 19 October 1945.
119 Hogg and Laucht, 'Introduction: British Nuclear Culture', p. 434.
120 Ralph Desmarais, 'Jacob Bronowski: A Humanist Intellectual for an Atomic Age, 1946–1856', *The British Journal for the History of Science* 45, 4 (December 2012), p. 574.
121 *Daily Mail*, 16 August 1945, p. 1.
122 *The Hull Daily Mail*, 12 January 1946, p. 3.
123 *Gloucestershire Echo*, 17 April 1947, p. 5.
124 *Daily Mail*, 20 August 1945, p. 3.
125 The Very Rev. C. C. Thicknesse, 'Why I Condemn the Atomic Bomb', *Daily Mail*, 22 August 1947, p. 2.
126 Willis, 'God and the Atom', p. 457.
127 Christoph Laucht, 'Atoms for the People: The Atomic Scientists' Association, the British State and Nuclear Education in the Atom Train Exhibition, 1947-1948', *British Journal for the History of Science* 45, 4 (December 2012), p. 599.
128 Hogg and Laucht, 'Introduction: British Nuclear Culture', p. 491.
129 John Hersey, *Hiroshima* (Harmondsworth: Penguin, 1946); Keiji Nakazawa, *Barefoot Gen* (London: Penguin, 1990). See extensive discussion of Hersey in Boyer, *By the Bomb's Early Light*, pp. 203–210.
130 C. S. Lewis, 'On the Atomic Bomb: Metrical Experiment' in Walter Hooper (ed.), *C. S. Lewis: Poems* (London: Geoffrey Bles, 1964), p. 64.
131 Hughes, 'What Is British Nuclear Culture?'
132 J. B. Priestley, 'Summer Day's Dream', in *The Plays of J.B. Priestley: Volume 3* (London: Heinemann, 1946).
133 *Derby Evening Telegraph*, 27 December 1947, p. 5.
134 C.S. Lewis, 'On Living in An Atomic Age', in Walter Hooper (ed.), *Present Concerns: Ethical Essays* (London: Fount, 1986), p. 23.
135 Walter Hooper, 'On Living in an Atomic Age', in Hooper (ed.), *Present Concerns*, p. 45.
136 Tony Shaw, *British Cinema and the Cold War: The State, Propaganda and Consensus* (London: I. B. Tauris, 2006), p. 117.
137 From Hogg and Laucht, 'British Nuclear Culture', p. 492.
138 Richard Hornsey, *The Spiv and the Architect: Unruly Life in Postwar London* (Minneapolis: University of Minnesota Press, 2010), p. 70.
139 Peter Hennessy, *The Secret State*; S. J. Ball, 'Military Nuclear Relations Between the United States and Great Britain Under the Terms of the McMahon Act, 1946–1958'.

Chapter 4

1   Parts of this chapter are based on a previously published article, Hogg, 'The Family That Feared Tomorrow', pp. 535–549. I thank Cambridge University Press for their permission to reproduce aspects of the article.

2   For histories of the early years of the CND, see Laurence S. Wittner, *Resisting the Bomb: A History of the World Disarmament Movement, 1954–70* (Stanford, CA: Stanford University Press, 1997); Richard Taylor, *Against the Bomb: The British Peace Movement, 1958–1965* (Oxford: Clarendon Press, 1988); Holger Nehring, 'The British and West German Protests Against Nuclear Weapons and the Cultures of the Cold War, 1957–64', *Contemporary British History* 19, 2 (2005), pp. 223–241.

3   Mathew Thomson, *Lost Freedom: The Landscape of the Child and the British Post-War Settlement* (Oxford: Oxford University Press, 2013); Mathew Thomson, *Psychological Subjects: Identity, Culture, and Health in Twentieth Century Britain* (Oxford: Oxford University Press, 2006).

4   Alan Sinfield, *Literature, Politics and Culture in Postwar Britain* (London: Continuum, 2000), p. 239.

5   See Len Scott, 'Labour and the Bomb', *International Affairs* 82, 4 (2006), pp. 685–700.

6   Jones, 'Great Britain, the United States, and Consultation over Use of the Atomic Bomb, 1950–1954', p. 826.

7   Ibid., p. 798.

8   Ibid., p. 799.

9   Baylis and Stoddart, *The British Nuclear Experience (Part 1)*, p. 340; Sir Norman Brook's policy review in 1956 is dealt with by Grant, *After the Bomb*, pp. 116–118.

10 *Agreement for Cooperation on the Uses of Atomic Energy for Mutual Defence Purposes* (London: HMSO, 1958).

11 Arnold, *Britain, Australia and the Bomb*, p. 7.

12 Jones, 'Great Britain, the United States, and Consultation over Use of the Atomic Bomb, 1950–1954', p. 827.

13 Ibid., p. 828.

14 Baylis and Stoddart, *The British Nuclear Experience (Part 1)*, p. 340.

15 Cmnd 124, *Defence: Outline of Future Policy: 1957* (London: HMSO).

16 Howard Ball, *Justice Downwind: America's atomic testing program in the 1950s* (New York: Oxford University Press, 1986).

17 Jones, 'Great Britain, the United States, and Consultation over Use of the Atomic Bomb, 1950–1954', p. 798.

18 Arnold and Pyne, *Britain and the H-Bomb*.

19 Lorna Arnold, *Windscale 1957: Anatomy of a Nuclear Accident* (Basingstoke: Palgrave: 2007).

20 Martin V. Melosi, *Atomic Age America* (London: Pearson, 2013), p. 161.

21 Ibid.

22 Dwight Eisenhower 'Atoms for Peace', full transcript can be found at <http://www.eisenhower.archives.gov/research/online_documents/atoms_for_peace/Binder13.pdf> [accessed 1 September 2014].

23 Hamblin, 'Fukushima and the Motifs of Nuclear History', pp. 289–292.

24 Oliver Tickell, 'Toxic Leak: the WHO and the IAEA', *The Guardian*, 28 May 2009 <http://www.theguardian.com/commentisfree/2009/may/28/who-nuclear -power-chernobyl> [accessed 1 September 2014].

25 Welsh, *Mobilising Modernity*, p. 74.

26 Gabrielle Hecht, *The Radiance of France: Nuclear Power and National Identity After World War II* (Cambridge, MA: MIT Press, 1998), p. 15.

27 TNA, INF 13/281, and described in Grant, *After the Bomb*, pp. 38–39; 48–51.

28 Philip Toynbee, *The Fearful Choice: A Debate on Nuclear Policy* (Detroit: Wayne State University Press, 1959).

29 Henry Hardy (ed.), *Enlightening: Letters 1946–1960* (London: Chatto & Windus, 2009), pp. 606–609. For Isaiah Berlin's Cold War role, see Jonathan Hogg, 'Locating Isaiah Berlin in the Cultural Cold War Context: Text and Ontology 1945–1989', unpublished PhD, 2007.

30 Hogg and Laucht, 'Introduction: British Nuclear Culture', pp. 488–489.

31 Hilgartner et al., *Nukespeak*, passim.

32 Grant, *After the Bomb*, pp. 104–105; 121.

33 Ibid., p. 34.

34 Ibid., p. 6, see also Jeff Hughes, 'The Strath Report', passim.

35 Grant, *After the Bomb*, pp. 66–69.

36 'If You Think It's Hopeless You're Wrong', *Daily Express*, 26 September 1957, p. 14.

37 *Home Defence and the Farmer*, London: Her Majesty's Stationery Office, 1958.

38 Grant, *After the Bomb*, pp. 34–35.

39 Jones, 'The Mushroom-Shaped Cloud', p. 15.

40 William Barkley, 'What Are We to Do If God Wearies of Mankind?', *Daily Express*, 2 March 1955, p. 4.

41 Ibid.

42 Official video of Operation Grapple, 6 June 1957, Imperial War Museum: <http://www.iwm.org.uk/collections/item/object/1060020933> [accessed 1 September 2014].

43 Michel Foucault, *The Will to Knowledge*, p. 176.

44 Michael Wall, 'Backroom Girl', *The Guardian*, 26 May 1962, p. 5.

45 *The Spectator*, 11 February 1955, p. 7.

46 Catherine Jolivette, 'Science, Art and Landscape in the Nuclear Age', *Art History* 35, 2 (April 2012), p. 260.

47 Nehring, *Politics of Security*.

48 The full transcript of the Russell-Einstein Manifesto, 9 July 1955, can be found at <http://scarc.library.oregonstate.edu/coll/pauling/peace/papers /peace6.007.5.html> [accessed 1 September 2014].

49 For a discussion of Schweitzer, see Lawrence S. Wittner, 'Blacklisting Schweitzer', *The Bulletin of the Atomic Scientists* (May/June 2005), pp. 55–61.

50 Albert Schweitzer, 'Declaration of Conscience', *The Saturday Review*, 18 May 1957, p. 20. Available at <http://www.unz.org/Pub/SaturdayRev -1957may18-00013> [accessed 1 September 2014].

51 *Manchester Guardian*, 12 April 1957, p. 3.

52 Richard Taylor and Colin Pritchard, *The Protest Makers: The British Nuclear Disarmament Movement of 1958–1965 Twenty Years On* (Oxford: Pergamon Press, 1980), p. 4.

53 See Scott, 'Labour and the Bomb', passim.

54 Taylor and Pritchard, *The Protest Makers*, p. 6.

55 Meredith Veldman, *Fantasy, the Bomb and the Greening of Britain: Romantic Protest, 1945–80* (Cambridge: CUP, 1994), p. 132.

56 Ibid., p. 133.

57 *The Spectator*, 11 February 1955, p. 12.

58 'Risks From Radiation', *The Spectator*, 14 June 1956, p. 4.

59 'Effects of Nuclear Tests on Human Bones', *The Times*, 22 February 1957, p. 5.

60 See Wilkinson, *Secrecy and the Media*; Hughes, 'The Strath Report'. For work in the American context, see Hiltgartner, Bell and O'Connor, *Nukespeak*.

61 Jenks, *British Propaganda and News Media in the Cold War*, p. 51.

62 *Daily Express*, 21 February 1955, p. 4.

63 *Daily Express*, 6 March 1957, p. 2.

64 *Daily Express*, 1 March 1957, p. 1.

65 *Daily Express*, 12 February 1958, p. 1.

66 Dir. Stanley Kubrick, *Dr. Strangelove Or: How I Learned to Stop Worrying and Love the Bomb*, Columbia Pictures, 1964.

67 On Pincher's active Cold War role, see Simone Turchetti, 'Atomic Secrets and Governmental Lies: Nuclear Science, Politics and Security in the Pontecorvo Case', *The British Journal for the History of Science* 36, 4 (December 2003), pp. 409–414.

68 *Daily Express*, 28 March 1957, p. 6.

69 *Daily Express*, 16 May 1957, p. 1.

70 *Daily Mirror*, 3 June 1957, p. 3.

71 The name of J. B. Priestley is mentioned on 11 March due to his TV play *Doomsday for Dyson*.

72 *Daily Express*, 10 March 1958, p. 6.

73 *Daily Express*, 11 March 1958, p. 8.

74 *Daily Express*, 11 March 1958, p. 8.

75 *Daily Express*, 10 March 1958, p. 6.

76 *Daily Mirror*, 14 October 1957, p. 1.

77 Newsreel from 13 April 1957. Gaumont British News, JISC.

78 ITV *Late Evening News*, 13 October 1957.

79 Brian Wynne, 'Misunderstood Misunderstandings: Social Identities and Public Uptake of Science', *Public Understanding of Science* 1, 3 (1992), pp. 281–304.

80 See 'A Revised Transcript of the Proceedings of the Board of Enquiry into the Fire at Windscale Pile No. 1, October 1957', released in 1989. Accessible at <http://news.bbc.co.uk/1/shared/bsp/hi/pdfs/05_10_07_ukaea.pdf> [accessed 18 July 2014].

81 *Daily Mail*, 13 August 1957, p. 4.

82 *Daily Express*, 20 September 1957, p. 10.

83 *Daily Express*, 5 October 1957, p. 6.

84 *Daily Express*, 10 September 1957, p. 13.

85 *Daily Express*, 26 February 1955, p. 4.

86 W. G. Hoskins, 'The Road Between', *The Listener*, 13 May 1954, p. 819.

87 Bill Paterson, *Tales From the Back Green* (London: Hodder and Stoughton, 2008), pp. 9–10.

88 Interview with Lily, by Sarah Hewitt 2010.

89 Interview with Barbara, by Sarah Hewitt 2010.

90 Interview with Vera, by Sarah Hewitt 2010.

91 Interview with Barbara, by Sarah Hewitt 2010.
92 Interview with Vera, by Sarah Hewitt 2010.
93 *West Lancashire Evening Gazette*, 10 August 1957, p. 1.
94 *Daily Mirror*, 16 August 1957, p. 7. See also *West Lancashire Evening Gazette*, 10 August 1957, p. 1; *Daily Express*, 14 August 1957, p. 5.
95 *Daily Mirror*, 16 August 1957, p. 7.
96 For scholarly debates concerned with the broader meanings of nuclear technology in British life, see especially Ian Welsh, *Mobilising Modernity*.
97 *The Daily Mirror*, 16 August 1957, p. 7.
98 *The Daily Mirror*, 16 August 1957, p. 7.
99 David Matless, *Landscape and Englishness* (London: Reaktion, 1998).
100 Jeff Nuttall, *Bomb Culture* (London: Paladin, 1968), p. 20.
101 'Sandys Warns of "'Annihilation"'', *Daily Mail*, 2 September 1957, p. 11.
102 Ibid.
103 'The Dangers, By the Atom Doctor', *Daily Mail*, 10 September 1957, p. 8.
104 For the historicization of fear and anxiety, see Joanna Bourke, 'Fear and Anxiety: Writing About Emotion in Modern History', *History Workshop Journal* 55 (2003), pp. 111–133; Jackie Orr, *Panic Diaries: A Genealogy of Panic Disorder* (Durham, NC: Duke University Press, 2005); Cathy Caruth, *Unclaimed Experience: Trauma, Narrative and History* (Baltimore, MA: John's Hopkins University Press, 1996); Mark Lafleur, 'Life and Death in the Shadow of the A-Bomb: Sovereignty and Memory on the 60th Anniversary of Hiroshima and Nagasaki', in Nico X. Carpentier (ed.), *Culture, Trauma and Conflict: Cultural Studies Perspectives on War* (Newcastle: Cambridge Scholars Publishing, 2007), pp. 209–229.
105 Caruth, *Unclaimed Experience*, p. 12.
106 G. Dawson and B. West, 'Our Finest Hour?: The Popular Memory of World War Two and the Struggle Over National Identity', in G. Hurd (ed.), *National Fictions: World War Two in British Films and Television* (London: BFI Books, 1984).
107 Paul K. Saint-Amour, 'Bombing and the Symptom: Traumatic Earliness and the Nuclear Uncanny', *Diacritics* 30, 4 (Winter, 2000), p. 60.
108 Frank Kermode, *The Sense of an Ending: Studies in the Theory of Fiction* (Oxford: Oxford University Press, 2000), p. 28.
109 Ibid., p. 95.
110 Anthony Giddens, *Modernity and Self-Identity: Self and Society in the Late Modern Age* (Cambridge: Polity, 1991), p. 4.
111 On the failure of the modern project in Europe, see Zygmunt Bauman, *Modernity and the Holocaust* (Cambridge: Polity Press, 1989); Theodore Adorno and Max Horkheimer, *Dialectic of Enlightenment* (London: Verso, 1979). On modernity and postwar Britain, see Becky Conekin, Frank Mort and Chris Waters, *Moments of Modernity: Reconstructing Britain 1945–1964* (London: Rivers Oram, 1999); Brian Appleyard, *The Pleasures of Peace: Art and Imagination in Postwar Britain* (London: Faber & Faber, 1989).
112 Peter B. Hales, 'The Atomic Sublime', *American Studies* (Spring 1991), p. 28.
113 *Daily Express*, 18 July 1950, p. 4.
114 *Daily Express*, 22 February 1955, p. 4.
115 *Daily Express*, 11 March 1958, p. 7.

116 Sinfield, *Literature, Politics and Culture in Postwar Britain*, p. 97. For useful outlines of 'high-culture' in the post-war era, see Robert Hewison, *In Anger*.

117 Marghanita Laski, *The Offshore Island* (London: Mayfair Books, 1961).

118 *Whizz for Atomms: A Guide to Survival in the 20th Century for Fellow Pupils, Their Doting Maters, Pompous Paters and Any Others Who Are Interested* (London: Parrish, 1956).

119 Hewison, *In Anger*, pp. 164–165.

120 On American government attempts to control the impact of the film, see Mick Broderick, 'Fallout *On the Beach*', *Screening the Past* (June 2013) <http://www.screeningthepast.com/2013/06/fallout-on-the-beach/> [accessed 1 September 2014].

121 Richard Hoggart, *A Sort of Clowning: Life and Times, Volume II: 1940–59* (Oxford: Oxford University Press, 1991), p. 197.

122 For a useful survey of post-war British society see Pat Thane, 'Family Life and "Normality" in Postwar British Culture', in Richard Bessell and Dirk Schimann (eds.), *Life After Death: Approaches to a Cultural and Social History of Europe During the 1940s and 1950s* (Cambridge: Cambridge University Press, 2003), pp. 193–210.

123 Jolivette, 'Science, Art and Landscape in the Nuclear Age', p. 253.

124 Catherine Jolivette (ed.), *British Art in the Nuclear Age*.

125 Jane Pavitt, *Fear and Fashion in the Cold War* (London: V&A Publishing, 2008); David Crowley & Jane Pavitt (eds.), *Cold War Modern*.

126 See Michael F. Hopkins, Michael D. Kandiah & Gillian Staerck (eds.), *Cold War Britain, 1945–1964: New Perspectives* (New York: Palgrave Macmillan, 2003).

Chapter 5

1 See Anthony Aldgate, James Chapman and Arthur Marwick (eds.), *Windows on the Sixties: Exploring Key Texts of Media and Culture* (London: I.B. Taurus, 2000).

2 Catherine Marsh and Colin Fraser, *Public Opinion and Nuclear Weapons* (Basingstoke: Macmillan, 1989), p. 184.

3 Robert S. Norris and Hans M. Kristensen, 'The British Nuclear Stockpile, 1953–2013', *Bulletin of the Atomic Scientists* 69, 2 (2013), pp. 69–75; John Walker, 'British Nuclear Weapons Stockpiles, 1953–78', *RUSI Journal* 156, 5 (October 2011), pp. 74–83.

4 See Aldgate, Chapman and Marwick (eds.), *Windows on the Sixties*; Robin Peel, *Writing Back: Sylvia Plath and Cold War Politics* (London: Associated University Presses, 2002).

5 Hennessy, *The Secret State*, p. 113.

6 Stoddart, *Losing an Empire and Finding a Role*.

7 Priest, 'In American Hands', pp. 353–376.

8 For parliamentary debate on this issue, consult Hansard, HC Deb 25 April 1963, Volume 676, cc. 414–416 <http://hansard.millbanksystems.com /commons/1963/apr/25/polaris-sales-agreement> [accessed 7 August 2014].

9 Offer details.

10 Home Defence Policy 1960 CAB/129/103; 'British Nuclear Policy', PM requests from FS in minute 94/67, 24 July 1967, TNA.

11 Baylis and Stoddart 'The British Nuclear Experience (Part 1)', p. 342.

12 Ibid.
13 Stephen Twigge, 'A Baffling Experience: Technology Transfer, Anglo-American Nuclear Relations, and the Development of the Gas Centrifuge 1964–70', *History and Technology* 19, 2 (2003), p. 151.
14 Grant, *After the Bomb*, p. 136.
15 See also Phythian, 'CND's Cold War'.
16 *Guardian*, 11 August 1965, p. 8.
17 Part of a speech by the British Foreign Secretary on the reasons for the crisis in Cuba, 23 October 1962, can be accessed at <http://www.nationalarchives .gov.uk/education/coldwar/G5/cs2/s2.htm> [accessed 6 August 2014].
18 See Len Scott, *The Cuban Missile Crisis and the Threat of Nuclear War* (London: Continuum, 2007).
19 Pauling's acceptance speech can be found here <http://www.nobelprize.org /nobel_prizes/peace/laureates/1962/pauling-acceptance_en.html> [accessed 9 August 2014].
20 *Daily Mirror*, 5 August, 1963, p. 7.
21 *Daily Mirror*, 9 August, 1963, p. 5.
22 *Guardian*, 31 July 1963, p. 4.
23 *Guardian*, 31 July 1963, pp. 8–9.
24 Science Reporter, 'Fall-Out Danger May Diminish', *Guardian* 17 August 1963, p. 8.
25 Masco, *Nuclear Borderlands*, p. 56.
26 Ibid.
27 Ibid.
28 Dir. Harold Baim, *Delta 8–3*, United Artists Corporation, 1960.
29 See the chapter on E. P. Thompson, in David Goodway, *Anarchist Seeds Beneath the Snow: Left-Libertarian Thought and British Writers from William Morris to Colin Ward* (Liverpool: Liverpool University Press, 2006), pp. 260–287.
30 John Minion and Philip Bolsover (eds.) *The CND Story: The First 25 Years of CND in the Words of the People Involved* (London: Allison & Busby, 1983), p. 17.
31 Ruth Brandon, *The Burning Question: The Anti-Nuclear Movement Since 1945* (London: Heinemann, 1987), pp. 44–46.
32 CND Archives, CND/1/15; *Guardian* 29 September 1960; *Time* 30 September 1960; *Daily Mail* 30 September, p. 3. See also Bertrand Russell, *Has Man a Future?* (Harmondsworth: Penguin, 1961), where Russell calls for world government and nuclear disarmament.
33 London School of Economics, CND Archives, CND/2008/8/4/5.
34 Christopher Booker, 'Miscellany', *The Guardian*, 18 July 1962, p. 5.
35 CND Archives, CND/10/1.
36 Adam Roberts, *Nuclear Testing and the Arms Race* (London: Peace News, 1962).
37 Stuart Hall, 'N.A.T.O. and the Alliances' (1960), CND Archives CND/2008/7/3/4.
38 Leonard Beaton, 'Would Labour Give Up the Bomb?', *Sunday Telegraph*, August 1964, p. 6.
39 *Sanity* (April 1963), p. 5.
40 'Caravan's noisy Send-off: Empire Loyalists at CND Meeting', *The Guardian*, 3 July 1962, p. 1.

41 CND Archives, CND/1/51/4 'Operation Peanuts', internal memo, 9 July 1962 from Peggy Duff.
42 CND Archives CND/1/51/14.
43 CND Archives CND/1/51/18.
44 CND Archives CND/1/51/19.
45 CND Archives, CND/1/19.
46 Lawrence S. Wittner, 'The Nuclear Threat Ignored: How and Why the Campaign Against the Bomb Disintegrated in the Late 1960s', in C. Fink, P. Gassert and D. Junker (eds.), *1968: The World Transformed* (Cambridge: Cambridge University Press, 1998), pp. 439–458.
47 Lawrence Wittner, 'Gender Roles and Nuclear Disarmament Activism', p. 214.
48 John Ezard, 'Japanese with Peace Mission in Britain', *The Guardian*, 4 April 1968, p. 5.
49 *Association of Jewish Refugees in Britain Information* XXIII, 6 (June 1968), p. 3.
50 *Morning Star.*
51 Anthony Arblaster, 'The Man From Hiroshima', *Tribune* 12 April 1968, p. 7.
52 Dir. Steven Okazaki, *White Light/Black Rain: The Destruction of Hiroshima and Nagasaki*, Home Box Office, 2007. *Hiroshima Maidens* – co-pilot had been drinking.
53 Ronald Bedford, 'More A-Dust: Fallout Tests on Babies', *Daily Mirror*, 22 March 1960, p. 3.
54 'Radio-Strontium Increase in Children's Bones: Little Chance of Overt Damage', *Guardian*, 14 October 1963, p. 3.
55 'Insurance Policies and Atomic Energy Risks', *Daily Mirror*, 8 January 1960, p. 15; *Guardian*, 8 January 1960, p. 12.
56 *Daily Mirror*, 18 April 1960, p. 4.
57 *Daily Mirror*, 18 October 1961, p. 7.
58 *Daily Mirror*, 19 September 1960, p. 12.
59 *Daily Mirror*, 5 October 1961, p. 16.
60 *Daily Mirror*, 19 November 1962, p. 4.
61 *Daily Mirror*, 20 May 1963, p. 5.
62 *Daily Express*, 31 May 1963, p. 6.
63 *Daily Mirror* 20 April 1965, p. 8.
64 *Guardian*, 7 May 1962, p. 14; *Guardian*, 13 May 1962, p. 4.
65 *Guardian*, 17 April 1964, p. 5.
66 ITV *Late Evening News*, 7 September 1962.
67 *Guardian*, 11 April 1964, p. 11.
68 Ibid., p. 8.
69 'Miss (Ban-the-Bomb) Britain Gives Up Title', *Daily Mirror*, 10 July 1962, p. 1.
70 'Landlord puts ban on CND', *Brighton Standard*, 16 October 1962, p. 5.
71 CND Archives CND/1/33.
72 *The Times* 1959, p. 6.
73 *Sanity*, May 1963, p. 7.
74 Ibid.
75 Liz Lochhead's memories of the Cuban Crisis in October 1962 can be read at The National Archives online: <http://www.nationalarchives.gov.uk/education /coldwar/G5/cs2/s6.htm> [accessed 10 September 2014].

76 <http://www.dailymail.co.uk/news/article-2205395/Cold-War-Russian
-scientists-tried-brainwash-Jodrell-Bank-telescope-founder-beam-focused
-radiation-claim-diaries-released-death.html> [accessed 11 December 2013].

77 ITV early evening news, 28 January 1962.

78 'Want a Fallout Shelter?' 1962 <http://www.britishpathe.com/video/want-a
-fallout-shelter-aka-fall-out-shelter> [accessed 1 September 2014].

79 *Life Magazine*, September 1962.

80 Sid Chaplin, 'Fear and Sorrow', *The Guardian*, 30 November 1963, p. 12.

81 Tom Stonier, *Nuclear Disaster* (London: Penguin, 1964).

82 Tony Shaw, *British Cinema and the Cold War*, pp. 134–136; I. Q. Hunter,
'The Day the Earth Caught Fire', in I. Q. Hunter (ed.), *British Science Fiction
Cinema* (London: Routledge, 2001), pp. 99–113.

83 Carpenter, *Dramatists and the Bomb*, pp. 30–1.

84 Ibid., p. 37.

85 Ibid., p. 39.

86 Sinfield, *Literature, Politics and Culture in Postwar Britain*, p. 239.

87 Walter M. Miller, *A Canticle for Leibowitz* (London: Corgi, 1974 [1960]).

88 Kingsley Amis, *Take a Girl Like You* (Harmondsworth: Penguin, 1965
[1960]).

89 B. S. Johnson, *Christie Malry's Own Double-Entry* (London: Picador, 2001
[1973]). Nuclear war is cited on p. 124.

90 Kit Pedler and Gerry Davis, *Brainrack* (London: Souvenir, 1974).

91 Dir. Joseph Losey, *These Are the Damned*, Hammer Films, 1963. The film was
based on H. L. Lawrence, *Children of Light* (London: World Distributors,
1960).

92 Penelope Gilliatt, 'Laughing at Annihilation', *Guardian*, 2 February 1964, p. 25.

93 *Guardian*, 2 March 1964, p. 5.

94 *Guardian*, 4 February 1964, p. 7.

95 Kenneth Tynan, 'Into the Apocalypse', *Guardian*, 25 April 1965, p. 24.

96 James Chapman, 'The BBC and the Censorship of *The War Game* (1965)',
Journal of Contemporary History 41, 1 (2006), pp. 75–94; Tony Shaw,
'The BBC, the State and Cold War Culture: The Case of Television's
The War Game (1965)', *English Historical Review* CXXI, 494 (2006),
pp. 1351–1384; Mike Wayne, 'Failing the Public: The BBC, *The War
Game* and Revisionist History, A Reply to James Chapman', *Journal
of Contemporary History* 42, 4 (2007), pp. 627–637; David Seed, 'TV
Docudrama and the Nuclear Subject: *The War Game, The Day After* and
Threads', in J. R. Cook and P. Wright (eds.), *British Science Fiction Television:
A Hitchhiker's Guide* (London: I.B. Tauris, 2006), pp. 154–173; James
Chapman, '*The War Game* Controversy – Again', *Journal of Contemporary
History* 43, 1 (2008), pp. 105–112.

97 A brief review of the play was published in the *Guardian*, 4 April 1967, p. 9.

98 Spike Milligan and John Antrobus, *The Bedsitting Room* (London: Star,
1970), p. 14.

99 *Guardian*, 26 March 1970, p. 12.

100 *Guardian*, 25 March 1970, p. 15.

101 Martin Amis, *Einstein's Monsters* (London: Vintage, 1999 [1987]), p. 35.

102 Nuttall, *Bomb Culture*, p. 73.

103 Amis, *Einstein's Monsters*, p. 22.

104 E. V. Cunningham, *Phyllis* (London: New English Library, 1969 [1962]),
     pp. 30–38.
105 Ibid.
106 Ibid., p. 124.

Chapter 6

1   Olav Njølstad, 'The Collapse of Superpower Detente, 1975–1980' in
     M. P. Leffler and O. A. Westad (eds.), *The Cambridge History of the Cold
     War: Volume 3, Endings* (Cambridge: Cambridge University Press, 2010),
     pp. 135–155.
2   For a useful overview of nuclear politics and diplomacy in this period, see
     Baylis, *Anglo-American Defence Relations 1939–1984*; for useful overviews
     up to 1975, see Matthew Grant (ed.), *The British Way in Cold Warfare*.
3   There are several articles on this in the *New Scientist*, 7 December 1978.
4   'What Windscale Row Is All About', *The Observer*, 19 June 1977, p. 13;
     'Unfair Play in the Nuclear Numbers Game', *Guardian* 31 October 1977, p. 2;
     Windscale Follies', *Guardian*, 31 October 1977, p. 12.
5   TNA, DEFE 19/275, Duff Mason Report on factors relating to the further
     consideration of the future of the UK nuclear deterrent, December 1978.
6   See 'I'll Throw Out Nuclear Missiles – Michael Foot', *Daily Mirror*,
     27 October 1980, p. 2.
7   Kate Hudson, *CND: Now More Than Ever* (London: Vision Paperbacks,
     2005), p. 150.
8   *Guardian*, 23 November 1981, p. 8.
9   'Maggie the Defender Hits Out at Labour over the Bomb', *Daily Express*,
     11 October 1986, p. 1.
10   Michael Quinlan, 'Preventing War', *Tablet*, 18 July 1981, p. 689.
11   Phythian, 'CND's Cold War'.
12   *Protect and Survive*, London: Central Office of Information, 1980; Cordle,
     'Protect/Protest', p. 656.
13   Ibid.
14   E. P. Thompson and Dan Smith (eds.), *Protest and Survive* (Middlesex:
     Penguin, 1980); Dorothy Thompson (ed.), *Over Our Dead Bodies: Women
     Against the Bomb* (London: Virago, 1983).
15   Gwyn Prins (ed.), *Defended to Death* (Middlesex: Penguin, 1983).
16   See also Peter Goodwin, *Nuclear War: The Facts* (London: Macmillan,
     1982); Gavin Scott, *How to Get Rid of the Bomb* (London: Fontana, 1982);
     E. P. Thompson, *Zero Option* (London: Merlin Press, 1982); Anthony Tucker
     and John Gleisner, *Crucible of Despair: The Effects of Nuclear Weapons*
     (London: Menard, 1982); Oliver Postgate, *Thinking it Through: The Plain
     Man's Guide to the Bomb* (London: Menard, 1981).
17   Owen Greene, *London After the Bomb: What a Nuclear Attack Really
     Means* (Oxford: Oxford University Press, 1982); Campbell, *War Plan, UK*,
     passim; The Report of the British Medical Association's Board of Science and
     Education, *The Medical Effects of Nuclear War* (London: Wiley, 1983).
18   Bingham, 'The Monster'?, pp. 609–625; Aubrey et al., *Nukespeak*.

19 The discursive links between nuclear fear and suicide have been discussed by Hogg, 'The Family That Feared Tomorrow', pp. 535–549.

20 'In Moscow's Sights: The Doomsday Village', *Daily Mirror*, 6 November 1980, p. 5.

21 Winston S. Churchill, 'This Sick Charade That Is Masterminded in Moscow', *The Sunday Express*, 6 June 1983, p. 7; *The Times*, 17 January 1980, p. 6; *Daily Mirror*, 8 August 1980, p. 5; *Daily Express*, 18 March 1982, pp. 20–21.

22 *The Times*, 19 January 1980, p. 3; *The Observer*, 12 July 1981, p. 31.

23 Peter B. Hales, 'The Atomic Sublime' pp. 5–31 (p. 28). See also, Peggy Rosenthal, 'The Nuclear Mushroom Cloud as Cultural Image', *American Literary History* 3, 1 (Spring 1991), pp. 63–92.

24 '"Nuclear Fear" Led Man to Kill Family and Himself', *The Guardian*, 28 April 1984, p. 2; 'Massacre Father's Atom Fear', *Daily Mirror*, 28 April 1984, p. 5.

25 *Guardian*, 19 November 1983.

26 Michael Evans, 'Scientists to Study Incredible Atom Man', *Daily Express*, 6 January 1979, p. 9.

27 Bel Mooney, 'Beyond the Wasteland', in *Over Our Dead Bodies: Women Against the Bomb* (London: Virago, 1983), pp. 9–10.

28 Peter Jones and Gordon Reece, *British Public Attitudes to Nuclear Defence* (London: Palgrave, 1990).

29 For example, data from Lindsay Brook et al. (eds.), *British Social Attitudes Sourcebook* (Aldershot: Gower, 1992) suggest that through the mid-1980s one in three people believed Britain should 'rid itself of nuclear weapons', at least one in two believed Britain was less safe due to 'American nuclear missiles in Britain'. Between 1,500 and 3,000 people contributed to the polls, most years between 1983 and 1989. The consistency of responses suggests that a significant portion of the national population did not agree with national nuclear policy, and were concerned about the danger of nuclear war.

30 'Mothers in A-War Death Pact', *Daily Mirror*, 5 March 1984, p. 1.

31 Heseltine was also attacked with red paint in Manchester (see *Daily Express*, 16 November 1983, p. 1).

32 Marsh and Fraser, *Public Opinion*, p. 56.

33 John Haines, 'A Nuclear Waste', *Daily Mirror*, 8 April 1988, p. 6.

34 *The Times*.

35 *Daily Mirror*.

36 Young, *Femininity in Dissent*, passim.

37 Young, *Femininity in Dissent*;'End This Greenham carnival', *Daily Express*, 13 December 1983, p. 8.

38 *Sunday Express* in June 1982, p. 6.

39 *Daily Express*, 14 November 1983, p. 5.

40 *Daily Mirror*, 6 November 1980, p. 5.

41 *Daily Mirror*, 6 May 1986, p. 2.

42 *Daily Mirror*, 29 May 1986, p. 1.

43 *Daily Mirror*, 21 June 1986, p. 7.

44 *Daily Mirror*, 29 May 1986, p. 6.

45 *Daily Mirror*, 2 July 1984, p. 5.

46 'Don't Panic: *Mirror* Gets the Facts After Atom Scare Meat Ban', *Daily Mirror*, 21 June 1986, p. 1.

47 Wynne, 'Misunderstood Misunderstanding', pp. 281–305.

48 Jon Agar, 'Sacrificial Experts? Science, Senescence and Saving the British Nuclear Project', *History of Science* 51, 1 (2013), pp. 63–84.

49 *Daily Mirror*, 17 June 1986, p. 1.

50 *Daily Mirror*, 19 November 1980, p. 5; See also Hansard, HC Deb 9 June 1980, Volume 986, cc26–31 <http://hansard.millbanksystems .com/commons/1980/jun/09/nuclear-alerts-united-states-of -america#S5CV0986P0_19800609_HOC_165> [accessed 1 September 2014].

51 'What Windscale Row Is All About', *Guardian*, 19 June 1977, p. 13.

52 'Windscale – It Seems Increasingly Like Pure Science Fiction', *Guardian*, 2 July 1977, p. 15.

53 Malcolm Pithers, 'The Windscale Follies', *Guardian*, 31 October 1977, p. 12.

54 Anthony Tucker, 'Unfair Play in the Nuclear Numbers Game', *Guardian*, 31 October 1977, p. 2; Malcolm Pithers, 'Source of Windscale Leak Not Traced', *Guardian,* 31 October 1977, p. 1.

55 'So How Safe Is Safe?', *Daily Express*, 9 August 1979, p. 8.

56 *Daily Express*, 2 April 1979, p. 8.

57 Richard Rashke, *The Killing of Karen Silkwood: The Story Behind the Kerr-McGee Plutonium Case*, 2nd edn. (Ithaca, NY: Cornell University Press, 2000 [1981]); Dir. Mike Nichols, *Silkwood*, 20th Century Fox, 1983.

58 Hilgartner et al., *Nukespeak*; Aubrey et al., *Nukespeak*.

59 Mooney, 'Beyond the Wasteland', p. 9.

60 See 'Letters to the Editor', *Guardian*, 8 December 1980, p. 12; See also Michael Pentz's chapter 'The Ban That Backfired', in Aubrey et al., *Nukespeak*, pp. 64–74.

61 Cordle, ' "That's Going to Happen to Us. It Is": Threads and the Imagination of Nuclear Disaster on 1980s Television', *Journal of British Cinema and Television* 10, 1 (2013), pp. 71–92.

62 This flippant use of nuclear references was common in satirical culture. One episode of *Spitting Image* represented a nuclear defence cabinet full of bumbling politicians with no realization of the wider consequences of their actions, and not a thought given for the masses of civilians that they represent (*Spitting Image*, ITV Studios, Series 1, Episode 6, 1984). One BBC *Only Fools and Horses* episode entitled 'The Russians are Coming', broadcast on 13 October 1981, is set mainly in a homemade fallout shelter.

63 Dir. Paul Jackson, 'Bomb', *The Young Ones*, BBC2, 30 November 1982; ITV Productions, *Spitting Image* (1984–1996).

64 Brian Bethell (ed.), *The Defence Diaries of W. Morgan Petty* (London: Viking, 1984).

65 Dir. Mick Jackson, *Q.E.D.: A Guide to Armageddon*, BBC, 1982.

66 This was commented upon in the national press, specifically in the *Daily Express* and the *Daily Mirror*.

67 Seed, 'TV Docudrama and the Nuclear Subject'.

68 Wr. John Pilger, 'The Truth Game', ITV, 1983. Other notable documentaries from this period include Jonathan Dimbleby's *The Bomb; The Journey* (1988), directed by Peter Watkins (who directed *The War Game*), is fourteen and a half hours long and is a sustained critique of nuclear weapons, and a self-conscious deconstruction of film-making etiquette. Watkins travels the world to investigate the effects of violence and state power, exploring

everyday testimony, sites of commemoration, war-torn areas of the world and hidden nuclear infrastructure. As an unofficial narrative, it dovetails with the broader argument of this chapter in serving to render visible the power of the nuclear state and its institutions and to disrupt the status quo in world affairs.

69 Dir. John Badham, *War Games*, MGM, 1983.
70 Hugh Gusterson, 'Short Circuit: Watching Television with a Nuclear Weapons Scientist', in H. Gusterson (ed.), *People of the Bomb: Portraits of America's Nuclear Complex* (Minneapolis, MN: University of Minnesota Press, 2004), p. 58.
71 J. G. Ballard, *Empire of the Sun* (London: Harper Collins, 2006), p. 267.
72 Christoph Laucht, 'Britannia Rules the Atom: The James Bond Phenomenon and Post War British Nuclear Culture', *The Journal of Popular Culture* 46, 2 (2013), pp. 359–360 (pp. 358–377).
73 The contributors to this debate were Robin Cook (Labour MP), George Walden (Conservative MP), John Cartwright (Alliance MP), Prof Paul Bracken (political science, Yale), Dr. Edward Luttwak, Dr. Phillip Steadman (Open University, author of *Doomsday*), Eric Alley (civil defence advisor), Dr. Gwin Prins (Cambridge) and General Sir Anthony Farrar-Hockley.
74 Cordle, pp. 654–655.
75 Michael Davie, 'The Painless Growth of Adrian Mole, Best-Seller: Notebook', *The Observer*, 16 December 1984, p. 40.
76 Sue Townsend, *The Secret Diary of Adrian Mole Aged 13¾* (1982) in the anthology *Adrian Mole from Minor to Major* (London: Methuen, 1991), p. 156.
77 Ibid., p. 337.
78 Ibid., p. 354.
79 Ibid., p. 366.
80 Ibid., p. 368.
81 Dorian Lynskey, *33 Revolutions Per Minute: A History of Protest Songs* (London: Faber and Faber, 2010), pp. 451–466.
82 *Sanity*, October 1982, p. 9.
83 This focus on Liverpool in the 1980s is expanded upon in Hogg, 'Cultures of Nuclear Resistance in 1980s Liverpool'.
84 David Hope, 'Blinding Flash of Destruction', *Liverpool Echo*, 10 January 1980, p. 6.
85 Hogg, 'Cultures of Nuclear Resistance in 1980s Liverpool', p. 2.
86 Ibid.
87 *Sanity*, March 1983, p. 20.
88 *Sanity*, May 1983, p. 41.
89 For more on the history of Liverpool, see Jon Murden, '"City of Change and Challenge": Liverpool since 1945' in J. Belchem (ed.), *Liverpool 800: Culture, Character and History* (Liverpool: LUP, 2006); Diane Frost and Peter North, *Militant Liverpool: A City on the Edge* (Liverpool: Liverpool University Press, 2013).
90 Campbell, *War Plan UK*.
91 Hogg, 'Cultures of Nuclear Resistance in 1980s Liverpool', p. 2.
92 Hogg, 'Cultures of Nuclear Resistance in 1980s Liverpool', p. 18.
93 Ibid.

94 See Hogg, 'Cultures of Nuclear Resistance in Liverpool', passim. Liverpool Central Library Archives (LCLA) and the papers of C. K. Wilson, County Solicitor and Secretary, Merseyside County Council, estate of C. K. Wilson were used alongside analysis of the local printed press and Liverpool culture more widely.

95 Grant, *After the Bomb*, p. 198.

96 Taylor, 'Nuclear Pictures and Metapictures', p. 568.

97 Ibid., p. 593.

98 Recent movements towards empathetic approaches to the nuclear century are best encapsulated by Brown, *Plutopia*; Masco, *Nuclear Borderlands*.

99 Taylor, 'Nuclear Pictures and Metapictures', p. 571.

100 Ibid.

Chapter 7

1 Norris and Kristensen, 'The British Nuclear Stockpile, 1953–2013', p. 70.

2 CND, 'Against the Tide: CND's response to the Trident Commission', 1 July 2014, published online <http://www.cnduk.org/cnd-media/item/1947-against-the-tide-cnd%E2%80%99s-response-to-the-trident-commission> [accessed 2 July 2014].

3 Lord Browne et al., *The Trident Commission: An Independent, Cross-party Inquiry to Examine UK Nuclear Weapons* (British American Security Information Council, July 2014), p. 10. Online at: <http://www.basicint.org/sites/default/files/trident_commission_finalreport.pdf> [accessed 2 July 2014].

4 Lord Browne et al., *The Trident Commission: An Independent, Cross-party Inquiry to Examine UK Nuclear Weapons* (British American Security Information Council, July 2014), p. 39. Online at: <http://www.basicint.org/sites/default/files/trident_commission_finalreport.pdf> [accessed 2 July 2014].

5 Lord Browne et al., *The Trident Commission: An Independent, Cross-party Inquiry to Examine UK Nuclear Weapons* (British American Security Information Council, July 2014), p. 41. Online at: <http://www.basicint.org/sites/default/files/trident_commission_finalreport.pdf> [accessed 2 July 2014].

6 Masco, *Nuclear Borderlands*, p. 4.

7 Dir. Justin Pemberton, *The Nuclear Comeback*, Docufactory, 2007.

8 Jacob Darwin Hamblin, 'Fukushima and the Motifs of Nuclear History', *Environmental History* 17, 2 (2012).

9 Boyer and Idsvoog argue that three main contextual factors shaped nuclear representation in the years after the Cold War ended: the persistence of nuclear hazards, the continued nuclear capability of nuclear states and the possibility of nuclear materials falling into the hands of 'unstable' states or 'terrorists'. Paul Boyer and Eric Idsvoog, 'Nuclear Menace in the Mass Culture of the Late Cold War Era and Beyond', in Paul Boyer (ed.), *Fallout: A Historian Reflects on America's Half Century* (Columbus: Ohio State University Press, 1998), p. 205.

10 Boyer and Idsvoog, 'Nuclear Menace', p. 224.

11 Jon Akass, 'Happily there's plenty for us to worry about', *Daily Express*, 20 November 1989, p. 9.

12 The Nuclear Threat Initiative online contains useful information on nuclear treaties <http://www.nti.org/treaties-and-regimes/treaties/> [accessed 8 August 2014].

13 For up-to-date nuclear information, see Ploughshares Fund <http://www.ploughshares.org/world-nuclear-stockpile-report> and the Nuclear Information Service <http://www.nuclearinfo.org> [both accessed 1 September 2014].

14 Hennessy, *Cabinets and the Bomb*, p. 5.

15 Imaginative but environmentally suspect solutions have been found. The documentary about Finnish nuclear waste, *Into Eternity* (2010), is a thought-provoking exploration of the long-term politics of nuclear waste.

16 Hamblin, *Poison in the Well*; Douglas Holdstock and Frank Barnaby (eds.) *The British Nuclear Weapons Programme, 1952–2002* (London: Frank Cass, 2003).

17 Hogg and Laucht, 'Introduction: British Nuclear Culture', p. 7.

18 For example, Donald MacKenzie, 'No Bomb Like an Old Bomb', *The Guardian*, 28 September 1995, p. B8; Christopher Zinn, 'Nuclear States Urged to Cut Stockpile', *The Guardian*, 15 August 1996, p. 11; 'Banning the Bomb', *The Guardian*, 22 May 2000, p. 19.

19 For example, 'Russia Foiled Bin Laden Nuclear Bid', *Daily Express*, 21 September 2001, pp. 6–7; 'The Kashmir Syndrome: A World Tiptoeing Towards the Horrors of Mass Destruction', *Sunday Express*, 9 June 2002, pp. 20–21.

20 *Daily Mirror*, 5 December 2006, p. 12.

21 *Daily Express*, 16 May 2004, p. 1.

22 *Daily Mirror*, 4 September 2004, p. 10.

23 'From Russia with Loath', *Daily Mirror*, 21 November 2006, p. 1.

24 'Nuked By A Cuppa', *Daily Mirror*, 25 November 2006, p. 1; 'Irradiated', *Daily Mirror*, 2 December 2006, p. 5; 'From Russia with Loath', *Daily Mirror*, 21 November 2006, p. 1.

25 Costandina Titus, 'The Mushroom Cloud as Kitsch' in Scott Zeman & Michael A. Amundson (eds.), *Atomic Culture: How We Learned to Stop Worrying and Love the Bomb* (Boulder, CO: University of Colorado Press, 2004), pp. 101–123. Peggy Rosenthal, 'The Nuclear Mushroom Cloud as Cultural Image', *American Literary History* 3, 1 (Spring 1991), pp. 63–92.

26 Boyer and Idsvoog, 'Nuclear Menace', p. 4.

27 See 'Homer Defined', episode 40, originally aired in 1991, where Homer saves Springfield nuclear power station from disaster.

28 Dir. Michael Cumming, *Toast of London*, Episode 4, 'Submission'. Objective Productions, 2013.

29 Ele Carpenter's 'Nuclear Culture' project website is a useful access-point to nuclear blogs and other links: <http://nuclear.artscatalyst.org/>

30 Adam Campbell, 'Is Sid Meier's *Civilisation* History?', *Rethinking History* 17, 3 (2013), p. 313.

31 Matthew Wilhelm Kapell and Andrew B.R. Elliot (eds.), *Playing with the Past: Digital Games and the Simulation of History* (London: Bloomsbury, 2013).

32 Campbell, 'Is Sid Meier's *Civilisation* History?', p. 328, n. 1.

33 Ibid., p. 314.

34 Ibid., p. 315.

35 Ibid., p. 316.

36 Peter Bacon Hales, *Outside the Gates of Eden: The Dream of America from Hiroshima to Now* (Chicago, IL: The University of Chicago Press, 2014), p. 372.

37 For other nuclear themed computer games, see *Crysis, World in Conflict, DEFCON 4/ Flight Simulator, Splinter Cell, GTA – San Andreas, RUSE, World in Conflict, Civilisation V, Command and Conquer* series *and Duke Nuke Em' 3D.*

38 William Knoblauch, 'The Pixilated Apocalypse: Video Games and Nuclear Fears, 1980–2012' in *The Silence of Fallout: Nuclear Criticism in a Post-Cold War World* (Newcastle: Cambridge Scholars, 2013); Mick Broderick and Robert Jacobs, 'Nuke York, New York: Nuclear Holocaust in the American Imagination from Hiroshima to 9/11', *The Asia-Pacific Journal* 10, 11, No 6 (12 March 2012). See more at: <http://www.japanfocus.org/-Mick -Broderick/3726#sthash.ftkZNkcd.dpuf>

39 Fredric Jameson, *Postmodernism: Or, The Cultural Logic of Late Capitalism* (London: Verso, 1991), p. 65.

40 The British Nuclear Test Veterans Association website contains useful and up-to-date information on the continuing fight to obtain compensation for nuclear veterans, as well as a repository of relevant reports and other documentation: <https://bntva.com/>

41 Sue Roff, 'UK Nuclear Veterans Timed Out?', *Bulletin of the Atomic Scientists*, 3 October 2012.

42 'Pacific Atomic Test Survivors Cannot Sue Ministry of Defence', *Guardian*, 12 March 2012.

43 Frank Walker, *Maralinga: the chilling expose of our secret nuclear shame and betrayal of our troops and country* (Sydney: Hachette, 2014); <http://www. theecologist.org/News/news_analysis/2476704/the_nuclear_war_against_ australias_aboriginal_people.html>; Bruno Barrillot, 'Human Rights and the Casualties of Nuclear Testing', *Journal of Genocide Research* 9, 3 (September 2007), pp. 443–459.

44 <http://www.hackgreen.co.uk/>

45 <http://www.secretbunker.co.uk/>

46 'CND membership booms after nuclear U-turn', *Independent*, 17 July 2006.

47 <http://actionawe.org/>.

48 James McKeon, 'Scottish Independence Could Leave UK Nuclear Weapons Homeless', *Bulletin of the Atomic Scientists*, 20 August 2014.

Chapter 8

1 Masco, *Nuclear Borderlands*, pp. 1, 24.

BIBLIOGRAPHY

Newspapers and periodicals consulted

Bath Weekly Chronicle and Herald, The Bookman, Brighton Standard, Bulletin of the Atomic Scientists, The Cheltenham Chronicle and Gloucestershire Graphic, The Cornishman, Derby Evening Telegraph, Encounter, English Review, The Evening News, The Evening Standard, Daily Express, Daily Mail, Daily Mirror, Daily Worker, The Garston and Woolton Weekly, Herald, Hull Daily Mail, The Listener, Liverpool Echo, London Illustrated News, The Manchester Guardian, Morning Star, Nash's Pall Mall Magazine, New Scientist, News Chronicle, The Observer, Pall Mall Gazette, Picture Post, Sanity, Scientific World, Spectator, Sunday Express, Sun Herald, Tamworth Herald, The Times, Times Literary Supplement, The Tribune, The Western Morning News

Archives

British Newspaper library at The British Library, Colindale
CND archives at the London School of Economics
Mass Observation Archives at the University of Sussex
The National Archives (TNA)
University of Liverpool, Cold War Collection/Science Fiction Foundation Collection
Merseyside CND (MCND)
Liverpool Central Library Archives (LCLA)
Papers of C. K. Wilson, County Solicitor and Secretary, Merseyside County Council
   (private collection)

Recommended online resources for nuclear history

Atomic Archive: http://www.atomicarchive.com/
Bulletin of the Atomic Scientists: http://thebulletin.org/
Chatham House: a policy document on 'nuclear near use' http://www.chathamhouse.
   org/sites/files/chathamhouse/home/chatham/public_html/sites/default/files
   /20140428TooCloseforComfortNuclearUseLewisWilliamsPelopidasAghlani.pdf

Comprehensive Nuclear Test Ban Treaty Organization (CTBTO) http://www.ctbto.org
Conelrad: http://www.conelrad.com/index.php/
CND: http://www.cnduk.org
Federation of American Scientists http://fas.org
Hansard: http://hansard.millbanksystems.com/commons/ and a useful reading
    list on recent British debates over the renewal of nuclear capability: http://
    www.parliament.uk/briefing-papers/SN04207/the-future-of-the-british-nuclear
    -deterrent-suggested-reading
Hibakusha testimony: http://www.hiroshima-nagasaki.com/
Hiroshima and Nagasaki memorial museums: http://www.pcf.city.hiroshima.jp
    /index_e2.html ; http://www.city.nagasaki.lg.jp/peace/english/index.html
Imperial War Museum: http://www.iwm.org.uk/collections/
IAEA http://www.iaea.org
National Archives Cold War section: http://www.nationalarchives.gov.uk/education
    /coldwar/
Nuclear Threat Initiative: http://www.nti.org/
Nuclear Information Service: http://www.nuclearinfo.org
Ploughshares Fund: http://www.ploughshares.org/
'Restricted Data', with Alex Wellerstein: http://blog.nuclearsecrecy.com/
Subterranea Britannica: http://www.subbrit.org.uk/category/nuclear-bunkers
Treaty on the Non-Proliferation of Nuclear Weapons: http://www.un.org
    /disarmament/WMD/Nuclear/NPT.shtml

Select bibliography

Although a wide variety of texts are cited throughout *British Nuclear Culture*, this
bibliography lists the texts directly related to nuclear history.

Abbott, Carl, 'The Light on the Horizon: Imagining the Death of American Cities',
    Journal of Urban History 32 (2006), pp. 175–196.
Abraham, Itty, 'The Ambivalence of Nuclear Histories', *Osiris* 21 (2006), pp. 49–65.
Adams, John Bertram, 'Four Generations of Nuclear Physicists', *Notes and Records
    of the Royal Society of London* 27, 1 (August 1972), pp. 75–94.
Agar, Jon, 'Sacrificial Experts? Science, Senescence and Saving the British Nuclear
    Project', *History of Science* 51, 1 (2013), pp. 63–84.
Agar, Jon, *Science in the Twentieth Century and Beyond*, Cambridge: Polity, 2012.
Aldrich, Richard J., *The Hidden Hand: Britain, America and Cold War Secret
    Intelligence*, London: Murray, 2001.
Alperovitz, Gar, *The Decision to Use the Atomic Bomb and the Architecture of an
    American Myth*, London: Fontana, 1996.
Arnold, Lorna, 'The History of Nuclear Weapons: The Frisch-Peierls Memorandum
    on the Possible Construction of Atomic Bombs of February 1940', *Cold War
    History* 3, 3 (2003), pp. 111–126.
Arnold, Lorna, *Windscale 1957: Anatomy of a Nuclear Accident*, Basingstoke:
    Palgrave Macmillan, 1995.
Arnold, Lorna and Pyne, Katherine, *Britain and the H-Bomb*, Basingstoke:
    Palgrave, 2001.

Arnold, Lorna and Smith, Mark, *Britain, Australia and the Bomb: The Nuclear Tests and Their Aftermath*, Basingstoke: Palgrave Macmillan, 2006.

Aubrey, Crispin (ed.), *Nukespeak: The Media and the Bomb*, London: Comedia, 1982.

Badash, Lawrence, 'Nuclear Fission: Reaction to the Discovery in 1939', *Proceedings of the American Philosophical Society* 130, 2 (June 1986), pp. 196–231.

Badash, Lawrence, 'Radium, Radioactivity, and the Popularity of Scientific Discovery', *Proceedings of the American Philosophical Society* 122, 3 (June 1978), pp. 145–154.

Badash, Lawrence, *Scientists and the Development of Nuclear Weapons: From Fission to the Limited Test Ban Treaty 1939–1963*, New Jersey: New Humanities Press, 1995.

Badash, Lawrence, 'From Security Blanket to Security Risk: Scientists in the Decade After Hiroshima', *History and Technology* 19, 3 (2003), pp. 241–256.

Badash, Lawrence, *A Nuclear Winter's Tale: Science and Politics in the 1980s*, Cambridge, MA: MIT Press, 2009.

Ball, Simon J., 'Harold Macmillan and the Politics of Defence: The Market for Strategic Ideas During the Sandys Era Revisited', *Twentieth Century British History* 6, 1 (1995), pp. 78–100.

Ball, Simon J., 'Military Nuclear Relations Between the United States and Great Britain Under the Terms of the McMahon Act, 1946–1958', *The Historical Journal* 38, 2 (1995), pp. 439–454.

Barnaby, Frank and Holdstock, Douglas (eds.), *The British Nuclear Weapons Programme*, London: Cass, 2003.

Barrillot, Bruno, 'Human Rights and the Casualties of Nuclear Testing', *Journal of Genocide Research* 9, 3 (September 2007), pp. 443–459.

Bartter, Martha, *The Way to Ground Zero: The Atomic Bomb in American Science Fiction*, New York: Greenwood Press, 1988.

Baylis, John, *Ambiguity and Deterrence: British Nuclear Strategy, 1945–1964*, Oxford: Clarendon, 1994.

Baylis, John, *Anglo-American Defence Relations 1939–1984: The Special Relationship*, London: Macmillan, 1984.

Baylis, John and MacMillan, Alan, 'The British Global Strategy Paper of 1952', *Journal of Strategic Studies* 16, 2 (1993), pp. 200–226.

Baylis, John and Stoddart, Kristan, 'The British Nuclear Experience: The Role of Ideas and Beliefs (Part One)', *Diplomacy and Statecraft* 23, 2 (2012), pp. 331–346.

Baylis, John and Stoddart, Kristan, 'The British Nuclear Experience: The Role of Ideas and Beliefs (Part Two)', *Diplomacy and Statecraft* 23, 3 (2012), pp. 493–516.

Berger, Albert, 'The *Astounding* Investigation: The Manhattan Project's Confrontation with Science Fiction', *Analog* 104, 9 (September 1984), pp. 125–137.

Berger, Albert, 'Love, Death and the Atomic Bomb: Sexuality and Community in Science Fiction, 1935–55', *Science Fiction Studies* 8, (1981), pp. 280–296.

Berger, Albert, 'The Triumph of Prophecy: Science Fiction and Nuclear Power in the Post-Hiroshima Period', *Science Fiction Studies* 3, 9 (July 1976), pp. 143–149.

Biess, Frank, '"Everybody Has a Chance": Nuclear Angst, Civil Defence, and the History of Emotions in Postwar West Germany', *German History* 27, 2 (2009), pp. 215–243.

Bingham, Adrian, '"The Monster"? The British Popular Press and Nuclear Culture, 1945–Early 1960s', *British Journal of the History of Science* 45, 4 (December 2012), pp. 609–625.

Blackett, Patrick M. S., *Fear, War, and the Bomb: Military and Political Consequences of Atomic Energy*, New York: McGraw Hill, 1948.

Booker, M. Keith, *Monsters, Mushroom Clouds and the Cold War: American Science Fiction and the Roots of Postmodernism*, Westport, CT: Greenwood Press, 2001.

Boorse, Henry Abraham, *The Atomic Scientists: A Biographical History*, 1989.

Bourantonis, Dimitris and Johnson, Edward, 'Anglo-American Diplomacy and the Introduction of the Atomic Energy Issue in the United Nations: Discord and Cooperation in 1945', *Contemporary British History* 18, 4 (2004), pp. 1–21.

Boyer, Paul, *By the Bomb's Early Light: American Thought and Culture at the Dawn of the Atomic Age*, Chapel Hill: University of North Carolina Press, 1994.

Brians, Paul, 'Dealing with Nuclear Catastrophe', *Science Fiction Studies*, 13, 39 (July 1986), pp. 198–199.

Boyer, Paul, *Fallout: A Historian Reflects on America's Half Century*, Columbus: Ohio State University Press, 1998.

Brians, Paul, *Nuclear Holocausts: Atomic War in Fiction, 1895–1984*, Kent, Ohio: Kent State University Press, 1987.

Broderick, Mick, *Nuclear Movies*, North Carolina: McFarland, 1991.

Brown, Andrew, *Keeper of the Nuclear Conscience: The Life and Work of Joseph Rotblat*, Oxford: OUP, 2012.

Brown, Andrew, *The Neutron and the Bomb: A Biography of Sir James Chadwick*, Oxford: OUP, 1997.

Brown, Kate, *Plutopia: Nuclear Families, Atomic Cities and the Great Soviet and American Plutonium Disasters*, Oxford: OUP, 2013.

Byrom, Andy, 'British Attitudes on Nuclear Weapons', *Journal of Public Affairs* 7 (2007), pp. 71–77.

Campbell, Duncan, *War Plan UK: The Truth About Civil Defence in Britain*, London: Burnett, 1982.

Canaday, John, *The Nuclear Muse: Literature, Physics, and the First Atomic Bombs*, Madison: University of Wisconsin Press, 2000.

Caputi, Jane, 'Nuclear Visions', *American Quarterly* 47, 1 (March 1995), pp. 165–175.

Carpenter, Charles A., *Dramatists and the Bomb: American and British Playwrights Confront the Nuclear Age, 1945–1964*, London: Greenwood Press, 1999.

Cathcart, Brian, *Test of Greatness: Britain's Struggle for the Atom Bomb*, London: Murray, 1994.

Chapman, James, 'The BBC and the Censorship of *The War Game* (1965)', *Journal of Contemporary History* 41, 1 (2006), pp. 75–94.

Chapman, James, '*The War Game* Controversy – Again', *Journal of Contemporary History* 43, 1 (2008), pp. 105–112.

Cirincione, Joseph, *Bomb Scare: The History and Future of Nuclear Weapons*, New York: Columbia University Press, 2007.

Clark, Ian, *Nuclear Diplomacy and the Special Relationship: Britain's Deterrent and America, 1957–1962*, Oxford: Clarendon, 1994.

Clark, Ronald W., *The Birth of the Bomb: The Untold Story of Britain's Part in the Weapon That Changed the World*, London: Phoenix House, 1961.

Cocroft, Wayne D. and Thomas, Roger J. C., *Cold War: Building for Nuclear Confrontation 1946–1989*, Swindon: English Heritage, 2003.

Conekin, Becky, *The Autobiography of a Nation: The 1951 Festival of Britain*, Manchester: Manchester University Press, 2003.

Cook, John R. and Wright, Peter, *British Science Fiction Television: A Hitchhiker's Guide*, London: I.B. Tauris, 2006.

Cordle, Dan, 'Protect/Protest: British Nuclear Fiction of the 1980s', *The British Journal for the History of Science* 45, 4 (December 2012), pp. 653–669.

Cordle, Dan, ' "That's going to happen to Us. It Is": Threads and the Imagination of Nuclear Disaster on 1980s Television', *Journal of British Cinema and Television* 10, 1 (2013), pp. 71–92.

Crawford, John, ' "A Political H-Bomb": New Zealand and the British Thermonuclear Weapon Test of 1957–58', *Journal of Imperial and Commonwealth History* 26, 1 (1998), pp. 127–150.

Croft, Stuart, 'Continuity and Change in British Thinking About Nuclear Weapons', *Political Studies*, XLII (1994), pp. 228–242.

Cross, Roger, 'British Nuclear Tests and the Indigenous People of Australia', in *The British Nuclear Weapons Programme 1952–2002*, ed. Douglas Holdstock and Frank Barnaby, London: Cass, 2003, pp. 76–90.

Crowley, David and Pavitt, Jane (eds.), *Cold War Modern: Design, 1945–1970*, London: V&A Publishing, 2010.

Daunton, Martin J. and Rieger, Bernhard (eds.), *Meanings of Modernity: Britain from the Late-Victorian Era to World War II*, Oxford: Berg, 2001.

Davies, Hunter (ed.), *Sellafield Stories: Life with Britain's First Nuclear Plant*, London: Constable, 2012.

Davies, Tracy, *Stages of Emergency: Cold War Nuclear Civil Defense*, Durham, NC: Duke University Press, 2007.

Derrida, Jacques, 'No Apocalypse, Not Now (Full Speed Ahead, Seven Missiles, Seven Missives)', *Diacritics* 14, 2 (1984), pp. 20–31.

Desmarais, Ralph, 'Jacob Bronowski: A Humanist Intellectual for an Atomic Age, 1946–1856', *The British Journal for the History of Science* 45, 4 (December 2012), pp. 573–589.

Dorsey, John T., 'The Responsibility of the Scientist in Atomic Bomb Literature', *Comparative Literature Studies* 24 (November 1985), pp. 277–290.

Dower, John W., 'Hiroshima, Nagasaki, and the Politics of Memory', *Technology Review* 98, 6 (1995), pp. 48–51.

Dowling, David, *Fictions of Nuclear Disaster*, Iowa City: University of Iowa Press, 1987.

Easlea, Brian, *Fathering the Unthinkable: Masculinity, Scientists and the Nuclear Arms Race*, London: Pluto Press, 1983.

Edgerton, David, *Shock of the Old: Technology and Global History Since 1900*, London: Profile Books, 2006.

Edgerton, David, *Warfare State: Britain, 1920–1970*, Cambridge: Cambridge University Press, 2006.

Epstein, Leon D., 'The Nuclear Deterrent and the British Election of 1964', *The Journal of British Studies* 5, 2 (May 1966), pp. 139–163.

Farrell, James J., 'American Atomic Culture', *American Quarterly* 43, 1 (March 1991), pp. 157–164.

Forgan, Sophie, 'Atoms in Wonderland', *History and Technology* 19, 3 (2003), pp. 177–196.

Franklin, H. Bruce, *War Stars: The Superweapon and the American Imagination*, New York: OUP, 1988.

Freedman, Lawrence, *Britain and Nuclear Weapons*, London: Macmillan, 1980.

Freedman, Lawrence, *The Evolution of Nuclear Strategy*, London: Macmillan, 1982.

Freedman, Michael I., 'Frederick Soddy and the Practical Significance of Radioactive Matter', *British Journal for the History of Science* 12, 42 (1979), pp. 257–260.

Fussell, P., 'Thank God for the Atom Bomb', in *Thank God for the Atom Bomb and Other Essays*, New York: Summit Books, 1988.

Gaddis, John Lewis, *We Now Know: Rethinking Cold War History*, Oxford: OUP, 1998.

Gamwell, Lynn, 'Atomic Sublime' in *Exploring the Invisible: Art, Science and the Spiritual*, Princeton, NJ: Princeton University Press, 2002.

Garrison, Dee, *Bracing for Armageddon: Why Civil Defense Never Worked*, Oxford: OUP, 2006.

Gay, William C., 'Myths About Nuclear War: Misconceptions in Public Beliefs and Governmental Plan', *Philosophy Social Criticism* 9, 116 (1982), pp. 117–144.

Gill, David James, 'Ministers, Markets and Missiles: The British Government, the European Economic Community and the Nuclear Non-Proliferation Treaty, 1964–68', *Diplomacy & Statecraft* 21, 3 (2010), pp. 451–470.

Goodman, Michael S., 'The Grandfather of the Hydrogen Bomb? Anglo-American Intelligence and Klaus Fuchs', *Historical Studies in the Physical and Biological Sciences* 34, 1 (2003), pp. 1–22.

Goodman, Michael S., 'Who Is Trying to Keep What Secret from Whom and Why?', *Journal of Cold War Studies* 7, 3 (2005), pp. 124–146.

Goodman, Michael S., *Spying on the Nuclear Bear: Anglo-American Intelligence and the Soviet Bomb*, Stanford: Stanford University Press, 2007.

Goodman, Michael and Pincher, Chapman, 'Research Note: Clement Attlee, Percy Sillitoe and the Security Aspects of the Fuchs Case', *Contemporary British History* 19, 1 (2005), pp. 66–77.

Gordin, Michael, *Five Days in August*, Princeton: Princeton University Press, 2007.

Gowing, Margaret, *Britain and Atomic Energy 1939–1945*, London: Macmillan, 1964.

Gowing, Margaret, 'James Chadwick and the Atomic Bomb', *Notes and Records of the Royal Society of London* 47, 1 (1993), pp. 79–92.

Gowing, Margaret assisted by Arnold, Lorna, *Independence and Deterrence: Britain and Atomic Energy, 1945–1952*, London: MacMillan, 1974.

Grant, Matthew, *After the Bomb: Civil Defence and Nuclear War in Cold War Britain, 1945–1968*, Basingstoke: Palgrave Macmillan, 2010.

Grant, Matthew (ed.), *The British Way in Cold Warfare*, London: Continuum, 2008.

Grant, Matthew, '"Civil Defence Gives Meaning to Your Leisure": Citizenship, Participation, and Cultural Change in Cold War Recruitment Propaganda, 1949–54', *Twentieth Century British History* 22, 1 (2010), pp. 52–78.

Grant, Matthew, 'Home Defence and the Sandys White Paper, 1957', *Journal of Strategic Studies* 31, 6 (2008), pp. 925–949.

Grant, Matthew and Ziemann, Benjamin (eds.), *Unthinking the Imaginary War: Intellectual Reflections of the Nuclear Age, 1945–1990*, Manchester: MUP, 2015.

Greene, Owen, *London After the Bomb: What a Nuclear Attack Really Means*, Oxford: OUP, 1982.

Gusterson, Hugh, *People of the Bomb: Portraits of America's Nuclear Complex*, Minneapolis, MN: University of Minnesota Press, 2004.

Hacker, Barton, *Elements of Controversy: the Atomic Energy Commission and Radiation Safety in Nuclear Weapons Testing, 1947–1974*, Berkeley, CA: University of California Press, 1994.

Hales, Peter B., 'The Atomic Sublime', *American Studies* 32, 1 (Spring 1991), pp. 5–31.

Hamblin, Jacob D., 'Fukushima and the Motifs of Nuclear History', *Environmental History* 17, 2 (2012), pp. 285–299.

Hamblin, Jacob D., *Poison in the Well: Radioactive Waste in the Oceans at the Dawn of the Nuclear Age*, New Brunswick, NJ: Rutgers UP, 2008.

Hecht, Gabrielle, *The Radiance of France: Nuclear Power and National Identity After World War II*, Cambridge, MA: MIT Press, 1998.

Hecht, Gabrielle, 'Nuclear Ontologies', *Constellations* 13, 3 (2006), pp. 320–331.

Hennessy, Peter, *Cabinets and the Bomb*, Oxford: OUP, 2007.

Hennessy, Peter, *The Secret State: Preparing for the Worst 1945–2010*, 2nd edition, London: Penguin, 2010.

Henriksen, Margot A., *Dr. Strangelove's America: Society and Culture in the Atomic Age*, Berkeley: University of California Press, 1997.

Herran, Néstor, 'Spreading Nucleonics: The Isotope School at the Atomic Energy Research Establishment, 1951–67', *British Journal of the History of Science* 39, 4 (2006), pp. 569–586.

Hersey, John, *Hiroshima*, Harmondsworth: Penguin, 1946.

Hewison, Robert, *In Anger: Culture in the Cold War, 1945–60*, London: Weidenfeld and Nicholson, 1981.

Hiltgartner, Stephen, Bell, Richard C. and O'Connor, Rory, *Nukespeak: Nuclear Language, Visions and Mindset*, San Francisco: Sierra Club Books, 1982.

Hogan, Michael J. (ed.), *Hiroshima in History and Memory*, Cambridge: CUP, 1996

Hogg, Jonathan, '"The Family That Feared Tomorrow": British Nuclear Culture and Individual Experience in the Late 1950s', *The British Journal for the History of Science* 45, 4 (December 2012), pp. 535–549.

Hogg, Jonathan and Laucht, Christoph, 'Introduction: British Nuclear Culture', *British Journal of the History of Science* 45, 4 (December 2012), pp. 479–493.

Holdstock, Douglas and Barnaby, Frank (eds.), *The British Nuclear Weapons Programme, 1952–2002*, London: Frank Cass, 2003.

Hopkins, Michael F., Kandiah, Michael D. and Staerck, Gillian (eds.), *Cold War Britain, 1945–1964: New Perspectives*, New York: Palgrave Macmillan, 2003.

Hornsey, Richard, '"Everything Is Made of Atoms": The Reprogramming of Space and Time in Post-War London', *Journal of Historical Geography* 34 (2008), pp. 94–117.

Hughes, Jeff, Deconstructing the Bomb: Recent Perspectives on Nuclear History',
  British Journal for the History of Science 37, 4 (2004), pp. 455–464.
Hughes, Jeff, 'The French Connection: The Juliot-Curies and Nuclear Research in
  Paris, 1925–1933', *History and Technology* 13, 4 (1997), pp. 325–343.
Hughes, Jeff, 'Radioactivity and Nuclear Physics', *The Cambridge History of
  Science*, Volume 5, Cambridge: CUP, 2002, pp. 350–374.
Hughes, Jeff, 'The Strath Report: Britain Confronts the H-Bomb, 1954–1955',
  History and Technology 19, 3 (2003), pp. 257–275.
Hughes, Jeff, 'What Is British Nuclear Culture?: Understanding Uranium 235',
  The British Journal for the History of Science 45, 4 (December 2012), p. 497
  (pp. 495–519).
Hughes, Michael, *Conscience and Conflict: Methodism, Peace and War in the
  Twentieth Century*, Peterborough: Epworth, 2008.
Hunter, Ian Q. (ed.), *British Science Fiction Cinema*, London: Routledge, 2001.
Irvine, Maxwell, *Nuclear Power: A Very Short Introduction*, Oxford: OUP, 2011.
Isaac, Joel and Bell, Duncan (eds.), *Uncertain Empire: American History and the
  Idea of the Cold War*, Oxford: OUP, 2012.
Jacobs, Robert A., *The Dragon's Tail: Americans Face the Atomic Age*, Amherst:
  University of Massachusetts Press, 2010.
Jacobs, Robert A., 'Nuclear Conquistadors: Military Colonialism in Nuclear
  Test Site Selection During the Cold War', *Asian Journal of Peacebuilding* 1, 2
  (November 2013), pp. 157–177.
Jasanoff, Sheila and Kim, Sang-Hyun, 'Containing the Atom: Sociotechnical
  Imaginaries and Nuclear Power in the United States and South Korea', *Minerva*
  47 (2009), pp. 119–146.
Jenks, John, *British Propaganda and News Media in the Cold War*, Edinburgh:
  Edinburgh University Press, 2006.
Jolivette, Catherine (ed.), *British Art in the Nuclear Age*, Surrey: Ashgate, 2014.
Jolivette, Catherine, 'Science, Art and Landscape in the Nuclear Age', *Art History*
  35, 2 (April 2012), pp. 252–269.
Jones, Greta, 'The Mushroom-Shaped Cloud: British Scientists' Opposition to
  Nuclear Weapons Policy, 1945–57', *Annals of Science* 43 (1986), pp. 1–26.
Jones, Matthew, 'Great Britain, the United States, and Consultation over Use of the
  Atomic Bomb, 1950–1954', *Historical Journal* 54, 3 (2011), pp. 797–828.
Jones, Peter and Reece, Gordon, *British Public Attitudes to Nuclear Defence*,
  London: Palgrave, 1990.
Josephson, Paul, *Red Atom: Russia's Nuclear Power Program from Stalin to Today*,
  Pittsburgh: University of Pittsburgh Press, 2000.
Kalaidjian, Walter, 'Nuclear Criticism', *Contemporary Literature* XL, 2 (1999),
  pp. 311–318.
Kelly, Cynthia (ed.), *Remembering the Manhattan Project*, London: World
  Scientific, 2004.
Kelly, Saul, 'No Ordinary Foreign Office Official: Sir Roger Makins and Anglo-
  American Atomic Relations, 1945–55', *Contemporary British History* 14, 4
  (2000), pp. 107–124.
Kimmage, Michael 'Atomic Historiography', *Reviews in American History* 38, 1
  (March 2010), pp. 145–152.
Kirby, Diane, 'The Church of England and the Cold War Nuclear Debate',
  Twentieth Century British History 4, 3 (1993), pp. 250–283.

Kirstein, Peter N., 'Hiroshima and Spinning the Atom: America, Britain, and Canada Proclaim the Nuclear Age, 6 August 1945', *The Historian* 71, 4 (2009), pp. 805–827.

Kohn, Richard H., 'History and the Culture Wars: The Case of the Smithsonian Institution's Enola Gay Exhibition', *The Journal of American History* 82, 3 (1995), pp. 1036–1063.

Kraft, Alison, 'Atomic Medicine: The Cold War Origins of Biological Research', *History Today*, 59, 11 (2009), pp. 26–33.

Kraft, Alison, 'Between Medicine and Industry: The Rise of the Radioisotope 1945–1965', *Contemporary British History* 20, 1 (2006), pp. 3–37.

Laucht, Christoph, 'Britannia Rules the Atom: The James Bond Phenomenon and Post War British Nuclear Culture', *The Journal of Popular Culture* 46, 2 (2013), pp. 359–360 (pp. 358–377).

Laucht, Christoph, *Elemental Germans: Klaus Fuchs, Rudolf Peierls and the Making of British Nuclear Culture 1939–59*, Basingstoke: Palgrave Macmillan, 2012.

Laucht, Christoph, '"An Extraordinary Achievement of the 'American Way':" Hollywood and the Americanization of the Making of the Atom Bomb in *Fat Man and Little Boy*', *European Journal of American Culture* 28, 1 (2009), pp. 41–56.

Lee, Sabine, '"In No Sense Vital and Actually Even Important"? Reality and Perception of Britain's Contribution to the Development of Nuclear Weapons', *Contemporary British History* 20, 2 (2006), pp. 159–185.

Leffler, Melvyn and Westad, Odd Arne (eds.), *The Cambridge History of the Cold War* (3 volumes), Cambridge: CUP, 2010.

van Lente, Dick (ed.), *The Nuclear Age in Popular Media: A Transnational History, 1945–1965*, Basingstoke: Palgrave, 2012.

Lifton, Robert Jay, 'On Death and Death Symbolism: The Hiroshima Disaster', *Psychiatry* 27 (August 1964), pp. 191–210.

Lifton, Robert Jay, *Death in Life: Survivors of Hiroshima*, New York: Random House, 1968.

Lifton, Robert Jay, *Indefensible Weapons: The Political and Psychological Case Against Nuclearism*, New York: Basic Books, 1982.

Lynskey, Dorian, *33 Revolutions per Minute: A History of Protest Songs*, London: Faber and Faber, 2010.

Mackby, Jenifer and Cornish, Paul, *U.S.-UK Nuclear Cooperation After 50 Years*, Washington, DC: Center for Strategic and International Studies Press, 2008.

Maddox, Robert J. (ed.), *Hiroshima in History: The Myths of Revisionism*, Columbia, Missouri: University of Missouri Press, 2007.

Maguire, Richard, 'Scientific Dissent amid the United Kingdom Government's Nuclear Weapons Programme', *History Workshop Journal* 63 (2007), pp. 113–135.

Maguire, Richard, '"Never a Credible Weapon": Nuclear Cultures in Government During the Era of the H-bomb', *The British Journal for the History of Science* 45, 4 (December 2012), pp. 519–534.

Maheffey, James, *Atomic Awakening*, New York: Pegasus, 2009.

Malloy, Sean L., '"The Rules of Civilised Warfare": Scientists, Soldiers, Civilians and American Nuclear Targeting 1940–1945', *Journal of Strategic Studies* 30 (2007), pp. 475–512.

Mandelbaum, Michael, *The Nuclear Revolution: International Politics Before and After Hiroshima*, Cambridge: Cambridge University Press, 1981.

Masco, Joseph, *Nuclear Borderlands: The Manhattan Project in Post-War New Mexico*, Princeton: Princeton University Press, 2006.

Masco, Joseph, '"Survival Is Your Business": Engineering Ruins and Affect in Nuclear America', *Cultural Anthropology* 23, 2 (2008), pp. 361–398.

Mariner, Rosemary B. and Piehler, G. Kurt (eds.), *The Atomic Bomb and American Society: New Perspectives*, Knoxville: University of Tennessee Press, 2009.

McNeill, John Robert (ed.), *Environmental Histories of the Cold War*, Cambridge: Cambridge University Press, 2010.

Melosi, Martin V., *Atomic Age America*, New York: Pearson, 2013.

Merricks, Linda, *The World Made New: Frederick Soddy, Science, Politics and Environment*, Oxford: Oxford University Press, 1996.

Messmer, Michael W., 'Nuclear Culture, Nuclear Criticism', *Minnesota Review* 30, 1 (1988), pp. 161–180.

Miles, Rufus E., 'Hiroshima: The Strange Myth of Half a Million Lives Saved', *International Security* 10 (Fall 1985), pp. 121–140.

Milliken, Robert, *No Conceivable Injury: The Story of Britain and Australia's Atomic Cover-Up*, Victoria, Australia: Penguin, 1986.

Miyamoto, Yuki, *Beyond the Mushroom Cloud: Commemoration, Religion, and Responsibility after Hiroshima*, New York: Fordham University Press, 2012.

Moore, Richard, *Nuclear Illusion, Nuclear Reality: Britain, the United States and Nuclear Weapons, 1958–1964*, Basingstoke: Palgrave Macmillan, 2012.

Moore, Richard, *The Royal Navy and Nuclear Weapons*, London: Cass, 2001.

Monteyne, David, *Fallout Shelter: Designing for Civil Defense in the Cold War*, Minneapolis: University of Minneapolis, 2011.

Nagel, Alan, *Containment Culture: American Narratives, Postmodernism, and the Atomic Age*, Durham, NC: Duke University Press, 1995.

Navias, Martin, *Nuclear Weapons and British Strategic Planning, 1955–1958*, Oxford: Clarendon, 1991.

Nehring, Holger, 'The British and West German Protests Against Nuclear Weapons and the Cultures of the Cold War, 1957–64', *Contemporary British History* 19, 2 (2005), pp. 223–241.

Nehring, Holger, *Politics of Security: British and West German Protest Movements and the Early Cold War, 1945–1970*, Oxford: OUP, 2013.

Newhouse, John, *The Nuclear Age: From Hiroshima to Star Wars*, London: M. Joseph, 1989.

Norris, Robert S. and Kristensen, Hans M., 'The British Nuclear Stockpile, 1953–2013', *Bulletin of the Atomic Scientists* 69, 4 (2013), pp. 69–75.

Nuttall, Jeff, *Bomb Culture*, London: Paladin, 1968.

O'Neill, Robert, 'Britain and the Future of Nuclear Weapons', *International Affairs* 71, 4 (October 1995), pp. 747–761.

Paul, Septimus H., *Nuclear Rivals: Anglo-American Atomic Relations, 1941–1952*, Columbus: Ohio State University Press, 2000.

Pavitt, Jane, *Fear and Fashion in the Cold War*, London: V&A Publishing, 2008.

Petersen, Stephen, 'Explosive Propositions: Artists React to the Atomic Age', *Science in Context* 17, 4 (2004), pp. 579–609.

Phythian, Mark, 'CND's Cold War', *Contemporary British History* 15, 3 (2001), 133–156.

Pierre, Andrew, *Nuclear Politics: The British Experience with an Independent Strategic Force, 1939–1970*, London: Oxford University Press, 1972.

Preston, Diana, *Before the Fallout: From Marie Curie to Hiroshima*, New York: Walker & Co., 2005.

Priest, Andrew, 'In American Hands: Britain, the United States and the Polaris Nuclear Project 1962–1968', *Contemporary British History* 19, 3 (September 2005), pp. 353–376.

Prins, Gwyn (ed.), *Defended to Death*, Middlesex: Penguin, 1983.

Quinlan, Michael, *Thinking About Nuclear Weapons: Principles, Problems, Prospects*, Oxford: OUP, 2009.

Rashke, Richard, *The Killing of Karen Silkwood: The Story Behind the Kerr-McGee Plutonium Case*, 2nd edition., Ithaca, NY: Cornell University Press, 2000 [1981].

Redford, Duncan, 'The "Hallmark of a First-Class Navy": The Nuclear-Powered Submarine in the Royal Navy 1960–77', *Contemporary British History* 23, 2 (2009), pp. 181–197.

Rentetzi, Maria, 'The Women Radium Dial Painters as Experimental Subjects (1920–1990)', *NTM* 12, 4 (September 2004), pp. 233–248.

Rhodes, Richard, *The Making of the Atomic Bomb*, London: Simon & Schuster, 1986.

Robinson, Derek, *Just Testing*, London: Collins Harvill, 1985.

Rose, Kenneth, *One Nation Underground: A History of the Fallout Shelter*, New York: New York University Press, 2004.

Rose, Paul Lawrence, *Heisenberg and the Nazi Atomic Bomb Project, 1939–1945*, Berkeley, CA: University of California Press, 1998.

Rosenthal, Peggy, 'The Nuclear Mushroom Cloud as Cultural Image', *American Literary History* 3, 1 (Spring 1991), pp. 63–92.

Rotter, Andrew J., *Hiroshima*, Oxford: OUP, 2009.

Ruston, Roger, *A Say in the End of the World: Morals and Nuclear Weapons Policy, 1941–1987*, Oxford: OUP, 1990.

Rutherford, Ernest, *Radioactivity*, London: Cambridge University Press, 1904.

Saint-Amour, Paul K., 'Bombing and the Symptom: Traumatic Earliness and the Nuclear Uncanny', *Diacritics* 30, 4 (Winter, 2000), pp. 59–82.

Schell, Jonathan, *The Fate of the Earth*, London: Picador, 1982.

Schrafstetter, Susanna, '"Loquacious … and Pointless as Ever?" Britain, the United States and the United Nations Negotiations on International Control of Nuclear Energy 1945–48', *Contemporary British History* 16, 4 (2002), pp. 87–108.

Sclove, Richard E., 'From Alchemy to Atomic War: Frederick Soddy's "Technology Assessment" of Atomic Energy, 1900–1915', *Science, Technology and Human Values* 14, 2 (Spring 1989), pp. 163–194.

Scott, Len, *The Cuban Missile Crisis and the Threat of Nuclear War*, London: Continuum, 2007.

Scott, Len, 'Labour and the Bomb', *International Affairs* 82, 4 (2006), pp. 685–700.

Seed, David, *American Science Fiction and the Cold War: Literature and Film*, Edinburgh: Edinburgh University Press, 1999.

Seed, David, 'H. G. Wells and the Liberating Atom', *Science Fiction Studies* 30, 1 (March 2003), pp. 33–48.

Shapiro, Jerome F., *Atomic Bomb Cinema*, London: Routledge, 2002.

Shaw, Tony, *British Cinema and the Cold War: The State, Propaganda and Consensus*, London: I.B. Tauris, 2001.

Shaw, Tony, 'The BBC, the State and Cold War Culture: The Case of Television's *The War Game* (1965)', *English Historical Review* CXXI, 494 (2006), pp. 1351–1384.

Sherwin, Martin J., *A World Destroyed*, New York: Knopf, 1975.

Simpson, John, *The Independent Nuclear State: The United States, Britain and the Military Atom*, London: Macmillan, 1983.

Sinfield, Alan, *Literature, Politics and Culture in Postwar Britain*, London: Continuum, 2000.

Siracusa, Joseph M., *Nuclear Weapons: A Very Short Introduction*, Oxford: OUP, 2008.

Smith, Joan, *Clouds of Deceit: The Deadly Legacy of Britain's Bomb Tests*, London: Faber, 1985.

Smith, Mark B., 'Peaceful Coexistence at All Costs: Cold War Exchanges Between Britain and the Soviet Union in 1956', *Cold War History* 12, 3 (2012), pp. 537–558.

Smith, Melissa, 'Architects of Armageddon: The Home Office Scientific Advisers' Branch and Civil Defence in Britain, 1945–68', *British Journal for the History of Science* 43, 2 (2010), pp. 149–180.

Soloman, James Fisher, *Discourse and Reference in the Nuclear Age*, Norman: University of Oklahoma Press, 1988.

Steege, Paul, *Black Market, Cold War: Everyday Life in Berlin, 1946–1949*, Cambridge: CUP, 2008.

Stoddart, Kristan, *Losing an Empire and Finding a Role: Britain, the USA, NATO and Nuclear Weapons, 1964–70*, Basingstoke: Palgrave Macmillan, 2012.

Szasz, Ferenc M., *British Scientists and the Manhattan Project: The Los Alamos Years*, New York: St. Martin's Press, 1992.

Taylor, Brian C., 'Nuclear Pictures and Metapictures', *American Literary History* 9, 3 (Autumn 1997), pp. 567–597.

Taylor, Richard, *Against the Bomb: The British Peace Movement, 1958–1965*, Oxford: Clarendon Press, 1988.

Taylor, Richard and Pritchard, Colin, *The Protest Makers: The British Nuclear Disarmament Movement of 1958–1965 Twenty Years On*, Oxford: Pergamon Press, 1980.

Thompson, Dorothy (ed.), *Over Our Dead Bodies: Women Against the Bomb*, London: Virago, 1983.

Thompson, Edward Palmer and Smith, Dan (eds.), *Protest and Survive*, Middlesex: Penguin, 1980.

Thorpe, Charles, 'Disciplining Experts: Scientific Authority and Liberal Democracy in the Oppenheimer Case', *Social Studies of Science* 32, 4 (August 2002), pp. 527–564.

Thorpe, Charles, *Oppenheimer: The Tragic Intellect*, Chicago: University of Chicago Press, 2006.

Titus, A. Costandina, *Bombs in the Backyard*, Reno: University of Nevada Press, 1986.

Toynbee, Philip, *The Fearful Choice: A Debate on Nuclear Policy*, Detroit: Wayne State University Press, 1959.

Tucker, Anthony and Gleisner, John, *Crucible of Despair: The Effects of Nuclear Weapons*, London: Menard, 1982.

Turchetti, Simone, 'Atomic Secrets and Governmental Lies: Nuclear Science, Politics and Security in the Pontecorvo Case', *The British Journal for the History of Science* 36, 4 (December 2003), pp. 409–414.

Twigge, Stephen, 'A Baffling Experience: Technology Transfer, Anglo-American Nuclear Relations, and the Development of the Gas Centrifuge 1964–70', *History and Technology* 19, 2 (2003), pp. 151–163.

Twigge, Stephen and Scott, Len, *Planning Armageddon: Britain, the United States and the Command of Western Nuclear Forces, 1945–1964*, Amsterdam: Harwood Academic, 2000.

Tyler-May, Elaine, *Homeward Bound: American Families in the Cold War*, New York: Basic, 1988.

Veldman, Meredith, *Fantasy, the Bomb and the Greening of Britain: Romantic Protest, 1945–80*, Cambridge: CUP, 1994,

Vincent, David, *The Culture of Secrecy: Britain, 1832–1998*, Oxford: Oxford University Press, 1998.

Walker, Frank, *Maralinga: The Chilling Expose of Our Secret Nuclear Shame and Betrayal of Our Troops and Country*, Sydney: Hachette, 2014.

Walker, J. Samuel, 'Recent Literature on Truman's Atomic Bomb Decision: A Search for Middle Ground', *Diplomatic History* 29, 2 (2005), pp. 311–334.

Walker, John, *British Nuclear Weapons and the Test Ban, 1954–1973: Britain, the United States, Weapons Policies and Nuclear Testing: Tensions and Contradictions*, Farnham: Ashgate, 2010.

Walker, John, 'British Nuclear Weapons Stockpiles, 1953–78', *RUSI Journal* 156, 5 (October 2011), pp. 74–83.

Warner, Frederick and Kirchmann, René J. C. (eds.), *Nuclear Test Explosions: Environmental and Human Impacts*, Chichester: John Wiley, 2000.

Wayne, Mike, 'Failing the Public: The BBC, *The War Game* and Revisionist History, a Reply to James Chapman', *Journal of Contemporary History* 42, 4 (2007), pp. 627–637.

Weart, Spencer R., *The Rise of Nuclear Fear*, Cambridge, MA: Harvard University Press, 2012.

Wellerstein, Alex, 'Patenting the Bomb: Nuclear Weapons, Intellectual Property and Technological Control', *Isis* 99 (2008), pp. 57–87.

Welsh, Ian, *Mobilising Modernity: The Nuclear Moment*, London: Routledge, 2003.

Welsh, Ian, 'The NIMBY Syndrome: Its Significance in the History of the Nuclear Debate in Britain', *British Journal for the History of Science* 26, 1 (1993), pp. 15–32.

Welsh, Ian and Wynne, Brian, 'Science, Scientism and Imaginaries of Publics in the UK: Passive Objects, Incipient Threats', *Science as Culture* 22, 4 (2013), pp. 540–566.

Whitfield, Stephen, *The Culture of the Cold War*, Baltimore, MD: Johns Hopkins University Press, 1996.

Wilkinson, Nicholas, *Secrecy and the Media: The Official History of the United Kingdom's D-Notice System*, London: Routledge, 2009.

Williams, Paul, *Race, Ethnicity and Nuclear War*, Liverpool: Liverpool University Press, 2011.

Williams, Robert C. and Cantelon, Philip L., *The American Atom: A Documentary History of Nuclear Policies from the Discovery of Fission to the Present*, Philadelphia: University of Pennsylvania Press, 1984.

Willis, Kirk, ' "God and the Atom": British Churchmen and the Challenge of Nuclear Power, 1945–1950', *Albion* 29, 3 (Fall 1997), pp. 442–457.

Willis, Kirk, 'The Origins of British Nuclear Culture, 1895–1939', *Journal of British Studies* 34 (January 1995), pp. 59–89.

Winkler, Allan M., *Life Under a Cloud: American Anxiety About the Atom*, New York: Oxford University Press, 1993; repr. Urbana: University of Illinois Press, 1999

Wittner, Laurence S., *Resisting the Bomb: A History of the World Disarmament Movement, 1954–70*, Stanford: Stanford University Press, 1997.

Wittner, Laurence S., 'Blacklisting Schweitzer', *The Bulletin of the Atomic Scientists* 51, 3 (May/June 1995), pp. 55–61.

Wittner, Laurence S., 'Gender Roles and Nuclear Disarmament Activism, 1954–1965', *Gender and History* 12, 1 (2000), pp. 197–222.

Wynne, Brian, 'Misunderstood Misunderstanding: Social Identities and Public Uptake of Science', *Public Understanding of Science* 1 (1992), pp. 281–305.

Young, Alison, *Femininity in Dissent*, London: Routledge, 1990.

Zeman, Scott C. and Amundson, Michael A. (eds.), *Atomic Culture: How We Learned to Stop Worrying and Love the Bomb*, Boulder, CO: University of Colorado Press, 2004.

APPENDIX: TIMELINE

1895:	Röntgen discovers X-rays
1898:	Radioactivity discovered
1911:	Rutherford proposed the existence of the neutron
1919:	Artificial disintegration of elements demonstrated by Rutherford
1932:	Cockcroft and Walton split the atomic nucleus of lithium into helium
1934:	Introduction of the 'tolerance dose'
1936:	Szilard patents the idea of the nuclear chain reaction with the British Admiralty
1939:	Einstein/Szilard letter to Roosevelt
1940:	Frisch-Peierls Memorandum
1941:	MAUD Committee report
1942–1946:	Manhattan Project
1943:	The Quebec Agreement
1944:	Churchill/Roosevelt Agreement
1945:	Atomic bombs are dropped at Hiroshima and Nagasaki
1945:	AERE established at Harwell
1945:	Washington Declaration on atomic energy
1946:	First UN atomic meeting held in London
1946:	Baruch Plan proposed by the United States
1946:	McMahon Act
1946:	First publicized atomic bomb tests, by the United States at Bikini
1947:	British nuclear weapons project formally begins
1947:	First British experimental reactor becomes operational at Harwell
1948:	Brussels Treaty
1948:	Berlin Blockade
1948:	UK Civil Defence Corps reactivated
1949:	Official announcement of British atomic bomb project
1949:	April, NATO established
1949:	Soviet Union tests an atomic bomb
1950:	Klaus Fuchs arrested, suspected spy

1950:   Atomic Weapons Research Establishment (AWRE) established at
          Aldermaston
1950:   US announce Hydrogen bomb project
1952:   First UK atomic bomb exploded
1953:   Bermuda Conference
1954:   Amendments to the McMahon Act agreed between the United
          States and the UK
1954:   Wilson-Sandys Agreement
1955:   Blue Streak initiated
1955:   UKAEA established
1956:   Suez Crisis
1956:   Calder Hall becomes the first commercial nuclear power station
          in the world
1956:   International Atomic Energy Agency (IAEA) formed
1956:   Bradwell Inquiry
1957:   Reactor fire at Windscale, and the Penney Enquiry that followed
1957:   The UK detonates first thermonuclear device
1958:   'Co-operation on the Uses of Atomic Energy for Mutual Defence
          Purposes' treaty signed between the UK and the United States
1958:   America starts supplying Thor missiles to Britain
1958:   Campaign for Nuclear Disarmament (CND) established
1961:   The first US nuclear submarine arrives at Holy Loch, Scotland
1962:   Cuban Missile Crisis
1962:   US and UK officials meet in Nassau to agree over the purchase of
          the US Skybolt system
1963:   Polaris sales agreement reached
1963:   Limited Test Ban Treaty
1963:   CND's 'Spies for Peace' campaign
1965:   *The War Game* is banned from terrestrial TV
1968:   UK tests Polaris, the country's first medium range nuclear missile
1968:   Nuclear Non-Proliferation Treaty
1974:   Chevaline programme initiated
1977:   Windscale Inquiry
1978:   Duff-Mason Report
1978:   Pochin Inquiry
1979:   Three Mile Island nuclear accident
1980:   Francis Pym confirms the existence of the Chevaline nuclear
          programme
1983:   US Cruise missiles arrive at Greenham
1983:   Able Archer incident
1986:   Chernobyl nuclear accident
2011:   Fukushima nuclear accident
2014:   Trident Commission Report published

INDEX

This index includes book, film, television and computer game titles, authors, and musical artists. Directors and producers of film, theatre and TV, song titles, and computer game creators are not indexed. Local newspapers are indexed, national newspapers are not.